The Ethnic Factor
in Family Structure
and Mobility

The Ethnic Factor in Family Structure and Mobility

Frances E. Kobrin
Brown University

Calvin Goldscheider
*The Hebrew University and
Brown University*

Ballinger Publishing Company • Cambridge, Mass.
A Subsidiary of J.B. Lippincott Company

This book is printed on recycled paper.

International Standard Book Number: 0-88410-358-7

Library of Congress Catalog Card Number: 77-25838

Printed in the United States of America

Library of Congress Cataloging in Publication Data

Kobrin, Frances E
   The ethnic factor in family structure and mobility.

   Bibliography: p. 251
   1. Marriage—Rhode Island—Case studies. 2. Ethnology—Rhode Island—Case studies. 3. Ethnic groups. 4. Social mobility—United States.
I. Goldscheider, Calvin, joint author. II. Title.
HQ536.K62   301.42'1   77-25838

ISBN 0-88410-358-7

To David and Barbara

Table of Contents

List of Tables

Foreword

This analysis of the ethnic factor in family structure and mobility processes merits recognition both for the ways in which it exploits a rich body of socio-demographic data and for the insights it provides on the extent to which ethnic continuity and ethnic convergence characterize the American scene today. It is the latest in a series of studies resulting from twenty-five years of research on Rhode Island's population. These efforts began with assessments of the historical patterns of development and changes in the size, distribution, and composition of the state's population, relying heavily on census statistics. These early analyses led to the recognition that the state offered particular advantages as a population laboratory. Demographic, social, and economic developments in Rhode Island often presaged those that came to characterize the United States as a whole. Moreover, the state's heterogeneous religious, ethnic, and class composition provided unusual opportunities for comparative analyses.

Reflecting this recognition, in 1966 the Population Research Laboratory was established at Brown University as part of the Population Studies and Training Center which is affiliated with the Department of Sociology. Three major comprehensive sample surveys undertaken by this Laboratory during the years 1967 through 1969, and annual follow-up interviews conducted through 1971, as well as specialized surveys taken since then, have resulted in a series of studies of mobility, fertility, and health in which the Rhode Island material has been used to investigate issues of general interest.

Yet a wealth of data from these surveys has remained unexploited, awaiting that unique combination of availability of talent and interest, together with conceptual and practical relevance of the specific problem area, that are essential for the success of a research undertaking. Our program at Brown was fortunate indeed that the appointment of Calvin Goldscheider of the Hebrew University, first as a visiting professor and subsequently as an adjunct professor, coincided with the presence on our faculty of Dr. Frances Kobrin. Her work on changing household structure in the United States had already earned for her the reputation as one of the leading experts on this topic. Dr. Goldscheider's general concern with population, modernization, and social structure, coupled with a particular interest in the sociology of minority groups, brings a unique combination of expertise to the analysis. Together, they recognized that major research gaps exist in our knowledge of the extent to which ethnic and religious identification affect the major life-cycle processes on which sociologists and demographers focus their attention and which, in themselves, are of such great importance to the strength and vitality of ethnic communities and ethnic identification in the United States.

This close coincidence of interests on the part of Drs. Kobrin and Goldscheider, together with their realization that a rich body of data relevant to examining some of these interests was available in Brown's Population Research Laboratory, led to an early and fortunate decision to use these data for the analysis undertaken in this monograph. The perspectives which Drs. Kobrin and Goldscheider bring to play on these data for investigating the interrelations of ethnicity, family structure, and mobility processes add immensely to the value of the research undertaken, to the sociological and demographic insights emanating from the analysis, and to the research questions identified as meriting further research.

Given the current concerns with ethnicity in the United States and the reinforcements, both demographically and socially, of certain ethnic groups through the comparatively large numbers of new immigrants arriving in the United States, attention to the variations and changes in family and mobility patterns among ethnic groups and their effect on the structure of ethnic communities and on ethnic continuity and convergence are indeed questions rating the highest priority. The opportunity to examine these questions for Catholics, Protestants, and Jews as well as for the Irish, French-Canadian, Italian, and Portuguese subgroups of the Catholic population enhances the richness of the analysis.

As the authors stress, perhaps the most important conclusion emerging from their analysis is the finding that ethnic pluralism remains a continuing feature of community life in America and that it must, therefore, be taken into account in any assessment of social, demographic, and economic processes. Concurrently, their analysis also emphasizes that both the extent and pattern of ethnic change varies over time and differently among ethnic subpopulations as well as for the various processes analyzed. On the substantive level, this argues strongly for recognition of the emergence of new forms of ethnic identity and ethnic cohesiveness, particularly since the changes that occur differ among the various subpopulations observed. The key roles of social class and life-cycle factors stand out in all the analyses; at the same time it is clear that other factors also help to account for the continuing ethnic differences in both family and mobility processes. Particularly intriguing is the finding, made repeatedly, that the variations at any given time and the changes over time are often sharper for the ethnic groups within the Catholic population than they are between Protestants and Catholics. Equally important as this specific finding is the strong interdependence identified among family, stratification, and residential mobility processes in the patterns of ethnic differentiation.

The study is not only of theoretical interest; its findings have practical implications for the specific religious-ethnic groups as well as for the community at large. The differential role, for example, which education plays in occupational success and in rates of out-migration from the community presents dilemmas that are not easily resolved if the goal is maintenance of ethnic identity. The recognition that patterns and levels of ethnic interaction provide more important channels in advancing individual members of certain ethnic groups than others helps to explain the lower incentives for continuing education in some groups as well as the closer ties that such individuals may maintain with their ethnic community. Similarly, more education may be a "mixed blessing" with respect to its impact on intermarriage and group cohesiveness in those subcommunities where maintenance of a "closed" community is a major value and continuity of ethnic identification a major goal.

But as in all solid research, the investigation raises as many questions as it provides answers. Some of these stem from the fact that the data were not originally collected for the analysis undertaken here. As a result, there is no opportunity to devote attention to attitudinal values rather than to the behavioral aspects of ethnic identity. Other questions relate to the decisionmaking process itself, particularly to the extent to which ethnic considerations enter into the decision to marry, to change neighborhoods, or to leave the community entirely, and the specific ways in which ethnic friendships and contacts play a role in job placement, residential location, and social participation generally. Perhaps most basic is the problem of how the values accruing to a particular ethnic identity are transmitted from one generation to another, especially in the face of counteracting pressures that stress the melting pot character of American society and equality of opportunity for members of all groups.

Beyond these concerns, there is still the more general and inevitable question of the extent to which the patterns noted for this particular community are typical of those that characterize other communities with different ethnic composition, different majority and minority groups, and different proportions of first, second, and third generation Americans. All community studies are faced with this question, and while one can have considerable confidence that what has been observed here is likely to be true of the society at large, comparable research undertaken in other settings is needed to test the validity of that expectation. This need in no way detract from the importance of the research undertaken here. Similarly, the fact that the data analyzed are largely cross-sectional argues strongly for pursuing, through longitudinal analysis, the lines of inquiry opened up in order to better identify and assess how ethnic factors actually operate at the time decisions are made and behavior initiated.

Even while recognizing these needs, one must be grateful to Drs. Kobrin and Goldscheider for the significant contributions they have made both in providing us with insights on the patterns that characterize their study community and in providing analytic frameworks which will prove useful in future research. Operating both as demographers and as sociologists, their resulting analysis of the ethnic factor in family structure and in mobility processes stands as a tribute to their ingenuity and persistence as well as an illustration of the advantages to be gained by bringing the perspectives of both disciplines to play on research topics which all too often suffer from too narrow an assessment.

Sidney Goldstein
George Howard Crooker Professor
of Sociology

Providence
October 1977

Brown University

Preface

This monograph presents a systematic examination of the role of ethnicity in major dimensions of family and mobility processes. One of the dominant themes emerging in American society is the continuing importance of ethnic communities and ethnic identification. It has become increasingly clear that the central life cycle processes associated with marriage and family formation, socioeconomic status and mobility, and residential patterns and migration vary significantly by ethnoreligious identification. Moreover, the velocity of change in these processes differs among ethnic groups and reflects factors associated with the structure and culture of ethnic communities. Despite the growing recognition among social scientists of the importance of ethnicity in American social life, few of these processes have been studied systematically or comprehensively. The general paucity of available data sources and the implicit assumption that ethnic group differentials are transitional in America have led to conspicuous gaps in our knowledge of major ethnic subpopulations in America.

This analysis of ethnic continuity and change is based on extensive materials collected as part of the sample surveys of Rhode Island obtained by the Population Research Laboratory of the Population Studies and Training Center, Brown University. These data provide detailed insights into family structure and change, social stratification and mobility, and residential patterns and migration of major religious groups (Protestants, Catholics, and Jews), and Catholic ethnic subcommunities (French Canadians, Irish, Italians, and Portuguese). Understanding these basic social processes for ethnic subpopulations is an essential first step in the analysis of variation and change in American society. The data available are excellent in quality and provide a fascinating case study of relationships discussed widely but rarely analyzed systematically.

Several questions serve as guidelines in the focus on the dynamics of the ethnic factor in social processes:

1. What are the family and mobility patterns of ethnic subpopulations and how have these changed over time?
2. Do ethnic differences in family and mobility processes reflect life cycle and social class factors and are there specific ethnic dimensions to these processes that transcend the social, demographic, and economic characteristics of ethnic groups?
3. How do variations and changes in family and mobility patterns affect ethnic continuity and the structure of ethnic communities?

The analysis is based on the assumption that the question of ethnic continuity and change is best examined at the community level, using empirical evidence to highlight the dynamics of ethnic change and variation in fundamental family, social mobility, and residential change processes.

The research is presented in four parts. Following a general introduction exploring the salience and meaning of ethnicity, Part I presents the basic dimensions of social stratification, marriage, and residential concentration patterns of religious and Catholic ethnic subpopulations. Part II examines in detail the processes of family formation and intermarriage. Parts III and IV deal with two separate but related issues of mobility. Differential social mobility between and within generations is analyzed in Part III, and the geographic mobility patterns of ethnic communities are investigated in Part IV.

None of the material presented in this book has ever been published before. Some of the data which form the basis for the analysis of Chapter 3, "The Marital Cycle," were used in a paper presented at the 1977 meetings of the Population Association of America in St. Louis under the title, "Ethnicity and Family Demography."

As the authors, we accept responsibility for the analyses and interpretations presented in this volume. However, we could never have accomplished this much without the guidance, support, encouragement, and help of many others. Our greatest debt is to the resources of the Brown University Population Studies and Training Center and to its director, Sidney Goldstein, for making available the data from the Brown Population Laboratory and for providing the occasion for our initiation of this project. Dietrich Rueschemeyer, chairman, and our many colleagues in the Brown University Department of Sociology provided essential support and encouragement throughout the entire period of this research project. In particular, the analysis of social mobility was greatly enhanced by the suggestions of Judah Matras, of the Hebrew University, and of Vincent Covello, of Brown. Ward Kingkade ranks first among the many helpful past and current Brown graduate students whose research in related areas using these data and thoughtful analyses have greatly benefited our project. Appreciation is also due the personnel of the Brown Computer Laboratory and the Social Science Data Center, particularly to Anneliese Greenier, whose advice was unfailingly cheerful and helpful when frustration seemed greatest. Valuable typing services were provided by Joyce Coleman, Gail Grossman, Norma MacDonald, Josephine De Hart, and Glenna Meade.

To all these, plus our friends who encouraged us and our families who loved us, we express our thanks.

Chapter 1

The Salience of Ethnicity

Ethnic pluralism is an integral feature of human societies and ethnicity continues to be an organic part of social and cultural changes. The major processes associated with industrialization and urbanization have not resulted in the disappearance of ethnic communities nor the eradication of ethnic differences in major social processes. Ethnicity cannot be viewed as a marginal phenomenon nor as a vestigal cultural legacy in the evolution toward societal homogeneity. Quite the contrary: some elements of modern society tend to reinforce ethnic continuity and emphasize ethnic differentiation. The conspicuousness of ethnic communities suggests that ethnic institutions and social networks even as they change remain major sources of group identification. Indeed, ethnicity varies and changes over time, reflecting variations and changes in the broader society. Hence, the sociological study of ethnic patterns highlights and reveals in microcosm more general social processes characterizing total societies.

The theoretical contexts within which ethnicity has been studied have emphasized either ethnic pluralism or ethnic assimilation. These theoretical constructs have often been used as opposing ideal types on a unidimensional continuum: ethnic groups either continue as separate entities or change in the direction of greater similarity to the broader society. Although the predictions differ, both perspectives are similarly limited by this unidimensionality in explaining the empirical complexities of ethnic phenomena. It is more accurate to consider pluralism and assimilation as processes that vary along many social and cultural dimensions. On the one hand, some processes associated with sociocultural change have clearly resulted in the greater similarity of disparate ethnic groups in modern society. However, such convergence often occurs simultaneously with the retention of structural separateness and societal pluralism (cf. Gordon, 1964). Hence, it seems more fruitful to view the dynamics of ethnic sociocultural change as a complex blend of elements of both continuity and transition. Ethnic groups differ in the extent of change in many social processes. Moreover, some ethnic groups have experienced different patterns of change over time. This ethnic variation reflects several external factors, including the different social origins of the group, the timing of the group's entrance into the society, competition with other ethnic groups, and the pace of social change in the society as a whole. In addition, the location of ethnic groups in selected social, economic, and ecological categories, in combination with the specific cultural heritages of communities, produce differential rates of change.

Of equal importance is the fact that there are often subgroupings within an ethnic population that are more receptive to social and cultural changes. For example, urban residents, the more educated, and the occupationally successful within ethnic groups are more likely to experience greater and more diverse types of changes. Hence, social differentials within the ethnic community provide clues to the determinants of social change and often foreshadow the future patterns that will characterize the group as a whole.

The view of ethnicity as a dynamic rather than an invariant characterisitic suggests that ethnic change does not necessarily imply that ethnicity is transient, unimportant, or temporal. Rather, the manifestation of ethnicity, its meaning and form, should be expected to change over time. Clearly, ethnic groups are different in contemporary America from what they were a century or half-a-century ago. Ethnicity is no longer pervasive in the sense of tribal loyalties and extensive control over resources. The shift away from ethnic dominance has not meant the disappearance of the ethnic factor but the emergence of a more specialized ethnic role in influencing social processes.

Most societies have become pluralistic through migration processes, colonialization, and status-caste systems that have established over time social, cultural, and political cohesion within (as well as tensions between) ethnic subpopulations (van den Berghe, 1971; Schermerhorn, 1969). Thus, the role of ethnicity in America shares many similarities with other societies. The unique manifestation of ethnicity in the United States relates to the particular political-ideological foundations and socioeconomic and demographic evolution of American society. Indeed, the examination of ethnicity in the United

States illustrates the complex coexistence of ethnic pluralism and assimilation. It has been argued that "even as groups attempt to assimilate into the social, political, and economic mainstream of a society, they must organize and develop a sense of their group distinctiveness in order to enter the social process" (Newman, 1973, p. 182; see also Greeley, 1974). Social forces in contemporary America maximize pressures and rewards for individual assimilation and integration but help preserve selected aspects of ethnic continuity. The tension between continuity and change is one of the essential themes in the analysis of ethnic groups in American society.

THE MEANING OF ETHNICITY

Beyond the assertion that ethnicity is a phenomenon that exists in America and requires systematic analysis, the question remains: what are the meanings of ethnicity? If ethnic factors continue to differentiate social processes and ethnic communities persist, then the social components, processes, and contexts associated with ethnicity must be clarified.

Several basic aspects of ethnicity have been emphasized in previous research. The major sociological argument has been that ethnic variation in social processes reflects the social class composition and urban concentration of ethnic groups. In extreme form this perspective reduces ethnicity to social class and related characteristics. Marxists, for example. tend to emphasize social class rather than ethnic cleavages as the basis for social differentiation. More specifically, ethnicity has been viewed as a manifestation of social class conflict and, therefore, the retention of ethnic distinctiveness represents a social problem that reflects class differences among ethnic groups. Hence, according to this formulation, only the poor, oppressed, lower socioeconomic groups retain ethnic identification. As ethnics move up socially and economically, ethnicity is shed as a major distinguishing characteristic. The more educated, occupationally successful, and middle and upper classes tend to be less ethnically identified. Thus, it is argued that, since ethnicity is the consequence of majority oppression, it is a remnant of an older social order that should be eliminated in modern society.

Undoubtedly, social class is an important element in ethnic community structure and affects the relationship between ethnicity and other social processes. Nevertheless, defining ethnicity solely in class terms raises the question: how and why are ethnic communities differentiated by social class, and what are the implications of such differentiation for major social processes? Furthermore, class factors may account for only part of the meaning of ethnicity. If so, an additional question must be posed: how do we explain the residual ethnic variations that go beyond social class?

A social class reductionist approach to ethnicity is inadequate for capturing its full meaning. Ethnicity and social class are different bases for making distinctions among groups and are not necessarily synonomous. Indeed, there are qualitative differences between ethnicity and class characteristics. Ethnic collectivities tend to be easier to organize than socioeconomic classes and ethnic boundaries are often more recognizable and rigid than are social class lines. Most importantly, social classes are by definition unequal and ranked, but such is not necessarily true for ethnic groups. Since ethnic group members are found at all levels of socioeconomic status, ethnicity is not reduceable solely to social class phenomena. The social class heterogeneity within ethnic groups, therefore, becomes an important research challenge for the systematic analysis of the ethnic factor.

Given the qualitative differences between ethnicity and social class, some have gone further and argued that ethnic group identification substitutes for a class identification where classes are not associated with strong affective ties and when issues are not class based (Bell, 1975). The recent reemergence (or recognition of the salience) of ethnicity suggests that with the blurring of class boundaries, ethnicity has become a more tangible basis for group cohesion in America. Ethnic identification may provide for many an alternative link to the broader society, compensating in part for the bureaucratic and impersonal qualities of modern life.

Although ethnic boundaries are more recognizable than class divisions and ethnic communities are more cohesive than social classes, the process of ethnic identification has a strong voluntary component. In this sense, ethnicity is neither an invariant ascriptive trait (at least for American whites) nor a primordial phenomenon from which deeply held identities emerge. Rather, ethnic group membership involves changing forms that, in turn, affect the ways in which identity is manifest (Horowitz, 1975). This is particularly important in defining ethnic group boundaries so that comparisons may be made between individuals and families who define themselves and are defined by others as members of specific ethnic groups.

An additional meaning of ethnicity derives from an emphasis on cultural factors associated with ethnic differences. Cultural change is one of the most conspicuous processes of ethnic assimilation and the most responsive to changing institutions and conditions of modern society. Nevertheless, acculturation does not necessarily imply the loss of ethnic identity or attachment to ethnic communities. The search, then, for the changing forms of ethnic identification must go beyond the isolation of cultural traits to consider structural elements that are the foundation of ethnic continuity. Indeed, one of the clearest findings of ethnic studies in America is that structural and cultural assimilation are different dimensions of ethnic change and there is no necessary conflict between structural pluralism and ethnic acculturation (Gordon, 1964; Barth, 1969; Greeley, 1974; Parsons, 1975).

Since ethnic continuity is not mainly dependent on cultural distinctiveness, some social scientists have identified the political dimension as the major factor in the maintenance of ethnic community structure. (See in particular, Glazer and Moynihan, 1970, 1975.) Ethnic group cohesiveness has been described as the result of conflict among ethnic groups and between ethnics and the majority over economic and social resources within the political system.

The community focus which results from attention to ethnic political interests is one approach which suggests the importance of directing research on ethnicity to the structural level. Other approaches which involve the structural level are the ecological (e.g., Lieberson, 1963) and, to some extent, those focusing on stratification and occupational concentration (Duncan and Duncan, 1968; Light, 1972). The ecological approach has been concerned primarily with analyzing residential segregation and concentration as indicators of ethnic continuity and community structure; occupational concentration has been used in similar fashion. Research combining these approaches at the structural level is rare (but see, especially, Smith, 1976; and Yancey et al., 1976). One important suggestion from this research is that structural-ecological circumstances in urban areas conditioned the evolution of ethnic communities and that new social-ecological configurations result in emerging new ethnic forms.

Two features of these research approaches are helpful in placing the analysis of ethnic continuity and change in a broader context: (1) emphasis is placed on the importance of ethnic communities as the bases for ethnic solidarity and (2) the social structural dimension is recognized as the key to understanding ethnic continuity. These two themes represent the theoretical underpinnings of the specific areas to be explored in our analysis of family and mobility processes among ethnic subpopulations.

THE RESEARCH FOCUS

The ensuing analysis of ethnicity focuses on systematic empirical evidence related to variation and change in family and mobility processes among white ethnic subcommunities. The community is the basic structural unit of society that has social qualities which cannot be analyzed fully either at the individual or national level. Overall patterns at the national level often fail to capture the nature of ethnic variation, since social processes associated with ethnicity are more localized and community oriented. The social structural component is often obscured by an emphasis on personal ethnic identification.

The analysis revolves around selected but fundamental processes of social life. These include marriage and family processes, stratification and social mobility, and residential concentration and residential change. These processes are examined individually and in their interdependence. If the ethnic factor emerges as a major differentiator of social processes, and if ethnicity has implications for community continuity and social life, then we should expect that ethnic variation and change will be reflected in these elementary but pervasive social phenomena.

Previous research for a variety of reasons, including the absence of basic data on ethnicity, has neglected an emphasis on systematic and comprehensive empirical evidence. A great deal of what is known about ethnic variation and change in America has been based on inferential rather than direct data or on evidence that is less than adequate for social scientific analysis. National surveys that have included data on ethnicity have been plagued by small numbers for specific ethnic groups and so have been unable to capture the rich details of ethnic heterogeneity. Furthermore, the necessarily broad geographic focus of research on the national level made it impossible to deal adequately with the community-level processes that are so central for the understanding of ethnicity. Thus, in many ways the study of ethnicity has a long tradition in American social science, yet little systematic empirical research has been carried out until quite recently. Previous research on ethnicity has been limited either in the weakness of the social structural data available or in the measures of ethnicity necessary for an adequate analysis.

The ethnic groups to be examined include three religious subpopulations—Protestants, Catholics, and Jews—and four Catholic ethnic groups—French Canadians, Irish, Italians, and Portuguese.[a] These ethnic subgroups present a wide range of social, economic, and cultural characteristics and some have never before been studied systematically and comparatively (particularly Portuguese and

---

[a]Nearly 98 percent of the total sample identified with one of the three religious groups and 79 percent of the Catholics belong to one of the four Catholic

French Canadians). The emphasis in these data is on white ethnics of basically European origins. Issues associated with racial, "deprived," or more conspicuous minorities (such as black, Chicano, Chinese, and Japanese Americans) will not be examined. The advantages of investigating white ethnics are that the extent of voluntary ethnic identification is greater and the timing of their community formation is sufficiently long to allow for an evaluation of ethnic continuity and change as well as the changing structure of ethnic communities.

In order to capture some of the dynamics of ethnic continuity, age cohorts will be used to infer retrospectively changes over time. Although generation has been more frequently used for this purpose, many problems in its interpretation have been encountered (Mannheim, 1952). Age seems to be both a more effective and more efficient single measure than generation, since it is not only highly correlated with generation, but also controls for both the effects of historical time periods and for life cycle effects that are fundamental in the examination of family and mobility processes.

As noted earlier, socioeconomic and class factors, while not synonymous with ethnicity, are crucial elements in understanding the ethnic factor. Measures of class position will be used in two ways in this research: (1) as a variable—i.e., in response to the analytic question, are the relationships between social class and the social processes of family formation, social mobility, and residential change differential within ethnic groups? and (2) as a control—to examine whether ethnic differences in social processes remain when the effects of socioeconomic status are controlled.

Similarly, life cycle processes relating age to family events such as marriage and childbirth have a powerful influence on the mobility processes considered in this research. The same questions may be raised for life cycle as for class: (1) Does life cycle affect social processes differentially for these ethnic subpopulations? and (2) do ethnic differences in these processes persist when the effects of life cycle are controlled?

The data on which this analysis of ethnic variation in family and mobility processes is based were drawn from three representative probability samples of the state of Rhode Island. These were household surveys conducted in 1967, 1968, and 1969, using a clustered, multistage stratified sample design. A total of 3,342 cases was available for analysis, resulting from an average response rate of 82

---

ethnic subcommunities. The remaining Catholics were too heterogeneous for classification as a separate subgroup. For group totals, see Appendix B.

percent.[b] (Varying portions of this total were used in this research. For details, see Appendix B.)

This data source is unusually valuable for the analysis of ethnicity, both because of the location of the study and its history, and because of the design of the surveys. Providence, the capital and dominant city in Rhode Island, was the eventual destination of many of the immigrants who came to the United States in the nineteenth and twentieth centuries. Like most of the cities of the eastern United States during this period, Providence developed large ethnic communities, first of the Irish, who left mid-nineteenth century Ireland for employment opportunities available abroad, and then, around the turn of the century, of Italians and Jews from Eastern Europe, who came in large numbers.

But ethnic heterogeneity in Rhode Island is not based as simply on the great pre-World War I trans-Atlantic movements as is the case in other areas. Beginning after the insurrection against the British in 1837, French Canadians moved southward into New England, so that in the period after the American Civil War a large community formed in Rhode Island, not in Providence, but in the more rural northern and northwestern parts of the state (Bouvier and Corless, 1968). In addition, the coastal fishing communities of Rhode Island and southeastern Massachusetts have attracted settlers from Portugal over a long period. As a result, separate ethnic communities, which were originally culturally, economically, and geographically distinct, have been characteristic of the Rhode Island population for several generations. And members of these communities have had several generations as well to respond to the changing economic and social opportunities of twentieth century America, as Rhode Island, like other parts of the country, has first urbanized and suburbanized (Mayer and Goldstein, 1958). One result of this long history is that those in both the Jewish and Catholic ethnic subpopulations are almost as likely to be native born as are the Protestants, with a distinctive proportion foreign born only among those age 65 and older.

Given this historical context, the design of the surveys was particularly valuable in several respects. By covering the entire state, ethnic communities which were not highly urban, such as the Portuguese and French Canadians, could be studied. This is important, since it has been a problem in ethnic research to separate the effects of urban residence and blue collar occupational status from more distinctively

---

[b]More details on these surveys are available in a report of the survey design and in the three monographs which have been based primarily on these data. See Organic and Goldstein, 1970; Speare et al., 1975; Bouvier and Rao, 1975; and Monteiro, 1976.

ethnic patterns. Further, many ethnic studies have been based on characteristics of a local ethnic community (Prior, 1932; Mindel and Habenstein, 1976). The inclusion of the entire state makes it possible in the analysis to distinguish those who remained in their communities from those who have moved out residentially, and thus to see how important ethnic residential concentration has been in the maintenance of other ethnic social characteristics. Finally, there is a wealth of detail on religion and national origin in these surveys, as well as data on the variety of social processes which form the basis for this study of ethnic continuity and community structure.

Since the data are drawn from a single state, the analysis shares many of the restrictions of case studies generally. However, although all case studies are unique, they may often shed a clearer light on more general social processes. As noted earlier, national data have been limited by the small number of cases available for the study of ethnicity, and by their lack of community focus. Moreover, the survey design includes the possibility of examining the differential characteristics of both in- and outmigrants, enabling the research to transcend somewhat its geographic restrictions (see, especially, Chapters 9 and 10). These data also present a unique theoretical opportunity. Many of the conclusions about ethnic social processes, particularly those on marriage and occupational choices, have been based on situations where the dynamics of minority status are operating. A substantial majority of the Rhode Island population is Catholic, thus making it possible to see how these social processes operate when majority-minority status is reversed from the national pattern.

For most of the analysis, ethnicity will be defined empirically for individuals by religious self-identification for Catholics, Protestants, and Jews, and for the other ethnics by the national origin of their father.[c] Because of the greater religious heterogeneity of French Canadians and Irish the analysis was limited to those whose fathers were Catholic. Only 1 to 2 percent of Italians or Portuguese had non-Catholic fathers. Using this definition, there were 396 Italian, 333 French Canadian, 202 Irish, and 108 Portuguese household heads in the sample.

The following analytic questions will be addressed in this research.

1. Are there ethnic variations in family and mobility processes?
2. Are there cohort differences in ethnic patterns reflecting changes over time that imply convergence or divergence in these processes?

---

[c]For intermarriage, where issues are somewhat more complex, ethnicity of both types is treated somewhat differently. For details, see Chapter 6.

3. Do family and mobility processes vary more among religious groups than among the Catholic ethnic groups?
4. How do class and life cycle factors affect these social processes within ethnic groups and are there socioeconomic subgroupings within ethnic groups that have been more characterized by change?
5. Does the ethnic factor remain salient in differentiating social processes when class and life cycle effects are controlled and is ethnic differentiation limited to particular socioeconomic subgroupings?
6. How do the social processes associated with family and mobility relate to ethnic continuity and ethnic community structure?

Answers to these questions are necessary if social science is to begin to understand the changing but continuing salience of ethnicity in modern life.

Part I

The Basic Structural Dimensions

✳ *Chapter 2*

Ethnic Stratification

In all societies individuals are differentiated and ranked hierarchically in a variety of ways. Age and sex are major elements of differentiation and ranking in most, if not all, societies. Similarly, social class and ethnicity (broadly defined) are sources of differentiation and have been the dominant sources of social stratification in American society. So powerful is the influence of social class that rarely is it meaningful to discuss ethnicity without considering elements of socioeconomic status. Moreover, analysis of the American class system is incomplete without considering the role of the ethnic factor. Perhaps the analysis of the intersection of social class and ethnicity provides the most fruitful direction for the systematic and comprehensive understanding of the nature of American social stratification (Gordon, 1964; Glazer and Moynihan, 1970; Greeley, 1974).

Most previous research has not focused directly on the complex intersections of class and ethnicity. Characteristic of most American social science is either the view that class and ethnic factors are alternative sources of strata formation or that ethnicity is but a subcategory of social class. In both views, ethnicity is treated as less significant and more transitory than social class. Clearly the focus on either factor to the exclusion of the other is truncated and incomplete. Moreover, despite the gray areas of overlap between ethnicity and class there may be significant dimensions of ethnicity that are independent of social class. To be sure, variation and change in ethnic communities are intimately tied to socioeconomic class factors. Differences between ethnic groups in a wide range of behavior and attitudes reflect these class factors. Assimilation, integration, and inequality of ethnic groups are related in part to their social class composition and to changes in their class structure. Nevertheless, the isolation of specific ethnic elements—cultural and structural— requires an extensive examination of the intersections of ethnicity and social class.

In this chapter several dimensions of the internal stratification of ethnic groups are explored. In particular, attention is directed to changes and variations in educational attainment, occupational status, and social class self-identification of different ethnic sub- populations. Comparisons of the social class composition of ethnic groups over time and relative to each other allow for an examination of differential patterns of social change and socioeconomic integra- tion. The analysis of the changing stratification of ethnic groups provides the foundation for understanding the dynamics of ethnic community change.

EDUCATIONAL ATTAINMENT

The first dimension of stratification that will be examined is the edu- cational pattern of ethnic groups. In general, education has been identified as a key factor affecting subsequent occupational status, income, and life-style. For ethnic minorities in America, education has been a major path toward integration and cultural assimilation.

The data on educational attainment will be presented separately for males and females; the dynamics of educational change for each of the ethnic subpopulations will be inferred from variation by two age cohorts—age 45 and over and below age 45. The distribution of education was divided into three categories: (1) at least some college education (high); (2) completed high school (medium); and (3) did not complete high school (low).

The focus of the ensuing analysis will be on educational variation and change among religious and Catholic ethnic subpopulations. Previous research has shown that educational differences between whites and blacks have widened over time. This has been the con- sequence of improvements among whites. Hence, the educational gap between races in America has increased. A second emerging pat- tern is the existence of sex differentials in educational attainment. Not only is the educational level of males higher than females but there has been little reduction in the gap between the sexes over time.

The patterns of educational differences by race are noteworthy not only for what they reveal about racial differences in America.

In the present context, the importance of these patterns lies in the questions they suggest about educational changes among ethnic populations over time and the distinctive trends for males and females. Have all ethnic groups increased their level of educational attainment? Has the gap between the educational level of men and women ethnics changed over time? Indeed, has there been educational divergence or convergence between ethnic subpopulations? Have educational inequalities been reduced for ethnic groups in the process of integration and change? These central issues are the focus of the ensuing analysis.

Education of Ethnic Men

The overall pattern of educational attainment of males of the three religious subpopulations shows a clear ranking of Jews in the highest levels followed by Protestants and Catholics (Table 2-1).[a] Almost 15 percent of the Catholic, 23 percent of the Protestant, and 57 percent of the Jewish males had at least some college education. Examining the lower end of the educational scale, 60 percent of the Catholic males did not complete high school compared to 40 percent of the Protestants and 14 percent of the Jews.

This overall educational ranking of Jews—Protestants—Catholics characterizes both age groups but differences among religious subgroups are accentuated for the older ages. While over half the Jewish males age 45 and over had at least some college education, about 20 percent of the Protestants and 8 percent of the Catholic older males had such high levels of education. Similarly, almost three-fourths of the older Catholic males did not complete high school and this was true of about half of the Protestants and less than one-third of the older Jewish males.

Over time, there has been a clear increase in the level of educational attainment for all three religious subpopulations. There has been a very sharp increase in college attendance among Catholics, from 8 percent to 22 percent, much sharper than among either Protestant or Jewish males. Thus, despite the retention of the third rank in educational level among the religious subpopulations, Catholics have narrowed the educational gap considerably. Differences between Protestant and Catholic males in college attendance have clearly diminished among the younger age cohorts. However, the gap between Protestants and Catholics at the lower end of the educational scale has increased: while there has been a decline in the

---

[a]These findings may be compared to those reported by Goldstein, 1969; Greeley, 1974.

Table 2-1. Educational Attainment by Ethnicity and Age: Males

Age and Education*	Protestants	Jews	Catholics	French Canadians	Irish	Italians	Portuguese
All Ages							
High	22.6	57.1	14.7	5.3	32.3	14.4	9.4
Medium	36.0	28.6	25.5	24.8	28.5	19.7	26.6
Low	41.4	14.3	59.8	69.9	39.2	65.9	64.1
Age 45 and Over							
High	19.9	52.9	8.2	5.0	20.0	8.9	3.2
Medium	25.6	17.6	17.7	15.0	22.9	13.0	16.1
Low	54.5	29.4	74.1	80.0	57.1	78.0	80.6
Below Age 45							
High	26.1	61.1	21.6	5.7	46.7	20.8	15.2
Medium	49.7	38.9	33.8	35.8	35.0	27.4	36.4
Low	24.2	0.0	44.6	58.5	18.3	51.9	48.5

*High = at least some college; medium = completed high school; low = did not complete high school.

proportion not completing high school for both Protestants and Catholics, the decline among Catholics has been slower. The combination of more rapid increase in the proportion of Catholics attending college and a slower decrease in the proportion not completing high school (relative to Protestants) suggests a trend toward educational bimodality or polarization among younger Catholics.

Part of this greater educational heterogeneity among younger Catholics may reflect ethnic variations within the Catholic subpopulation. Indeed, an examination of the data on the four ethnic Catholic subpopulations reveals considerable variations in educational levels and patterns of change over time. Overall, French Canadian, Italian, and Portuguese Catholic males are characterized by low levels of educational attainment (64-70 percent have not completed high school). The Irish stand out as the best educated among Catholic ethnic males. While there are no conspicuous differences between non-Irish Catholics at the lower end of the educational scale, there is some variation at the upper end of the educational scale. Examining the proportion having some college education shows that Italian males are better educated than Portuguese; French Canadians rank the lowest among all Catholic ethnics in the sample.

This overall educational ranking of Catholic ethnics (Irish, Italian, Portuguese, and French Canadian) holds in large part controlling for age. For both age groups, the Irish clearly stand out in terms of higher educational attainment and Italians rank higher than Portuguese or French Canadian males. French Canadians rank somewhat higher than the Portuguese in the older age cohort but improvements in education over time have been much slower for the French Canadians. In contrast, the Portuguese have tripled the proportion having some college education and reduced substantially the proportion not completing high school. Hence, among the younger ages the Portuguese have surpassed the educational level of the French Canadians and rank third among Catholic ethnics after Irish and Italians. Indeed, the high proportion of the younger French Canadian males who have not completed high school (60 percent) and the low proportion with some college education (6 percent) ranks this group the lowest educationally of all ethnic groups.

A closer look at the Italian pattern reveals significant heterogeneity. While the proportion having attended some college has more than doubled to 21 percent among the younger males, over half of the young Italians have not completed high school. Hence, the educational differences characterizing Italian, French Canadian, and Portuguese Catholics are mainly in the higher proportion of Italians attending college.

Of equal importance is the fact that the Irish level of educational attainment is higher than the general pattern noted earlier among Protestants. This is not true for the older ages where there are few educational differences between Protestant and Irish Catholic males. For the younger age cohort, 47 percent of the Irish have some college education and 18 percent have not completed high school. This compares to about one-fourth of the Protestants at both the high and low levels of the educational scale. This finding in combination with the noted educational heterogeneity among Catholic ethnics points unmistakably to the inadequacy of comparing educational levels between the broad categories of Protestants and Catholics. Moreover, educational variation within the Catholic subpopulation is significantly greater than between Catholics and Protestants. This is true when the level of education is compared controlling for age as well as when the patterns of educational change are examined over time.

Education of Ethnic Women

As with males, educational variation and change for ethnic women adds an important dimension to the understanding of ethnic stratification and social structure. Moreover, differences in the educational achievements of men and women over time reflect changing inequalities by sex within ethnic subpopulations. Of no less importance, the patterns of educational attainment for ethnic women may have significant implications for social processes associated with marriage and mobility. Data in Table 2-2 allow for a detailed examination of variation and change in the level of education of ethnic women.

The general pattern of educational differences between religious subpopulations noted for males characterizes females as well: Jewish women are much more concentrated in the higher educational categories than are Protestant or Catholic women. Educational differences between Protestant and Catholic women are much sharper than for males—over three times as many Protestant women have some college education compared to Catholic women. Catholic women clearly lag behind Catholic men in educational attainment relative to the Protestant pattern.

The overall sharp Protestant—Jewish differences in the educational attainment of women is much more conspicuous for the younger age cohort than among the older women: 56 percent of the Jewish women below age 45 had some college education compared to less than 20 percent of the Protestant women. An important point emerges when the pattern of educational change is examined over time for men and women. For Jewish men concentration in higher

Table 2-2. Educational Attainment by Ethnicity and Age: Females

Age and Education*	Protestants	Jews	Catholics	French Canadians	Irish	Italians	Portuguese
All Ages							
High	16.5	33.3	5.0	2.9	11.7	4.0	2.9
Medium	39.3	41.0	34.8	28.3	48.0	30.4	28.4
Low	44.2	25.6	60.2	68.8	40.2	65.6	68.6
Age 45 and Over							
High	14.7	17.4	1.9	1.1	4.1	0.7	0.0
Medium	32.5	43.5	20.8	13.6	40.2	14.6	10.5
Low	52.8	39.1	77.3	85.2	55.7	84.7	89.5
Below Age 45							
High	18.7	56.3	7.9	5.1	20.7	7.6	4.7
Medium	47.2	37.5	48.5	47.1	57.3	47.7	39.1
Low	34.1	6.3	43.6	47.8	22.0	44.7	56.3

*High = at least some college; medium = completed high school; low = did not complete high school.

19

educational levels characterizes the older age cohort—i.e., there appears to have been a relatively early emphasis of at least some college education among Jewish men. For Jewish women the move to college took longer than for men. For the older age cohort of women, the shift was clearly toward high school completion. The decline in the percentage not completing high school has been very sharp among women and virtually none of the young Jewish men or women do not complete high school.[b]

The difference in educational attainment between Protestant and Catholic women has diminished at the younger ages, particularly at the upper end of the educational scale. Of equal significance is the decline among Catholic women in the proportion not completing high school and a parallel increase in the proportion completing high school. While about one out of five older Catholic women at least completed high school, almost three out of five younger Catholic women at least completed high school. It is interesting to note that Catholic women below age 45 are in the approximate position of Jewish women of earlier generations (age 45 and over).

The educational heterogeneity within the Catholic subpopulation noted for males in large part characterizes female Catholic ethnics, with some important qualifications. Overall, Irish women are clearly further ahead educationally than other Catholic ethnics, with Italian women ranked second and no differences in the educational level of French Canadian and Portuguese women. The latter two Catholic ethnic groups are characterized by very low educational levels with seven out of ten women not completing high school and only 3 percent having some college education. Irish women are better educated than Protestants but only among the younger age cohort, a pattern paralleling males. The higher levels of education attained by Irish women relative to other Catholic ethnics characterizes both age groups but Italian women are ranked higher than French Canadian and Portuguese women only for the younger cohort. Unlike the male pattern, there are few systematic differences in the educational levels of French Canadian and Portuguese women. Even among the younger cohort, only 5 percent of these ethnic women go to college and about half do not complete high school.

Clearly the Irish Catholic women have increased their education to a level higher than other American Catholic ethnics. However, Italian women have made the most dramatic progress educationally, given their initial low levels of education. The proportion of Italian women not completing high school declined from 85 percent to

---

[b]For similar trends based on other data sources cf. Goldstein and Goldscheider, 1968; Goldstein, 1969.

45 percent and the proportion completing at least high school increased from 15 percent to 55 percent when older and younger women are compared.

A final type of comparison that may be made relates to the relative educational levels of men and women of various ethnic subpopulations. A simple comparison of the data in Tables 2-1 and 2-2 shows that for every ethnic and age category a higher proportion of men compared to women have had at least some college education. The reverse pattern, i.e., the greater concentration of women at the lower end of the educational scale, is true generally but with exceptions of Protestants and Irish among the older cohort and French Canadian and Italian Catholics among the younger cohort.

Two general issues may be addressed in the educational comparisons of men and women: First, what are the patterns of ethnic variation in the relative magnitude of differences in educational levels attained by men and women? Second, have there been differential changes over time in the educational gap between men and women of various ethnic subpopulations?

To answer these questions, data in Table 2-3 show the proportion of women relative to men who have had some college education. The higher the proportion, the greater the relative gap in educational levels between men and women in favor of the former. For example, about 50 percent fewer white women have had some college education compared to white men and that relative gap has remained fairly constant over time despite increases for both sexes in the proportion attending college. An examination of these data points to several major findings:

1. The educational gap between Protestant men and women has been relatively steady over time and smaller than the gap between Catholic men and women. The relatively large educational gap between Jewish men and women has been reduced considerably for the younger age cohort.

2. The educational achievement of Jewish women (relative to Jewish men) has improved mainly because of the sharper increase in college attendance among Jewish women. Over time an even more dramatic decline in the educational gap between men and women characterizes French Canadians, but this is the result of a very different pattern of change. The reduced educational gap for French Canadian men and women emerges because the proportion of French Canadian women having some college education increased significantly while the proportion of French Canadian males having some higher education has been fairly stable and low over time.

3. There has been a general narrowing of the sex gap in educational attainment for all ethnic groups but the gap is still larger for

Table 2-3. Relative Differences between the Proportion of Males and Females Having Attended College by Ethnicity and Age*

	All Ages	Age 45 and Over	Below Age 45
Total	49.7	51.8	50.2
Protestants	27.0	26.1	28.4
Jews	41.7	67.1	7.9
Catholics	66.0	76.8	63.4
French Canadians	45.3	78.0	10.5
Irish	63.8	79.5	55.7
Italians	72.2	92.1	63.5
Portuguese	69.2	100.0	69.1

*This represents the absolute difference in the proportion of males having attended college minus the proportion of females having attended college divided by the proportion males having attended college (M-F÷M).

Catholics than Protestants and has become larger for Protestants than Jews. For older age cohorts the gap in the educational attainment of men and women is greater between Protestants and Catholics than between Catholic ethnic subpopulations and this is the case for the younger cohort, as well, except for French Canadians. Hence, it appears that religion may play a more important role in differentiating male and female roles (at least in terms of education) than ethnic variations within religious groups.

OCCUPATIONAL STATUS

The second major dimension of ethnic stratification that will be examined relates to occupational status. Unlike educational attainment, which is relatively concentrated in the life cycle and less affected by marriage and childbearing, occupation shifts may occur throughout a larger portion of the adult life cycle. Moreover, because of the complications of childbearing and the possibility of status competition with the husband (see Oppenheimer, 1977, for an examination of these issues), the analysis of occupational status will be limited to males. Occupations may shift not only within the life cycle but are responsive to macro economic changes that characterize society. Hence, examination of occupational changes for various age cohorts spread over a fifty-year period may reflect a combination of intragenerational, intergenerational as well as occupational distribution shifts within society (see Chapters 7 and 8).

These overall difficulties of analysis are accentuated among ethnic groups that differ in terms of age and life cycle and have various patterns of occupational concentration and change. Two measures of occupational status will be used in an attempt to overcome or standardize for some of these methodological difficulties. For each ethnic group we shall examine measures of current occupation as well as occupation at age 25 (initial occupation). Clearly for the older age cohorts current occupation is problematic, while examination of occupation at age 25 for younger cohorts is not very different from current occupation. The use in this chapter of both measures is to examine the relative consistency of the patterns of ethnic occupational status.[c] Current occupation and occupation at age 25 were coded to allow for a general subdivision into four occupational prestige rankings based on the Duncan scale (Reiss, 1961). While such a ranking is not without limitations, it appears to be a more reliable way of capturing prestige than the use of broad occupational categories.

It should be noted that there is a strong relationship between these four occupational ranks and the more standard occupational classification. For example, 84 percent of those occupations in the highest rank were high white collar and 88 percent of those occupations in the lowest rank were low blue collar. Over 90 percent of the low white collar occupations were ranked in the higher two ranks and 87 percent of the high blue collar occupations were ranked in the middle two levels. Thus, the four occupational ranks are closely related to divisions into high and low white and blue collar. The total white population was used as a basis for classifying the occupational distributions into four ranks of nearly equal size.

Comparing the distributions of current occupational status of Protestants and Catholics there are remarkably few differences (Table 2-4). Only a slightly higher proportion of Catholics are ranked at the lower end of the occupational scale when compared to Protestants. In contrast to the occupational similarity of Protestants and Catholics, Jews are more heavily concentrated at the upper ranks with only an insignificant proportion at the lower end.

These overall patterns of occupational similarity of Protestants and Catholics are distorted by cohort differences.[d] Indeed, comparing the occupational distributions of Protestants and Catholics shows that over time there has not only been a narrowing of the differences but among the young, Catholics appear to be located in higher ranked occupations than Protestants. For example, among the oldest age cohort twice as many Catholics as Protestants are concentrated in the lowest ranked occupations and twice as many

---

[c]A comparison of current and past occupational patterns will be made in Chapter 8 to measure intragenerational career mobility.

[d]Unlike the educational distribution which could be presented by two age groupings without distortions, the distribution of occupation showed differential patterns by detailed age groupings. Hence, a fourfold age breakdown will be used.

Table 2-4. Occupational Rank,* Current and at Age 25, by Religion and Age: Males

Age and Occupational Rank	Protestants Current	Age 25	Jews Current	Age 25	Catholics Current	Age 25
All Ages						
I	21.0	18.9	67.2	52.3	21.2	14.2
II	23.5	29.0	25.0	36.4	25.7	24.8
III	27.2	23.1	6.3	6.8	27.8	26.7
IV	18.3	29.0	1.6	4.5	25.3	34.3
65 and Over						
I	22.9	15.7	—	—	8.9	4.1
II	23.7	32.5	—	—	19.3	17.6
III	32.2	19.3	—	—	27.7	22.3
IV	21.2	32.5	—	—	44.1	56.1
45-64						
I	32.1	16.0	58.1	40.9	16.7	9.4
II	23.2	30.8	29.0	45.5	26.7	25.2
III	26.6	23.6	9.7	9.1	28.8	26.9
IV	18.1	28.6	3.2	4.5	27.8	38.5
35-44						
I	39.2	23.2	84.6	—	25.5	14.8
II	20.8	24.4	15.4	—	26.5	25.8
III	24.6	23.2	0.0	—	27.0	31.7
IV	15.4	29.3	0.0	—	20.9	27.7
25-34						
I	27.6	22.2	66.7	—	31.7	30.6
II	26.8	25.9	25.0	—	26.9	27.7
III	26.8	25.9	8.3	—	26.9	22.8
IV	18.9	25.9	0.0	—	14.5	18.9

*I = Duncan scale values 59 to 97; II = 34 to 58; III = 18 to 33; IV = 1 to 17.

Protestants as Catholics are concentrated in the highest ranked occupations. In contrast a higher proportion of young Catholics compared to Protestants are concentrated in the highest ranked jobs and a higher proportion of young Protestants compared to Catholics are concentrated in the lowest ranked jobs. Similarly, while 55 percent of the Protestants in both the 45-64 and 25-34 age cohorts were concentrated in the top two ranked occupational categories, the Catholic proportion increased from 43 percent to almost 60 percent. Hence, the initial gap in current occupation favoring Protestants has been clearly eliminated and in fact reversed for the youngest age cohort.

The same patterns emerge using occupation at age 25 as a measure of occupational status. Differences between Protestants and Catholics are somewhat sharper overall using initial occupation but are in the same direction. For the youngest age cohort, 58 percent of the Catholics enter the labor force in the top half of the occupational ranks (at age 25) compared to 48 percent of the Protestants. The higher occupational prestige of Catholics is clearly a recent phenomenon. Comparing older age cohorts it becomes evident that Catholics entering the labor force (occupation at age 25) in the late 1940s and 1950s (who were age 35-44 in the late 1960s) had lower initial occupational ranks than Protestants and this is certainly the case for Catholics who were age 25 and entering the labor force in the 1920s through World War II (i.e., age 45 and over in the late 1960s).

To the extent that these reconstructed data on occupations at age 25 are reliable, they suggest unequivocally that the occupational gap between Protestants and Catholics was characteristic only up to the end of the 1950s. Beginning in the 1960s Catholic males entering the labor force were ranked in terms of occupational status equal to or better than Protestants, on the average. Thus, in contrast to the educational data that show a closing but not yet closed gap between Protestant and Catholic levels, occupational status data show a closed gap and an improved ranking of Catholics over Protestants among the youngest cohort. These aggregate patterns suggest that education for Catholics is not as important a vehicle for status attainment as it is for Protestants. Particularly in a community where Catholics predominate, family-ethnic ties may play a more important role than education in occupational achievement—at least at initial occupational levels. It is clear from these aggregate data that Catholic occupational rank (relative to Protestants) is less directly related to education and that the path to occupational status for Catholics differs from that of Protestants and Jews.

In an attempt to clarify the relationship between education and occupation for Protestants and Catholics, data were prepared showing the educational origins of those in the highest occupational ranks (current and initial) and the initial and current occupational achievements of those with at least some college education. These inflow and outflow data relating to education and occupation are presented in Table 2-5 for two cohorts of Protestants and Catholics— age 25-34 and age 45-64. The patterns that emerge from these data are remarkable evidence for the power of ethnic factors in facilitating occupational achievements.

The first indication of differential paths to occupational achievement for religious subpopulations comes from an analysis of inflows to the highest occupational rank from various levels of education. Protestants in the highest ranked occupation are more likely to have

Table 2-5. Inflows to Highest Occupational Rank* (Current and Initial) from Education and Outflows from Highest Educational Level to Occupational Rank (Current and Initial) by Religion and Age

	Protestants		Catholics	
	25–34	45–64	25–34	45–64
Inflows to Highest Current Occupational Rank				
Education				
High	60	65	60	47
Medium	41	25	32	29
Low	0	10	8	4
Inflows to Highest Initial Occupational Rank				
Education				
High	53	79	53	44
Medium	47	17	39	21
Low	0	4	9	35
Outflows from Highest Educational Level				
Current Occupational Rank				
I	59	65	77	69
II	19	17	21	24
III & IV	22	10	3	7
Outflows from Highest Educational Level				
Initial Occupational Rank				
I	42	63	77	39
II	32	30	18	50
III & IV	26	7	5	11

*I = Duncan scale values 59 to 97; II = 34 to 58; III = 18 to 33; IV = 1 to 17.

high educational levels than are Catholics. Almost eight out of ten Protestants age 45-64 whose initial occupation (at age 25) was in the highest rank had some college education compared to 44 percent of the Catholics; none of the younger Protestants whose initial or current occupational rank was high had less than a complete high school education compared to 8-9 percent of the Catholics. Moreover, the cohort patterns show differential changes over time in this relationship for Protestants and Catholics. While the proportion of Catholics in the highest ranked occupations who have high education increases over time (from 47 percent to 60 percent for current occupational rank and from 44 to 53 percent for initial occupational rank), the reverse characterizes the Protestants (declining from 65 percent to 60 percent for current occupational rank and from 79 percent to 53 percent for initial occupational rank). Hence, while the educational path to higher occupational achievement seems to characterize Catholics less than Protestants, the trend over time is clearly toward convergence.

For Protestants of the older cohort, the proportion with higher education in the highest initial and current occupational rank was about the same; for Catholics, education plays a more significant role in current than in initial occupational rank. The contrasts in the importance of high education for high occupational rank between Protestants and Catholics are therefore greater for initial than current occupations and for older than younger cohorts and most pronounced for initial occupational rank of the older cohort.

The fact that the path to higher occupational rank for Catholics is less associated with high education than for Protestants does not imply that Catholics with high education do not have high ranked occupations. To the contrary: Catholics with at least some college education are more likely than similarly educated Protestants to have high ranked occupations, initially and currently. Over three-fourths of the younger Catholics with at least some college education enter the labor force and are currently in the highest ranked occupations compared to 42 percent (initial occupational rank) and 59 percent (current occupational rank) of the better educated Protestants. Over time the proportion of better educated Catholics entering and currently in the highest ranked occupations has increased (more for initial than for current occupational rank) while for Protestants the reverse has occurred: fewer young, educated Protestants enter or are currently in high ranked occupations than older Protestants. Moreover, while only 39 percent of the older Catholics with high educations entered the labor force in the highest occupational rank, 69 percent are currently in the highest occupational rank. Hence, high education did not automatically mean the best initial jobs for Catholics of an older generation nor does the lack of some college education preclude the achievement initially or subsequently of a high ranked occupation among young Catholics.

Thus, these data strongly support the suggestion emerging from the aggregate data that education is less necessary a mechanism for occupational success for Catholics than for Protestants. This finding combined with the fact that over three-fourths of better educated Catholics enter and are currently in the highest occupational rank (much higher than for Protestants) points in the direction of the importance of specific ethnic factors in Catholic occupational success. This is particularly the case where Catholics have become a majority and when the control over resources may have moved from Protestants to Catholics. Not only do these ethnic factors operate in moving the less educated into the highest ranked jobs but facilitate greatly the entrance of the better educated into the highest occupational ranks.

Part of the higher occupational status of young Catholics relative to Protestants may be clarified by examining ethnic variation among Catholics. The pattern of occupational variation among Catholic ethnics is of significance because of the differential changes that have occurred and because of the growing dichotomy developing between Irish and Italian Catholics, on the one hand, and French Canadian and Portuguese Catholics, on the other.

Examining the overall patterns of occupational distribution for the four Catholic ethnic groups reveals a clear and unmistakable fourfold ranking for both current occupation and occupation at age 25 (Table 2-6). The proportion in the top two occupational categories is Irish (61 percent), Italian (48 percent), French Canadian (37 percent), and Portuguese (31 percent). The same Catholic ethnic pattern emerges when occupation at age 25 is used and when the top occupational level alone is examined.

These patterns, however, are clearly distorted by age variations within these ethnic Catholic populations and the different relationships between cohort generation (as indicated by age) and occupational status among ethnic Catholics. The Irish stand out as being at the top of the occupational hierarchy among ethnic Catholics. For the oldest age cohorts, over half of the Irish are in the upper ranks of the status hierarchy, over twice the proportion of any other ethnic Catholic group. There was little change among the Irish in this ranking between the 65 and over and 45-64 age groups. The significant shifts from the second to the top occupational rank and out of the bottom two ranks occur for the 35-44 age group and continue for the youngest cohort. Thus, fully 70 percent of the Irish age 25-34 are in the top two occupational ranks and only 10 percent are in the lowest occupational rank.

Italian Catholics generally occupy the second rank among ethnic Catholics but have a pattern of changes in occupational distribution distinct from the Irish. There has been a decrease for Italians in the lowest rank occupations from the 65 and over age group to the 45-64 age group, and their concentration at the highest occupational rank has more than doubled. This occupational redistribution process toward the higher ranks continues for the 35-44 cohort to a growing

Table 2-6. Occupational Rank,* Current, and at Age 25, by Catholic Ethnic Groups and Age: Males

Age and Occupational Rank	French Canadians		Irish		Italians		Portuguese	
	Current	Age 25	Current	Age 25	Current	Age 25	Current	Age 25
All Ages								
I	16.4	9.0	30.0	22.2	21.7	12.5	13.4	6.3
II	21.0	19.5	30.8	40.9	26.8	23.3	17.6	12.5
III	35.3	34.1	23.3	19.9	24.8	24.4	27.5	25.0
IV	27.3	37.5	15.8	17.0	26.8	39.7	41.5	56.3
65 and Over								
I	10.1	4.0	15.2	8.0	6.0	2.9	0.0	0.0
II	14.5	20.0	36.4	36.0	18.0	8.6	5.6	0.0
III	31.9	34.0	30.3	20.0	38.0	20.0	22.2	14.3
IV	43.5	42.0	18.2	36.0	48.0	68.6	72.2	85.7
45-64								
I	16.2	6.1	22.0	16.4	15.3	5.6	7.0	8.1
II	19.1	13.3	29.0	43.3	29.0	26.3	19.3	10.8
III	36.8	30.6	28.0	22.4	25.7	23.4	26.3	21.6
IV	27.9	50.0	21.0	17.9	30.1	44.4	47.4	59.5
35-44								
I	15.8	6.9	43.9	32.6	27.9	11.7	16.7	0.0
II	24.2	23.6	31.6	41.9	25.4	20.8	13.3	10.0
III	35.8	44.4	14.0	16.3	24.6	33.8	33.3	25.0
IV	24.2	25.0	10.5	9.3	22.1	33.8	36.7	65.0
25-34								
I	23.4	23.4	40.0	30.6	34.4	37.3	27.0	12.0
II	26.0	25.5	30.0	38.9	29.0	29.4	24.3	24.0
III	35.1	25.5	20.0	19.4	21.5	15.7	27.0	36.0
IV	15.6	25.5	10.0	11.1	15.1	17.6	21.6	28.0

*I = Duncan scale values 59 to 97; II = 34 to 58; III = 18 to 33; IV = 1 to 17.

equalization among all four occupational ranks and an increase in the top rank from 15 to 28 percent. Thus, the change over time toward the highest ranked occupations for Italians has been much less abrupt than for the Irish.

The French Canadian occupational pattern shows very slow changes upward that start with the 45-64 age cohort. The changing proportion in the top two ranked occupational categories for French Canadians is 35 percent to 40 percent to 50 percent for the youngest three cohort age groupings. The most conspicuous change for French Canadians is for the youngest cohort and contrasts to the Italian experience where the 35-44 age cohort experienced the most rapid increase in occupational rank and to the Irish where the most dramatic shift was for the 45-64 age cohort.

The Portuguese start out with a very high concentration in the lowest occupational categories (72 percent of the oldest Portuguese are in the lowest ranked occupation measured by current occupation and 85 percent measured by initial occupation). The significant shift among the Portuguese has been out of this lowest occupational category from 72 percent for the oldest to 22 percent for the youngest cohort. While there has also been a shift into the top ranked occupations (from 7 percent of the 45-64 cohort to 27 percent of the 25-34 cohort), the redistribution has been mainly toward the middle two ranks.

In cohort terms, the Catholic ethnic patterns imply that the Irish have been on top occupationally throughout the period under examination. The Italians move into the second rank only for the cohorts below age 45. The youngest cohort of Italian males is rapidly approaching the occupation level of the Irish. The Portuguese have been on the bottom but are reducing the gap in occupational status with the French Canadians. Moreover, the almost equal distribution of Portuguese age 25-34 in the four occupational levels parallels the distribution of Italians age 35-44 and the distribution of the Irish age 45-64. These occupational patterns clearly reflect the differential socioeconomic integration of these Catholic ethnic subpopulations over time.

Thus, while the overall ethnic Catholic rankings in occupational status reveal an unambiguous fourfold ranking, younger Catholics tend to be ranked occupationally into two patterns—Irish-Italian and French Canadian-Portuguese. It should be noted that the French Canadian rank in occupation contrasts with their poorer educational ranking vis-à-vis the Portuguese. In general, the emerging dichotomous occupational ranking of young Catholic ethnics and the retention of a fourfold rank of Catholic ethnics in educational attainment suggests again that the role of education is differential *within* the Catholic population as is the case *between* Catholics and Protestants.[e] Indeed, it is clear that the superior Catholic occupational concentration relative to Protestants that was noted earlier is an Irish-Italian pattern and does not hold for the other two Catholic ethnic subgroups. Irish Catholics have a greater concentration in the better ranked current and initial occupations compared to Protestants starting with the 35–44 age cohort and this pattern characterizes Italians of the youngest cohort.

An examination of the relationship between education and occupation for Catholic ethnic groups is limited by the small number of Portuguese in the highest occupational rank and educational level. However, the educational origins of French Canadians, Irish, and Italians in the highest occupational rank reveal significant differences (Table 2-7). Less than one-fourth of the young French Canadians

Table 2-7. Inflows to Highest Current Occupational Rank* from Education** and Outflows from Highest Educational Level to Current Occupational Rank for Catholic Ethnic Groups by Age

Catholic Ethnic Group and Age	Inflows to Highest Current Occupational Rank			Outflows from Highest Educational Level		
	Education			*Current Occupational Rank*		
	High	*Medium*	*Low*	*I*	*II*	*III&IV*
French Canadians						
25–34	22.2	66.7	11.1	—	—	—
45–64	19.0	47.6	33.3	—	—	—
Irish						
25–34	90.5	9.5	0.0	90.5	4.8	4.8
45–64	83.3	0.0	16.7	55.6	33.3	11.1
Italians						
25–34	62.1	27.6	10.3	66.7	29.6	3.7
45–64	50.0	19.2	30.8	76.5	23.5	0.0

*I = Duncan scale values 59 to 97; II = 34 to 58; III = 18 to 33; IV = 1 to 17.
**High = at least some college; medium = completed high school; low = did not complete high school.

---

[e]A direct examination of these patterns appears in Chapter 8.

in the highest occupational rank have at least some college education compared to 62 percent of the Italians and 90 percent of the Irish. The same pattern holds for the older cohort. Clearly the French Canadians have not attained their higher ranked occupations through higher educational levels. For all three ethnic groups, there has been an increase in the level of education by occupational rank between the older and younger cohorts.

Not only are the educational origins of the Irish in higher ranked occupations very high but the proportion of those with at least some college education who are in the highest occupational rank is high as well. Furthermore, there has been a very sharp increase in the proportion of the better educated Irish who are in the highest ranked occupations: from 56 percent for those 45-64 years of age to 90 percent for the youngest cohort. The pattern for Italians is reversed: somewhat fewer educated Italians are in the highest occupational ranks for the younger than the older ages.

Although the range of occupations within the highest rank is substantial and only some require higher education, it is clear that the role of education in occupational success is substantially different for the three Catholic ethnic groups. Moreover, the relationship between education and occupational achievement for Catholic ethnics differs from the overall Protestant pattern.

SUBJECTIVE SOCIAL CLASS

In addition to the standard variables of educational attainment and occupational status that measure objectively different dimensions of stratification, the subjective perceptions of individuals of their social class ranking may be used as a basis for analyzing social class. Undoubtedly, there are limitations and ambiguities in using subjective social class identification as the sole or major criterion of stratification. However, the lack of consistency between dimensions of stratification—objective and subjective—may not necessarily imply that some measures are "better" than others but that different measures capture various aspects of a complex social ranking that is inherently multidimensional (Matras, 1975, pp. 103-107; Hodge and Treiman, 1968; Runciman, 1966).

In an attempt to examine ethnic variation and change in a wide range of stratification contexts data were obtained on self-identification of social class.[f] This self-assignment of social class adds an important subjective criterion in the analysis of ethnic groups since they may

---

[f]For specific questions see Appendix A.

exhibit tendencies toward inconsistencies for several dimensions of social stratification. For all ethnic and age groupings, subjective social class tended to be defined by respondents into one of two distinct categories: (1) middle class and (2) working class, with but a marginal percentage of the population defining themselves as either upper or lower class.[g] Hence, the analysis will focus on the proportion defining themselves as at least middle class (including the small proportion defining themselves as upper class). These data by age and ethnicity are presented in Table 2-8.

In general, the pattern of subjective social class reveals very little relative variation by age for each of the various ethnic subpopulations. Hence, the use of age as an indicator of generation and, more particularly, the use of cross-sectional data by age to infer longitudinal patterns may be less appropriate for subjective social class measures than for measures such as education that change relatively little after age 25.

Despite the relative stability of subjective social class between age groups within ethnic subpopulations, considerable variation by ethnicity (controlling for age) emerges. First, religious differences in the proportion defining themselves as middle or upper class are quite pronounced. Almost nine out of ten Jews define themselves as upper or middle class compared to about six out of ten Protestants and five out of ten Catholics. This rank in subjective social class (Jewish, Protestant, Catholic) holds for each age group. The smallest relative differences among religious subpopulations in social class self-identification occur for the youngest cohort, but differences remain

Table 2-8. **Proportion Defining Self as Upper or Middle Class by Ethnicity and Age**

	All Ages	65 and over	45-64	35-44	25-34
Total	54.7	55.1	53.0	54.5	57.8
Protestants	63.0	69.6	57.5	66.3	61.4
Jews	87.8	85.7	86.2	94.1	85.7
Catholics	49.5	45.1	48.6	48.6	55.0
French Canadians	43.0	36.1	40.8	47.2	50.5
Irish	62.3	71.0	56.2	59.7	66.7
Italians	50.6	41.3	50.7	46.6	64.0
Portuguese	37.2	41.2	27.3	40.5	45.5

[g]Similar findings have been reported in national American surveys. See, for example, Hodge and Treiman, 1968.

substantial: Among those 25–34 years of age, 86 percent of the Jews, 61 percent of the Protestants, and 55 percent of the Catholics define themselves as middle or upper class. Part of the narrowing of the Protestant-Catholic gap in self-identification is a clear increase in the proportion of Catholics defining themselves as upper or middle class. Of no less significance is the decline in the proportion of Protestants defining themselves as middle or upper class: from 70 percent of the older cohort of Protestants to 61 percent of the Protestants age 25–34.

Second, ethnic variation within the Catholic subpopulation in the proportion defining themselves as upper or middle class is substantial. The proportion of Irish defining themselves as upper or middle class is similar to the Protestant level; among the youngest cohort a larger proportion of Irish Catholics define themselves as middle or upper class than do Protestants. Lower ranked than the Irish are the Italians who, in turn, are followed by French Canadians and Portuguese. With some variation this subjective social class rank within the Catholic subpopulation holds by age. Finally, there is an unmistakable convergence in the proportion defining themselves as middle or upper class among the four Catholic ethnic subpopulations. The diminishing differences among Catholic ethnic subpopulations are the result of slow but steady increases among French Canadian and Portuguese ethnics, sharper changes among Italians with minor alterations among the Irish.

Hence, the youngest age cohort is characterized by a growing dichotomy among ethnic Catholics that parallels the pattern noted for occupational status. There are relatively small differences between young Italian and Irish Catholics in the proportion defining themselves as upper or middle class. Subjective social class differences between young Portuguese and French Canadians are also small but lag behind the Irish-Italian pattern. Indeed, for the younger age cohort, the Catholic ethnic gap in subjective social class is wider than the gap between Protestants and Catholics.

The analysis of the several dimensions of ethnic stratification points clearly in the direction of variation and differential change for the various subpopulations examined. Although some trend toward the reduction of inequalities has been observed, there still remains enormous diversity among ethnic groups in the patterns of educational attainment, occupational status, and social class self-identification. Since social class is a major differentiator of social processes, it follows that class factors must be treated as central variables in the examination of ethnic variation and change in social processes. To the extent that differences in marriage and mobility vary by ethnicity, the differential social class composition of ethnic sub-populations must be taken into consideration as factors explaining such variation. If ethnic differences are solely a function of social class concentration, our analytic questions are directed to understanding the evolution of differential internal stratification and inequality in ethnic communities. If ethnic differences in social processes persist within social class categories, the analytic focus shifts to other, more specifically ethnic elements—cultural or structural—that may account for differences between ethnic groups. In either case, social class factors must be viewed as critical dimensions in the analysis of ethnic communities.

※ *Chapter 3*

The Marital Cycle

The formation and dissolution of families through marriage, separation, divorce, and remarriage are basic processes of social life. Group continuity and demographic survival have been based on the extent of marriage and the transmission to the next generation of cumulative social and cultural patterns. For ethnic groups the extent of marriage takes on additional significance as a mechanism for subgroup continuity, structurally and culturally. Of equal importance are the consequences of variation and change in marriage formation and dissolution patterns for other social processes. Not only is the extent of marriage shaped by the socioeconomic and demographic conditions in society but it has obvious implications for a wide range of social processes.

There is a long tradition of research in marriage patterns, particularly among social scientists using census materials (see in particular, Glick, 1957; Glick and Parke, 1965; Glick and Norton, 1973). The focus has usually been on changes in the extent of marriage as one response to population pressures and rising economic opportunities in the early stages of modernization (cf. Davis, 1963; Dixon, 1971; Chamratrithirong, 1976), on the contrasts between Western and non-Western patterns of celibacy (Hajnal, 1965), or on differentials in marital stability for socioeconomic and racial subpopulations (Carter and Glick, 1976; Bernard, 1966; Billingsley, 1968). The detailed analysis of broader ethnic differentials and changes in marriage formation and dissolution has been neglected, mainly because of the absence of adequate data.

This chapter focuses on variation in the extent and stability of marriage among Protestants, Jews, and Catholics, and among Catholic ethnic subgroups (French Canadians, Irish, Italians, and Portuguese).[a] Specifically, variations and changes in the proportions ever-marrying and remaining celibate (never-marrying), the velocity of remarriage, and separation will be investigated for the seven ethnic subpopulations. Moreover, the interaction of social class and ethnicity in affecting variation and changes in the formation and dissolution of families will be analyzed.

THE EXTENT OF MARRIAGE[b]

The first dimension of marriage that may be examined with the data available is the proportion ever-marrying. Data in Table 3-1 show very high rates of ever-marriage for all subgroups and for men and women. As is true of the United States as a whole, over 90 percent of men and women over the age of 25 have been married at least once. Stated in reverse form, the proportion never-marrying is very low for both sexes and all ages.

If getting married is almost universal, how does it vary by religious and Catholic ethnic subpopulations? Differences in the proportions ever-marrying between Protestants and Catholics are very small and no systematic pattern by cohort emerges. Nevertheless, the Catholic pattern is heterogeneous. In particular, the Irish stand out in terms of lower ever-marriage rates compared to all other groups considered. Overall, 15 percent of Irish men and women never marry, a pattern that is more pronounced for the older cohorts. Fully 20 percent of the Irish over age 65 have never married, a level that is four times that of other subgroups for males and about twice as high as other female ethnics. At the opposite end of the continuum are the older Italians where only a small proportion (none of the Italian males over age 65 and only 4 percent of the Italian females) have never been married.

The Jewish pattern does not differ substantially from that of Protestant and Catholic males, but there is a very high level of marriage among Jewish women: 97 percent of Jewish women in the sample have been married. The virtually universal marriage pattern among Jewish women is higher than that for non-Jewish women and higher than for Jewish males. For both Jewish men and women, the proportion ever-married has increased over time.

---

[a] Age at marriage is the subject of Chapter 5.

[b] An earlier version of the analysis of these data on the marital cycle was presented at the 1977 meetings of the Population Association of America (Kobrin and Goldscheider, 1977).

Table 3-1. Percentage Ever-Married by Ethnicity, Sex, and Age

Sex and Age	Total	Protestants	Jews	Catholics	French Canadians	Irish	Italians	Portuguese
Males								
Total	92	92	92	93	95	85	96	94
25–44	91	92	95	91	95	85	93	94
45–64	92	90	88	94	95	89	98	92
65+	95	95	—	95	95	80	100	—
Females								
Total	92	92	97	93	93	85	94	97
25–44	95	94	100	95	94	93	94	100
45–64	91	93	100	91	93	83	92	94
65+	88	89	91	88	91	80	96	—

This has not been the pattern for non-Jews. Over time there has been a clear increase in the proportions ever-marrying among Protestant and Catholic women but a reverse tendency among men. Hence, among the older cohorts, women are more likely never to have married, while among the younger age groups the proportion never-married is significantly higher among males. Among the Irish, a significant decline may be noted in the proportion never-marrying— sharper among women than men. Indeed, for the youngest cohort of women, there are no differences between religious or Catholic ethnic groups (including the Irish) in the extent of ever-marrying; for males age 25–44, the Irish continue to have higher rates of celibacy than the non-Irish. With but minor exceptions, non-Irish Catholics have higher rates of ever-marriage compared to Protestants of both sexes and all ages, while the Irish have lower rates of ever-marriage when compared to Protestants.

Thus, a trend toward ethno-religious convergence in the proportion never-married may be discerned, with the exception of the youngest cohort of Irish males. This may reflect somewhat later age at marriage among Irish males (see Chapter 5). Judging by the experience of the 45–64 age cohort, it appears likely that the 15 percent never-married among the youngest cohort of Irish males may decline to around the same level as other ethnic subgroups as some of the Irish males delaying marriage marry.

The convergence in the proportion married by ethnicity is complemented by convergence by sex. Among older women of each ethnic group, the proportion never-married is higher than the proportion never-married among older males. In contrast, the proportion never-married among the youngest cohort is consistently lower for females than males.

SEPARATION AND REMARRIAGE

If marriage is almost universal among all ethnic subpopulations, how stable are these marriages? Using retrospective data we are able to examine not only those who are currently divorced but also those who have divorced and subsequently remarried. Combining the divorced and remarried, separation ratios (per 100 ever-married persons) have been calculated for males and females of each ethnic subpopulation. In general, males have lower separation ratios than females, and Protestants have higher separation ratios than Catholics for both sexes (Table 3-2). Irish and Italians have the lowest separation ratios among Catholic ethnics and this is true for both sexes. Portuguese males have the highest separation ratios of all ethnic groups considered: about one-fourth of all ever-married Portuguese males are either divorced or remarried. This does not characterize the Portuguese women, whose separation ratios are lower than for Protestant women and the same as French Canadian women (but higher than the Irish or Italians).

Female separation ratios are generally higher than those for males except for French Canadians and Portuguese. Most importantly, Catholic ethnic variation in separation ratios is greater than interreligious differences, but this is mainly a male pattern.

Another dimension of the extent of marriage is the question of remarriage: of all those who have been formerly married, what proportion are remarried? Generally, these remarriage velocities show significant variation by sex and ethnicity. Overall, 47 out of 100 formerly married males have remarried, about three times the rate for women. For both men and women, remarriage is higher for Protestants than Catholics: over half the formerly married Protestant males and one-fifth of the formerly married Protestant females remarry compared to 44 percent and 15 percent, respectively, of the formerly married Catholics. Among male Catholic ethnics, Portuguese have high remarriage velocities—even higher than Protestant males. Irish and Italian males and females have the lowest remarriage velocities among all ethnic subpopulations considered. French Canadian women have the highest remarriage velocities among Catholic ethnics and resemble the Protestant women in this regard.

In general, the range of variation in remarriage is higher among Catholic ethnics than between Protestants and Catholics, and this is true for both sexes. The Catholic ethnic difference in remarriage is exaggerated among males because of the very high rates for the Portuguese and among females because of the very low rates for the Irish. Examining the male-female ratio in remarriage velocities shows

Table 3-2. Separation Ratios and Remariage Velocities by Ethnicity and Sex

	Separation Ratio*		Remarriage Velocity**	
	Male	Female	Male	Female
Total	14	16	47	17
Protestants	17	20	51	20
Catholics	13	15	44	15
French Canadians	15	15	47	20
Irish	8	11	35	6
Italians	8	11	34	11
Portuguese	24	15	60	14

*Separation ratio is the ratio of remarried and divorced per 100 ever-married.
**Remarriage velocity is the ratio of remarried per 100 formerly married.

that sex differences are greater for Catholics than Protestants and higher for Irish and Portuguese than other Catholic ethnics.

FIRST MARRIAGE

The combined effects of the variation and change in the extent and stability of marriage may be seen in the proportions who are in first marriages by ethnicity, age, and sex (Table 3–3). Catholic males and females are more likely to be in first marriages than Protestants: 76 percent of the Catholic men and 59 percent of the Catholic women are in first marriages compared to 69 percent and 53 percent of Protestant men and women, respectively. Although a sufficient number of Jews was not available for an analysis of remarriage velocities and separation ratios, the data show a higher proportion of Jews than non-Jews in first marriages for both sexes and controlling for cohort. Combined with the earlier data on percentage ever-married, these data imply a high level of marriage and marital stability for Jews, higher than most if not all of the ethnic groups examined.

Overall, differences in the proportion in first marriage by religion are not as great as the variation for Catholic ethnic groups. While the proportion of Irish and Portuguese men in first marriages is similar to the Protestant level (70 percent), Italian men have a very high proportion in first marriages (83 percent) and French Canadian men are in an intermediate position (73 percent). The range in first marriage among women is between 52 percent for Irish women to 73 percent for Portuguese women compared to 53 percent, 59 percent, and 64 percent for Protestant, Catholic, and Jewish women, respectively.

In general, the proportion in first marriages is significantly lower for women than for men (except for the Portuguese) for a variety of reasons associated with the effects of sex differences in marriage age and mortality on widowhood and the effect, in turn, on remarriage. Since women tend to marry at younger ages than men, live longer, and remarry at lower rates, the percentage of males in first marriages is higher than for females. These sex differences increase sharply with age and hold even when controlling for variation in celibacy, i.e., when the proportion in first marriages is related to the ever-married.

Part of these interethnic differences in the proportion in first marriage are clarified by examining age cohorts. There is a very strong negative life cycle effect on the proportion in first marriages. Among men, for example, the proportion in first marriage declines from 82 percent to 51 percent and among women from 76 percent to 22 percent from the youngest to the oldest age cohorts.

Table 3-3. Percentage in First Marriages by Ethnicity, Sex, and Age

Age and Sex	Total	Protestants	Jews	Catholics	French Canadians	Irish	Italians	Portuguese
Males								
Total	73	69	79	76	73	70	83	71
25–44	82	77	89	83	87	80	87	81
45–64	72	67	76	75	69	66	87	68
65+	51	53	—	52	48	35	60	—
Females								
Total	58	53	64	59	60	52	63	73
25–44	76	71	83	77	76	75	86	82
45–64	58	57	69	58	65	54	56	75
65+	22	24	36	21	27	14	30	—

In general, this life cycle effect characterizes each of the ethnic subpopulations. Nevertheless, some variations in the proportion in first marriage by ethnicity are noteworthy: For the oldest age cohort, about half the men and slightly over one-fifth of the women are in their first marriage. The major exceptions are the Irish, with a much lower proportion in first marriages, and the Italians, with a significantly higher proportion in first marriages. For the younger age cohorts, the Irish men and women lose their distinctiveness, while the Italians retain a slightly higher proportion in first marriages.

A significant part of the distinctive Irish and Italian patterns is the result of differential celibacy by age, noted earlier. When the proportion of the first married is calculated from a base excluding the never-married (i.e., percentage in first marriages among the ever-married), the proportion of Irish males and females in first marriages is very close to other ethnic subpopulations. Although the ever-married Italians tend to have a higher proportion in first marriages, the differences are smaller than when the never-married are included.

SOCIAL CLASS AND MARRIAGE

In general, the relationship between social class and marriage patterns is complex and varies in significant ways by sex. Oversimplifying, there tends to be an inverse relationship between celibacy and social class for males and a positive relationship for females, i.e., higher rates of nonmarriage characterize males in the lower classes, while the higher the social class, the higher the rate of celibacy for females. Previous research suggests that the higher level of nonmarriage for better educated women is particularly characteristic of Catholics. Remarriage tends to follow the same patterns as marriage, with higher remarriage characterizing higher social class males and lower social class females. Generally, there is an inverse relationship between social class and marital separation—the higher the social class the lower the separation rate. (See, for example, Ross and Sawhill, 1975; Carter and Glick, 1976).

In this section, these general relationships between social class and marriage will be examined for each of the ethnic subpopulations. Moreover, attention will be focused on whether ethnic variations and changes in marriage patterns are diminished when social class factors are controlled.

Data in Table 3–4 show the relationship between social class (measured subjectively and by educational attainment) and the proportion ever-married for ethnic males. Overall, differences between the percentage ever-married of middle and working class males are

Table 3–4.   Percentage Ever-Married by Ethnicity, Age, Subjective Social Class, and Education: Males

Age	Total	Protestants	Catholics	French Canadians	Irish	Italians	Portuguese
*Social Class**							
Total							
Middle	93	92	95	96	87	95	95
Working	92	91	92	95	81	97	94
25–44							
Middle	91	90	92	92	89	92	—
Working	91	95	90	97	81	94	90
45–64							
Middle	94	92	94	98	89	98	—
Working	91	87	93	93	87	98	94
65+							
Middle	95	96	93	100	80	100	—
Working	95	94	96	94	—	100	—
*Education***							
Total							
High	89	90	88	82	87	94	—
Medium	93	96	91	95	81	95	93
Low	93	90	95	96	89	97	95
25–44							
High	90	90	89	—	93	91	—
Medium	92	96	91	95	78	92	90
Low	91	88	93	97	80	94	94
45–64							
High	89	87	86	—	82	100	—
Medium	94	96	94	100	89	100	—
Low	93	88	94	95	88	97	94
65+							
High	91	100	67	—	—	—	—
Medium	87	100	71	—	—	—	—
Low	96	93	97	97	94	100	—

*Middle = middle or upper class; working = working or lower class.
**High = some college; medium = completed high school; low = did not complete high school.

small for all subpopulations and cohorts. For every ethnic group (except Italians) middle class males have slightly higher rates of marriage than working class males. There are some exceptions by cohort but the overall pattern is consistent with previous research. More important in the present context are variations by ethnicity in the proportion ever-marrying *within* social class categories. Middle and working class Catholics tend to marry more than Protestants, with minor exceptions by cohort. Furthermore, the higher rate of celibacy among Irish males characterizes both the middle and working classes, although the pattern is more pronounced among the latter. With but one exception (working classes, age 45–64), the Irish celibacy level is higher than that for Protestants, controlling for subjective social class. There are, however, few systematic differences among non-Irish Catholic ethnics when class and age are controlled and a very high proportion are ever-married.

The patterns by education are much less clear. Differences are small, but the tendency is for the better educated males to marry somewhat less than the less educated males; there are numerous exceptions by cohort. The Irish pattern by education and age suggests that greater nonmarriage characterizes all educational levels and cohorts except for the youngest cohort at the highest educational level. Among the Irish age 25–44 with less than a completed high school education, the proportion never-marrying is higher than any other ethnic group—about 20 percent of the Irish remain celibate, double the level of the non-Irish. However, for the young, college educated Irish, the level of celibacy is low and comparable to the non-Irish, suggesting a strong trend toward convergence. Another emerging pattern from these data is that the higher rate of marriage among Catholics compared to Protestants characterizes only the less educated groups within age cohorts.

A somewhat different picture of the impact of social class on marriage patterns characterizes women and is again consistent with previous research (Table 3–5). With but minor exceptions, mainly among Italian women, middle class women marry at lower rates than working class women for all ethnic groups by cohort. Differences between middle and working class women are significantly greater than the class contrast for men, and the trends are in opposite directions. The Protestant-Catholic contrast for women is not clear by subjective social class when cohort is controlled. Irish women tend to marry less than non-Irish women of both social classes and, as with the male patterns, differences tend to be greater among working class women and the older cohorts. Despite the trends toward convergence over time in the proportion of women never-marrying, the extent of

Table 3-5. Percentage Ever-Married by Ethnicity, Age, Subjective Social Class, and Education: Females

Age	Total	Protestants	Catholics	French Canadians	Irish	Italians	Portuguese
*Social Class**							
Total							
Middle	91	89	91	90	84	94	100
Working	94	97	93	95	88	93	94
25–44							
Middle	94	92	94	92	90	95	100
Working	96	98	95	96	100	94	100
45–64							
Middle	90	90	89	88	81	91	—
Working	92	96	92	96	84	93	92
65+							
Middle	85	85	85	86	77	100	—
Working	93	100	91	94	85	93	—
*Education***							
Total							
High	86	88	80	73	73	—	—
Medium	91	93	90	95	87	85	96
Low	94	93	94	94	87	97	97
25–44							
High	90	84	90	—	94	—	—
Medium	94	99	93	98	93	100	100
Low	97	93	97	93	100	98	100
45–64							
High	73	85	53	—	—	—	—
Medium	88	95	83	89	83	74	—
Low	95	95	95	95	93	97	97
65+							
High	92	94	75	—	—	—	—
Medium	81	75	87	—	79	—	—
Low	89	90	88	92	77	94	—

*Middle = middle or upper class; working = working or lower class.
**High = at least some college; medium = completed high school; low = did not complete high school.

convergence between Irish and non-Irish women is less than among men. For example, even among young Irish middle class women, 10 percent have not married compared to 5 percent among Italians.

More educated women have systematically higher rates of celibacy than less educated women for most comparisons by age. Overall, for example, 86 percent of women who have some college education marry compared to 91 percent among those who have completed high school and 94 percent of those with less than a high school education. These patterns characterize all the religious and Catholic ethnic subpopulations and are exaggerated among French Canadian and Irish women: 27 percent of the college educated French Canadian and Irish women are celibate compared to 6 percent (French Canadian) and 13 percent (Irish) with low education. The same pattern holds within age cohorts.

The data by education also show convergence over time in the proportion ever-marrying among Irish and non-Irish women. High rates of celibacy for Irish women are much more characteristic of the older cohorts and the less educated. Catholic women are less likely to marry than Protestant women for most social class and educational levels, but the pattern is more pronounced at the highest education level. Thus, despite a potentially larger marriage market for educated Catholic women (the ratio of highly educated males to females is much higher among Catholics than Protestants, as shown earlier in Table 2–3), more educated Catholic women marry less. Education implies greater opportunities for nonfamilial roles and the conflict between these opportunities and marriage may be greater for Catholic women.

The general pattern of an inverse relationship between social class and separation holds for the various ethnic groups (Table 3–6). For both males and females and for subjective social class as well as education, the higher the social class, the lower the separation ratio. The differences between social classes are substantial for some groups. For example, almost one-fourth of the ever-married working class Portuguese males have remarried or are divorced compared to less than 10 percent of the middle class Portuguese males. The pattern by education is equally clear. For example, 22 percent of the ever-married, less educated Protestants are divorced or remarried compared to 9 percent of the more educated; the contrast for Catholics is 15 percent to 2 percent. This pattern holds for all comparisons by education. There are some exceptions with subjective social class, primarily for French Canadian men and Italian and Portuguese women.

Almost without exception, Protestant women and men have

Table 3-6. Separation Ratios and Remarriage Velocities by Ethnicity, Subjective Social Class,* Education, and Sex**

Separation Ratios	Total	Protestants	Catholics	French Canadians	Irish	Italians	Portuguese
Males							
Social Class							
Middle	13	16	10	21	7	6	10
Working	15	20	13	12	11	11	24
Education							
High	6	9	2	—	3	0	—
Medium	13	17	10	15	13	12	31
Low	26	22	15	16	8	9	31
Females							
Social Class							
Middle	12	15	12	10	10	11	19
Working	19	29	16	11	11	9	8
Education							
High	14	11	13	—	5	—	—
Medium	12	16	12	8	8	9	19
Low	18	27	17	18	4	12	13
Remarriage Velocities							
Males							
Social Class							
Middle	50	53	45	57	30	45	100
Working	45	49	43	39	40	28	54
Education							
High	50	—	—	—	—	—	—
Medium	70	68	70	—	—	—	—
Low	41	41	40	41	8	32	62
Females							
Social Class							
Middle	15	16	13	14	5	15	10
Working	19	27	17	21	8	7	17
Education							
High	24	17	20	—	—	—	—
Medium	17	17	16	7	5	—	—
Low	17	22	16	19	7	9	12

*Middle = middle or upper class; working = working or lower class.
**High = at least some college; medium = completed high school; low = did not complete high school.

higher separation ratios than Catholics and the differences tend to be greater for the lower classes, particularly among women. For the Catholic ethnics, separation ratios tend to be highest among French Canadian and Portuguese men and women whose pattern is most unlike other ethnic Catholics or the overall Catholic low level of separation. Irish and Italians are characterized by the lowest rates of separation among all ethnic subpopulations and for all class levels.

Remarriage velocities by class measures are consistent with the overall data presented earlier and with general marriage patterns. Remarriage velocities are higher among middle class males (except for the Irish) and among working class females (except for the Italians). The patterns by education are somewhat less clear and the small number of cases prevents detailed analysis. The subjective social class data show that Protestant males and females have higher remarriage velocities for both classes when compared to Catholics. Remarriage tends to be highest among Portuguese and working class French Canadians and lowest generally for Irish and Italian women and men of all class and eduational levels.

Data showing the interrelationships of social class, ethnicity, sex and age on proportions in first marriages are presented in Tables 3-7 and 3-8. These data reflect the complex effects on both the extent and stability of marriages. Briefly, the following patterns emerge:

1. A higher proportion of middle class males tend to be in first marriages than working class males, reflecting their higher rates of marriage, and remarriage and lower separation ratios. There are some exceptions to these patterns by cohort and there is a general tendency for the least variation by social class to characterize the youngest age cohort. A similar pattern emerges with education: the higher the education, the higher the proportion in first marriages. The Protestant male pattern by education is illustrative: 80 percent of Protestant males with at least some college education are in their first marriages compared to 76 percent of those who completed high school and 57 percent of the least educated. This pattern characterizes all the ethnic groups for the three age coherts, with minor exceptions.

2. Middle class women are also more likely to be in first marriages than are working class women, but differences are small with a number of exceptions when cohort is controlled. The reason for this mixed pattern relates to the different relationship of class and marriage for women compared to men. Middle class women are less likely to marry but are more stable in those marriages than working class women. Hence, the picture that emerges for the proportions in first marriages reflects these opposite patterns. Only for the oldest

Table 3-7. Percentage in First Marriages by Ethnicity, Age, Subjective Social Class, and Education: Males

	Total	Protestants	Catholics	French Canadians	Irish	Italians	Portuguese
Social Class*							
Total							
Middle	76	72	79	70	75	86	86
Working	69	62	63	74	64	81	64
25–44							
Middle	84	77	86	85	68	90	90
Working	80	79	81	88	72	83	76
45–64							
Middle	74	75	76	58	80	88	—
Working	68	55	74	80	—	85	65
65+							
Middle	57	57	61	67	40	50	—
Working	46	48	46	41	—	65	—
Education**							
Total							
High	82	80	83	73	82	91	—
Medium	78	76	80	79	68	83	87
Low	67	57	72	72	65	82	59
25–44							
High	85	85	85	—	93	87	—
Medium	83	80	85	90	71	89	90
Low	77	68	82	86	70	87	71
45–64							
High	79	80	81	—	71	100	—
Medium	72	73	73	56	67	73	—
Low	69	55	74	73	81	88	67
65+							
High	64	—	—	—	—	—	—
Medium	56	—	—	—	—	—	—
Low	49	51	51	47	39	59	—

*Middle = middle or upper class; working = working or lower class.
**High = at least some college; medium = completed high school; low = did not complete high school.

Table 3-8.   Percentage in First Marriages by Ethnicity, Age, Subjective Social Class, and Education: Females

	Total	Protestants	Catholics	French Canadians	Irish	Italians	Portuguese
*Social Class**							
Total							
Middle	59	53	61	69	52	64	73
Working	56	53	56	53	51	62	74
25–44							
Middle	79	76	79	86	73	85	76
Working	71	73	74	63	82	88	88
45–64							
Middle	57	53	57	67	49	52	—
Working	60	62	58	64	59	59	71
65+							
Middle	26	27	24	25	20	40	—
Working	17	13	18	24	0	22	—
*Education***							
Total							
High	59	58	63	55	62	—	—
Medium	70	63	69	76	64	75	70
Low	52	43	54	56	35	60	71
25–44							
High	77	74	80	—	81	—	—
Medium	80	82	79	89	80	85	77
Low	70	53	73	64	73	87	82
45–64							
High	44	58	27	—	—	—	—
Medium	61	56	62	67	63	59	—
Low	58	60	57	67	41	54	76
65+							
High	21	19	25	—	—	—	—
Medium	23	31	13	—	14	—	—
Low	24	21	24	30	14	36	—

*Middle = middle or upper class; working = working or lower class.
**High = at least some college; medium = completed high school; low = did not complete high school.

cohort of women is the pattern clear for all ethnics: middle class women are more likely to be in first marriages than are working class women. It is for this age cohort that differences in the proportion never-married between social classes are small and the differential proportion in first marriages reflects the effects of separation by social class.

3. The proportion of Protestant men and women in first marriages is low compared to Catholics for both social classes by cohort. The pattern seems to be stronger for middle than working classes and several exceptions characterize women, when cohort is controlled. This generally holds when the effects of education are controlled but again the pattern is clearer for men than for women and for the less than the more educated. Most of the differences between Protestants and Catholics in the proportion in first marriages reflects differential separation patterns by religion.

4. The proportion in first marriages is higher for Portuguese and Italians compared to Irish and French Canadians. For the Portuguese this is largely a middle class pattern since working class Portuguese are characterized by high separation ratios and, hence, low levels of proportions in first marriage. Most importantly, the lower proportions of Irish and French Canadians in first marriages stem from different processes: for the Irish it is the lower proportion ever-married; for the French Canadians it is the higher proportion separated. Thus, for example, 64 percent of the Irish and Portuguese working class are in first marriages and 70 percent of the French Canadian middle class are in first marriages—low proportions compared to other Catholic ethnics. For the Irish, however, this reflects the fact that 19 percent of the working class males have never married (compared to 5 percent, 6 percent, and 3 percent of the French Canadians, Portuguese, and Italians, respectively). For the French Canadian middle class and Portuguese working class the critical factor in the low proportion in first marriage is their high separation ratios—21 percent for French Canadians and 24 percent for Portuguese (over twice as high as other Catholic ethnics of the same class level).

5. The lower extent of Irish marriages also affects the proportion in first marriage for the younger cohorts of males but is much less conspicuous for the two older cohorts of females. These data suggest again that the changes over time in Irish marriage patterns characterize women more than men of both social classes. The same is true for education.

It is clear that in order to assess differences in the role of marriage in group life, two different dimensions must be considered: (1) the

extent of marriage that appears in the proportions remaining celibate
and the velocity of remarriage; (2) the *stability* of marriage that
underlies the separation ratio and the proportions in first marriages.
These two dimensions affect marriage in different ways for various
ethnic subpopulations. For example, Protestants and Catholics have
very similar proportions married but Catholics tend to have higher
stability and somewhat lower extent when remarriage velocities and
ever-married patterns are combined.

Among the ethnic groups, deviation from the basic Catholic
pattern, which the Italians most resemble in exaggerated form,
occurs in two directions. The Irish have the lowest proportions currently married because of their high proportion who never marry.
The Portuguese and French Canadians also have lower proportions
married than the Italians because of their high separation rates.
Since overall, both extent and instability are increasing, the low,
stable pattern typified by older Irish is giving way to the high extent,
low stability pattern of Protestants. Schematically, the situation
looks like this:

Proportion ever-married

		High	Low
	High	Portuguese French Canadians Protestants	
Separation ratio	Low	Italians Catholics	Irish

To the extent that a direction of change can be discerned with
these data, it seems that the flow is clockwise, starting with the Irish.
It might be hypothesized that the empty cell will be filled by the
next generation. The Irish are reducing their proportions celibate so
that younger Irish resemble Italians. And, although age data were less
reliable for the other comparisons, there is some tendency, especially
among women and the higher socioeconomic groups, toward higher
rates of marital dissolution among younger people.

Within this pattern, however, the persistent sex interactions are
significant. The relationships between marriage and economic in-
dependence for women seem to be operating differentially. This is
the case for the Protestant-Catholic and the Italian-Irish comparisons.
Higher education reduces proportions married more for Catholic
and Irish than for Protestant or Italian women. Since marriage and
family may be considered a major source of ethnic solidarity, these

class differences take on particular significance. The extent and stability of marriage have differential consequences for the structure of ethnic social life and for social processes associated with ethnic continuity. Continuity and change emerge clearly from this analysis of ethnic variation in the marital cycle.

✳ *Chapter 4*

Residential Concentration
and Dispersal

A dominant theme in American social science research has been the residential segregation or integration of ethnic groups. Focusing on first and later generations of immigrant groups and, in more recent research, on racial and ethnic subpopulations, social scientists have tended to view residential concentration as one of the major indicators of assimilation and integration. In large part, ethnic residential segregation has been considered not only as an index of social class differences between minority and majority groups but as a reflection of either undesirable status traits of ethnic-racial groups (involuntary segregation) or as a facilitating factor in immigrant adjustment to American society (cf. Lieberson, 1963). For white ethnics, residential concentration has most often been conceptualized as a transitional stage in the assimilation process and as a vehicle for cultural and structural separateness.

However, ethnic residential concentration must be viewed as more than a process of immigrant adaptation related to initial cultural differences upon arrival and conditions of settlement (Yancey et al., 1976). Residential concentration of ethnic groups clearly maintains the visibility and awareness of ethnic identification for members of the ethnic community as well as for others. In particular, ethnic residential concentration reinforces ethnic community institutions and distinctive ethnic consciousness and behavior. Most importantly, residence in areas of relatively high ethnic density may be expected to have a major impact on ethnic socialization, interaction, marriage, and mobility patterns. In short, the ethnic factor is likely to be most pronounced when ethnics are clustered residentially.

Ethnic residential concentration may be considered to be one of the central mechanisms for the continuity and survival of ethnic communities.

Most previous research on ethnic residential segregation has focused on census data with the advantages and limitations inherent in that source. This chapter combines data from the 1960 census on ethnic stock with the sample survey data to provide an in-depth look at ethnic residential segregation.[a] More specifically, each census tract in Rhode Island was classified in terms of the proportion of ethnic stock, defined as immigrants and their children. Ethnic residential concentration was classified as high when the proportion of ethnic stock was 25 percent or over in the census tract. Low ethnic residential concentration characterizes census tracts of less than 5 percent ethnic stock, while medium levels of ethnic concentration were assigned to tracts with between 5 and 25 percent ethnic stock. Three ethnic classifications were available from census data that closely approximate the ethnic groups in the sample survey—Canadians (French), Irish, and Italians. Thus, for example, Irish in the survey who were living in an area of low ethnic concentration were those whose residence was in a census tract where fewer than 5 percent of the population were of Irish stock. Census tract data were not available for the Portuguese and the proportion of total foreign stock (foreign born plus children of foreign born parentage) was used as our measure for the Portuguese. No data are available from the census on religious affiliation and this chapter will focus only on the Catholic ethnic subpopulations.

The major issues to be addressed with these combined census tract and sample data are (1) What are the patterns of residential segregation for the four ethnic groups? (2) How have these patterns changed over time (as measured by age cohorts)? (3) How does ethnic residential segregation vary by social class and education? and (4) What are the residential patterns of intermarried and nonintermarried ethnics?

ETHNIC RESIDENTIAL CONCENTRATION

According to the definition of ethnic concentration used, about half of the sample live in areas where ethnic concentration is less than 5 percent and slightly over one-fifth live in areas of high ethnic concentration. The remaining 30 percent of the sample live in areas of

---

[a]It was necessary to use 1960 tract information since the surveys were conducted before the 1970 census, and cases were coded by 1960 tract locations. Rhode Island is unique in that the entire state is tracted by the Bureau of the Census.

medium ethnic concentration. How do these overall patterns of
ethnic residential concentration vary by ethnicity and age cohort?
Data in Table 4-1 show substantial ethnic variation in residential
concentration. Overall, the Irish are least ethnically concentrated
followed by Italians, French Canadians, and Portuguese. None of the
Irish were in census tracts where 25 percent or more of the population were of Irish stock, while 80 percent lived in census tracts
containing less than 5 percent Irish stock.[b] At the other end of the
residential concentration continuum are the Portuguese: 44 percent
of the Portuguese live in areas estimated to be of high Portuguese
residential concentration and less than 40 percent are in areas of low
Portuguese residential concentration. French Canadians and Italians
are in an intermediate position in terms of residential concentration.
The Italians are more likely than French Canadians to be living in
low ethnic concentration areas (but significantly less than the Irish

**Table 4-1. Ethnic Residential Concentration by Ethnicity and Age (Per-
centage)**

Ethnicity and Age**	Residential Concentration*			Total Percent
	Low	Medium	High	
French Canadians	40.7	39.8	19.5	100.0
25–44	44.6	36.9	18.5	100.0
45–64	36.9	45.1	18.0	100.0
65+	40.4	36.2	23.4	100.0
Irish	79.7	20.3	0.0	100.0
25–44	77.4	22.6	0.0	100.0
45–64	84.6	15.4	0.0	100.0
65+	61.1	38.9	0.0	100.0
Italians	44.7	28.3	27.0	100.0
25–44	43.1	32.4	24.5	100.0
45–64	45.8	26.2	28.0	100.0
65+	45.7	17.1	37.1	100.0
Portuguese	39.4	16.5	44.0	100.0
25–44	40.0	20.0	40.0	100.0
45–64	38.6	13.6	47.7	100.0
65+	—	—	—	—

*For this and subsequent tables low concentration is less than 5 percent ethnic
stock; medium concentration is 5–24 percent ethnic stock; high concentration
is 25 percent or more ethnic stock.
**Age refers to males.

[b]In fact, the Irish are concentrated at the lower end of the medium level. No
census tract in Rhode Island contains more than 15 percent Irish stock. Part of
the low concentration of Irish is due to the census definition used, since if third
and later generations were included, a higher proportion of the tract population
would have been classified as Irish.

and more than the Portuguese), but they are also somewhat more concentrated than French Canadians in areas of high ethnic density (27 percent compared to 20 percent).

Previous research has suggested that ethnic residential concentration declines over time with distance from the immigrant generation. The data on residential concentration by age cohort support this finding for each of the four ethnic groups. The pattern for French Canadians illustrates this cohort effect on ethnic residential concentration most clearly. French Canadians age 25-44 are less concentrated in French Canadian areas and more likely to be in areas of low ethnic residential concentration compared to the oldest cohort of French Canadians. The 45-64 cohort is more concentrated in areas where 5-25 percent of the population is French Canadian. Thus, the inferred transition from these cohort patterns is from areas of high to medium to low ethnic residential concentration for the three age cohorts of French Canadians.

A majority of Irish of all ages are in areas where Irish residential concentration is less than 5 percent. For the older cohort there is a significantly higher percentage of Irish in areas of medium Irish concentration compared to the two younger cohorts. It is interesting to note that the youngest cohort of Irish is somewhat more likely to reside in medium areas of Irish concentration compared to the Irish age 45-64. This exception for the youngest cohort and the fact that overall only 20 percent of the Irish are concentrated in areas where 5-24 percent of the population are of Irish stock suggest that when residential integration is high, differentiation within the ethnic group (by cohort in this case) is less clear-cut (at least for those below age 65). The possibility of a small reversal toward somewhat greater ethnic residential concentration for the younger cohort should not, however, be dismissed and may indicate a real tendency toward increased residential concentration.

Italians follow the general pattern of declining ethnic residential concentration as age decreases. However, the decline in high Italian ethnic concentration is not toward the lowest but toward medium levels of residential concentration. The proportion of Italians living in areas where less than 5 percent of the population are of Italian stock has remained relatively unchanged for the three age cohorts and even declines somewhat for the youngest cohort. In contrast, Italian residence in areas of medium levels of concentration increases from 17 percent to 32 percent when the oldest and youngest age cohorts are compared.

A sufficient number of cases is not available for the oldest age cohort of Portuguese ethnics, but the patterns for the two younger cohorts are as expected: high ethnic residential concentration declines and low ethnic residential concentration increases among the young. Similar to the Italian pattern, the youngest cohort of Portuguese has experienced sharper increases in areas of medium residential concentration.

Hence, while the overall pattern for all ethnic groups has been away from high ethnic residential concentration, the trend has not been toward total residential integration in areas where the proportion of ethnic concentration is below 5 percent. The trend has been much more to areas of medium levels of ethnic residential concentration. Thus, despite the confirmation of the general hypothesis of diminishing ethnic residential concentration over time, the fact remains that a majority of young Italians, Portuguese, and French Canadians continues to live in areas of medium to high ethnic concentration. Of no less significance is the persistence of ethnic differences in the extent of residential concentration. For ethnics of the youngest cohort, the Irish are significantly more integrated residentially than are the Portuguese, with Italians and French Canadians in an intermediate position. For all cohorts, the most striking differences in residential concentration are between the Irish and non-Irish. There has been a tendency toward greater residential concentration for young Italians compared to French Canadians, a reversal of the pattern that characterizes the oldest cohort. Nevertheless, there has been little convergence over time between ethnic groups in residential concentration, implying that the rate of change over time has been about the same for the four ethnic groups considered.

STRATIFICATION AND ETHNIC RESIDENTIAL CONCENTRATION

Previous research suggests that ethnic residential concentration is more characteristic of the least educated and the working (and lower) classes. The survey data available allow for an examination of the relationship between two measures of social class and ethnic residential concentration: (1) subjective class identification and (2) educational attainment. The overall patterns are clear: ethnics who define themselves as middle (or upper) class are more likely to live in areas of low ethnic concentration compared to working (or lower) class (55 percent compared to 45 percent) and are less concentrated in areas of high ethnic density (17 percent compared to 25 percent).

Similarly, an inverse relationship exists between education and residential concentration: the higher the level of education, the lower the ethnic concentration. Among ethnics with some college education

63 percent are in low ethnic concentrated areas compared to 59 percent of the high school graduates and 42 percent of those who have not completed high school. At the other end of the ethnic concentration continuum, over one-fourth of those who have not graduated from high school live in areas of high ethnic concentration compared to 15 percent of those who graduated from high school and 11 percent of those with at least some college education.

As shown in Chapter 2, the socioeconomic composition of ethnic groups varies substantially. How do patterns of social class affect ethnic residential concentration for each of the ethnic groups? More importantly, are ethnic differences in residential concentration diminished when social class differences are controlled? Is ethnic residential concentration a lower class phenomenon or do middle class, educated ethnics continue to reside in ethnically concentrated areas? How does the relationship between social class and ethnic residential concentration vary by age cohort? Data in Tables 4-2 and 4-3 provide some preliminary answers to these issues.

Data on relationship between subjective class identification and ethnic residential concentration (Table 4-2) show the proportion in high ethnically concentrated areas is higher for working than middle class Italians, French Canadians, and Portuguese. The proportion in low ethnic residential areas is higher for middle class than

Table 4-2.   Ethnic Residential Concentration by Ethnicity, Age, and Subjective Social Class* (Percentage)

	Middle Class Residential Concentration			Working Class Residential Concentration		
	Low	Medium	High	Low	Medium	High
French Canadians	46.4	36.4	17.1	36.9	42.2	20.9
25–44	55.7	30.0	14.3	35.6	42.5	21.8
45–64	36.7	49.0	14.3	37.0	42.5	20.5
65+	40.0	30.0	30.0	40.7	40.7	18.5
Irish	78.7	21.3	0.0	81.9	18.1	0.0
25–44	77.6	22.4	0.0	83.3	16.7	0.0
45–64	82.6	17.4	0.0	87.5	12.5	0.0
65+	71.4	28.6	0.0	—	—	—
Italians	49.8	28.9	21.3	38.3	27.8	33.9
25–44	47.3	30.0	22.7	37.2	35.9	26.9
45–64	53.5	27.9	18.6	37.8	24.4	37.8
65+	46.7	26.7	26.7	45.0	10.0	45.0
Portuguese	39.6	20.8	39.6	41.4	13.8	44.8
25–44	28.6	28.6	42.9	51.9	11.1	37.0
45–64	53.3	6.7	40.0	31.0	17.2	51.7
65+	—	—	—	—	—	—

*Middle = middle or upper class; working = working or lower class.

Table 4-3. Ethnic Residential Concentration by Ethnicity, Age, and Education (Percentage)

	Less than High School Residential Concentration			High School Residential Concentration			Some College Residential Concentration		
	Low	Medium	High	Low	Medium	High	Low	Medium	High
French Canadians	35.3	41.9	22.8	49.4	39.8	10.8	56.5	30.4	13.0
25–44	37.1	41.6	21.3	51.9	37.0	11.1	66.7	25.0	8.3
45–64	31.5	45.7	22.8	45.8	41.7	12.5	—	—	—
65+	41.2	32.4	26.5	—	—	—	—	—	—
Irish	74.6	25.4	0.0	85.9	14.1	0.0	80.0	20.0	0.0
25–44	80.0	20.0	0.0	78.9	21.1	0.0	80.4	19.6	0.0
45–64	76.9	23.1	0.0	95.5	4.5	0.0	83.3	16.7	0.0
65+	58.3	41.7	0.0	—	—	—	—	—	—
Italians	38.2	29.4	32.5	52.2	28.3	19.6	56.3	28.1	15.6
25–44	32.5	37.3	30.1	53.3	26.7	20.0	51.1	31.9	17.0
45–64	41.2	27.2	31.6	48.4	32.3	19.4	70.6	17.6	11.8
65+	41.9	16.1	41.9	—	—	—	—	—	—
Portuguese	41.3	12.7	46.0	46.4	10.7	42.9	—	—	—
25–44	37.0	18.5	44.4	50.0	11.1	38.9	—	—	—
45–64	43.3	10.0	46.7	40.0	10.0	50.0	—	—	—
65+	—	—	—	—	—	—	—	—	—

working class French Canadians and Italians. Differences between middle and working class Portuguese are greater in areas of medium residential concentration. Sixty percent of the Portuguese middle class live in medium or low ethnically concentrated areas compared to 55 percent of the working class. The Irish deviate from the non-Irish in this pattern and slightly fewer Irish middle class ethnics live in low ethnic concentrated areas than working class Irish.

The same patterns emerge when ethnic residential concentration by educational attainment is examined (Table 4-3). For French Canadian, Italian, and Portuguese ethnics, the higher the education, the lower the ethnic residential concentration; the lower the education, the greater the concentration in high ethnic residential areas. The Italians are a representative illustration of these patterns: 56 percent of the better educated Italians are in areas of low Italian concentration compared to 38 percent of the Italians who have not completed high school; about one-third of the lower educated Italians live in areas where over 25 percent of the population are of Italian stock compared to less than one-sixth of the more educated Italians.

The relationship between education and residential concentration is much less clear for the Irish. About one-fourth of the less educated Irish reside in areas of medium ethnic concentration and 75 percent are in areas of low concentration. This compares to 14 percent and 86 percent of the Irish high school graduates. This pattern is not consistent for the Irish with at least some college education. It should be emphasized again that the Irish exhibit a pattern of residential integration unmatched at any class or educational level by other ethnics. Moreover, the pattern of ethnic difference in residential concentration is maintained *within* class and educational categories: The Irish and Portuguese remain at polar ends of the residential concentration continuum with Italians and French Canadians in intermediate positions.

The introduction of age controls affects not only the extent of ethnic residential concentration but the relationship between social class and residential concentration for ethnic groups. This is because the composition of ethnic groups by class variables and ethnic residential concentration has changed over time.

Young French Canadians are less concentrated in high ethnic areas for both educational levels and, without exception, the higher the education, the lower the ethnic residential concentration by cohort where comparisons are possible. Middle class, young French Canadians are more concentrated in low ethnic areas than are the other two age cohorts and older French Canadians who define themselves as middle class are more concentrated in high ethnic areas compared to the younger two cohorts (30 percent compared to 14 percent). However, among French Canadians who define themselves as working class, differences by cohort are much narrower and there is a tendency for younger working class French Canadians to reside in areas of high French Canadian concentration compared to older working class French Canadians. The shift toward less residential concentration among the younger French Canadians noted earlier is therefore largely a middle class phenomenon and most characteristic of the more educated. A comparison of the proportion of French Canadians living in low ethnic areas by age and subjective social class reveals that differences appear only for the youngest cohort.

The Irish pattern of residential concentration is again mixed when class variables and age are controlled. The classic pattern of reduced ethnic residential concentration by age emerges only for the Irish who have not completed high school. Among the middle class Irish, the oldest cohort has a higher concentration in medium ethnic areas, but, as in the overall pattern, the youngest cohort of Irish is more concentrated in the medium areas of residential concentration compared to those age 45–64. This latter pattern characterizes the working class Irish as well. For the two cohorts where comparisons are possible, working class Irish are less residentially concentrated than are middle class Irish.

The decline over time in Italian residential concentration characterizes clearly the Italian population that did not go to college. For example, 42 percent of the older Italians who did not complete high school live in areas of high ethnic concentration compared to 30 percent of the youngest cohort of Italians of the same educational level. In almost every case where comparisons are possible within cohorts, the higher the education, the lower the ethnic concentration of Italians. Similar patterns emerge using the subjective social class measure. Working class Italians show clear reductions in ethnic residential concentration, but the age pattern is less clear for middle class Italians. For each age group, middle class Italians are more concentrated in low ethnic areas than are working class Italians, with differences substantially greater among the younger two cohorts.

The relationship between age and residential concentration of Portuguese of the two lower levels of education follows the Italian pattern of declining concentration. The same emerges for subjective social class among working class Portuguese. Interestingly, this age pattern does not characterize the middle class Portuguese—the younger class tend to be more concentrated in ethnically dense areas than those 45-64 years of age. Only among the Portuguese age 45-64 do the middle classes have less ethnic residential concentration than the working classes. These age patterns suggest that it may take middle class Portuguese a longer time in their life cycles to move out of Portuguese areas—i.e., age may reflect life cycle rather than generational effects.

Examining the general patterns of change over time in ethnic residential concentration reveals a general convergence, particularly for the more educated and middle classes. For example, differences in residential concentration among younger French Canadians, Irish, and Italians with at least some college education are smaller than among those with less than a high school education. This is due not to changes in residential concentration among the Irish but to changes in the level of residential concentration of French Canadians and Italians. The proportion in areas of low concentration increases among the young from 32 percent to 51 percent (Italians) and from 37 percent to 62 percent (French Canadians) from the lowest to the highest educational level; it declines from 30 percent to 17 percent (Italian) and from 21 percent to 8 percent (French Canadians) in areas of high residential concentration. In general, there seems to be less difference in residential concentration among middle class than among working class ethnics. For both measures of social class, change in residential concentration has been less conspicuous for Italians than French Canadians.

INTERMARRIAGE AND ETHNIC RESIDENTIAL CONCENTRATION

One of the interesting areas of analysis that has been neglected in previous research relates to the residential concentration and dispersal of intermarried ethnics. Most research has focused on the effects of residential segregation on intermarriage rates (see, for example, Lieberson, 1963, pp. 156-158). The focus here is on the residential patterns of intermarried couples. Some studies have shown that the intermarried tend to live in more integrated, less ethnically concentrated areas (cf. Goldstein and Goldscheider, 1968, pp. 161-163). More generally, the argument has been that ethnic residential concentration varies by the strength of ethnic ties. Thus, for example, ethnic residential concentration among the younger cohorts has generally diminished. In part, this may be because younger ethnics are less "ethnic" than previous generations or because residential segregation may no longer represent the way ethnicity is expressed as it had in the past. A similar argument may be made for intermarriage. To the extent that marriage between persons of different ethnic backgrounds represents a dilution of ethnic content, intermarried ethnics should be less concentrated in ethnic areas than nonintermarried ethnics.

The combination of sample data on intermarriage (for details and definitions see Chapter 6) and census tract data on ethnic residential concentration provides a unique opportunity to examine the relationship between interethnic marriage and the extent of ethnic residential concentration. Overall, there is a significant pattern of variation in ethnic concentration that relates to homogamy: Intermarried ethnics are much less likely to reside in areas of high ethnic concentration than are nonintermarried ethnics (Table 4-4). For example, the proportion of homogamous French Canadians residing in areas of high ethnic concentration is three times as high as intermarried French Canadians. The ratio of homogamous to heterogamous Italians living in areas of high ethnic concentration is 2 to 1. Even among the Irish, a larger proportion of the inmarried live in medium areas of Irish concentration compared to the intermarried Irish. The Portuguese are clearly an exception to this pattern: A larger proportion of in-married Portuguese are in areas of low ethnic concentration than intermarried Portuguese and a higher proportion of intermarried Portuguese are in areas of high ethnic

Table 4-4. Ethnic Residential Concentration by Ethnicity, Age, and Intermarriage (Percentage)

	Intermarried Residential Concentration			Nonintermarried Residential Concentration		
	Low	Medium	High	Low	Medium	High
French Canadians	42.2	48.9	8.9	39.7	33.7	26.6
25–44	47.4	42.1	10.5	41.0	33.7	25.3
45–64	36.2	57.4	6.4	37.2	35.9	26.9
65+	36.4	63.6	0.0	42.1	28.9	28.9
Irish	80.7	19.3	0.0	78.5	21.5	0.0
25–44	80.0	20.0	0.0	79.5	20.5	0.0
45–64	83.3	16.7	0.0	84.2	15.8	0.0
65+	—	—	—	62.5	37.5	0.0
Italians	56.3	27.4	16.3	38.7	28.7	32.6
25–44	51.8	31.3	16.9	37.0	33.3	29.6
45–64	66.0	20.0	14.0	37.3	28.8	33.9
65+	—	—	—	48.6	14.3	37.1
Portuguese	32.2	16.9	50.8	48.0	16.0	36.0
25–44	32.4	18.9	48.6	52.6	21.1	26.3
45–64	25.0	15.0	60.0	48.0	12.0	40.0
65+	—	—	—	—	—	—

concentration. It is not clear why the Portuguese pattern of residential concentration is exceptional for the intermarried. One hypothesis relates to the possibility that intermarried Portuguese tend to identify with the Portuguese ethnic group. However, subsequent analysis points in the opposite direction, i.e., lower rates of Portuguese identification characterized the Portuguese intermarried. Perhaps, the measure used for Portuguese residential concentration (the proportion of total foreign stock in the census tract rather than the proportion of Portuguese stock that was not available) distorts the pattern for the intermarried.

The general pattern of higher rates of ethnic residential concentration among the homogamously married holds for almost all comparisons by age (except again for the Portuguese and for the Irish age 45–64). It is significant to note that for French Canadian, Irish, and Italian intermarried ethnics, the proportion living in areas of high ethnic concentration has increased for the younger age cohort. For Italians and Irish, the increase is from 14 percent to 17 percent and from 17 percent to 20 percent, respectively. For the French Canadian intermarried, the increase is monotonic from none among those age 65 and over to 6.4 percent among those age 45–64 to 10.5 percent among the youngest cohort. This increase among the intermarried in ethnic concentration contrasts with the consistent decline among the homogamously married in the proportion of high ethnic residential concentration (from 29 percent to 25 percent for the French Canadians and from 37 percent to 30 percent for Italians). This may suggest the greater acceptance today of the intermarried in areas of ethnic residential concentration compared to the past or the emergence of greater ethnic consciousness among younger intermarried ethnics.

Is the general pattern of lower ethnic residential concentration among the intermarried a middle class phenomenon and is it characteristic of the more educated? Data in Table 4–5 show that the relationship between ethnic residential concentration and intermarriage characterizes all class and educational levels; controlling for subjective class identification and years of school completed, the intermarried have lower rates of ethnic residential concentration than the homogamously married for each ethnic group (except the Portuguese). Among middle class French Canadians, for example, 23 percent of the in-married are in areas of high ethnic concentration compared to 9 percent of the intermarried. The respective proportions for working class French Canadians are 29 percent and 9 percent. Moreover, for both intermarried and nonintermarried French Canadians the middle classes are less ethnically concentrated than are the working classes. The same pattern emerges with education: almost three times as many homogamous French Canadians with less than a high school education or with a high school education are in areas of high ethnic residential concentration compared to the intermarried of similar educational levels. Differences in ethnic

Table 4-5. Ethnic Residential Concentration by Ethnicity, Subjective Social Class,* Education,** and Intermarriage (Percentage)

	Intermarried Residential Concentration			Nonintermarried Residential Concentration		
	Low	*Medium*	*High*	*Low*	*Medium*	*High*
French Canadians						
Subjective Class Identification						
Middle Class	44.8	46.6	8.6	47.6	29.3	23.2
Working Class	40.0	50.7	9.3	34.8	36.6	28.6
Education						
High	53.3	33.3	13.3	62.5	25.0	12.5
Medium	59.5	35.1	5.4	41.3	43.5	15.2
Low	32.5	57.5	10.0	37.0	32.6	30.4
Irish						
Subjective Class Identification						
Middle Class	79.3	20.7	0.0	78.3	21.7	0.0
Working Class	83.7	16.3	0.0	78.3	21.7	0.0
Education						
High	81.3	18.8	0.0	78.8	21.2	0.0
Medium	86.8	13.2	0.0	84.6	15.4	0.0
Low	76.3	23.7	0.0	72.7	27.3	0.0
Italians						
Subjective Class Identification						
Middle Class	68.0	24.0	8.0	39.7	31.6	28.7
Working Class	40.7	32.2	27.1	37.2	25.6	37.2
Education						
High	60.7	28.6	10.7	52.8	27.8	19.4
Medium	57.9	34.2	7.9	48.1	24.1	27.8
Low	52.9	23.5	23.5	31.9	31.9	36.3
Portuguese						
Subjective Class Identification						
Middle Class	28.1	15.6	56.3	62.5	31.3	6.3
Working Class	38.5	19.2	42.3	43.8	9.4	46.9
Education						
High	20.0	40.0	40.0	—	—	—
Medium	33.3	11.1	55.6	70.0	10.0	20.0
Low	39.3	7.1	53.6	42.9	17.1	40.0

*Middle = middle or upper class; working = working or lower class.
**High = some college; medium = completed high school; low = did not complete high school.

residential concentration are small between college educated French Canadians in homogamous and heterogamous marriages and are in a different direction compared to other educational levels.

The same consistent finding, with smaller differences, character-izes the Irish, i.e., the homogamously married Irish are more likely to be in areas of greater Irish residential concentration compared to the intermarried of all educational levels and both social classes. For both the intermarried and nonintermarried Irish, those with at least some college education are more concentrated in more dense ethnic areas than those completing high school. Nevertheless, the highest level of residential concentration characterizes the least educated Irish, irrespective of whom they marry.

In-married Italians of all classes and educational levels are more residentially concentrated than intermarried Italians and differences are substantial (comparable to the French Canadians). For example, 29 percent of the middle class, homogamously married Italians are in areas of high ethnic concentration compared to 8 percent of the intermarried Italians; 28 percent of homogamously married Italians who completed high school are in high ethnic areas compared to 8 percent of the intermarried with similar levels of educational attainment. There is a clear inverse relationship between education and ethnic residential concentration for both the intermarried and nonintermarried Italians. For homogamously married Italians, 53 percent of those with some college education are in areas of low ethnic concentration compared to 48 percent of high school gradu-ates and 32 percent of those with less than a high school education. The comparable proportions for the intermarried Italians are 61 per-cent, 58 percent, and 53 percent, respectively. The same pattern may be observed with subjective social class.

Controlling for both class and age simultaneously does not alter this overall picture. Data in Table 4-6 show that the in-married French Canadians and Italians are more concentrated in ethnic areas for both age cohorts and within cohorts for both social class categories. Within the intermarried and nonintermarried subgroups, working class French Canadians and Italians have higher rates of areal concentration than the middle classes for both age cohorts. Differences between intermarried and nonintermarried middle class Italians are greater than between working class Italians, a pattern that does not characterize the French Canadians. Moreover, there is an increase between the two youngest cohorts in the proportion of intermarried couples who are concentrated in high ethnic areas—a pattern that characterizes all three ethnic groups and is particularly pronounced among the middle classes. The overall patterns of residential concentration for the Irish intermarried and noninter-married controlling for class and age are much less consistent than for Italians and French Canadians.

Controlling for both education and cohort, data on the residential concentration of the intermarried and nonintermarried show the same patterns (Table 4-7). Nonintermarried ethnics are more concentrated residentially than intermarried ethnics within all educational categories, without exception, for Italians and French Canadians and with one exception for the Irish. Similarly, the more educated within the intermarried and nonintermarried Italians and French Canadians of both cohorts are less residentially concentrated in ethnic areas than the less educated. This is true for the Irish

Table 4-6. Ethnic Residential Concentration by Ethnicity, Subjective Social Class,* Age, and Intermarriage (Percentage)

	Intermarried Residential Concentration			*Nonintermarried Residential Concentration*		
	Low	*Medium*	*High*	*Low*	*Medium*	*High*
French Canadians						
25-44						
Middle Class	57.6	33.3	9.1	54.1	27.0	18.9
Working Class	39.5	48.8	11.6	31.8	36.4	31.8
45-64						
Middle Class	28.6	66.7	0.0	42.9	35.7	21.4
Working Class	40.0	52.0	8.0	35.4	37.5	27.1
Irish						
25-44						
Middle Class	76.3	23.7	0.0	—	—	—
Working Class	85.2	14.8	0.0	77.8	22.2	0.0
45-64						
Middle Class	85.0	15.0	0.0	80.8	19.2	0.0
Working Class	85.0	15.0	0.0	91.7	8.3	0.0
Italians						
25-44						
Middle Class	60.5	30.2	9.3	38.8	29.9	31.3
Working Class	41.0	33.3	25.6	33.3	38.5	28.2
45-64						
Middle Class	83.3	13.3	3.3	37.5	35.7	26.8
Working Class	40.0	30.0	30.0	37.1	22.6	40.3
Portuguese						
25-44						
Middle Class	19.0	23.8	57.1	—	—	—
Working Class	50.0	12.5	37.5	54.5	9.1	36.4
45-64						
Middle Class	40.0	0.0	60.0	—	—	—
Working Class	—	—	—	40.0	10.0	50.0

*Middle = middle or upper class; working = working or lower class.

with one exception. Finally, the increase in residential concentration among those 25–44 compared to the older age cohort is evident among the intermarried French Canadians and Italians while there is a decrease among the homogamously married for each of the educational levels.

Table 4-7. Ethnic Residential Concentration by Ethnicity, Education,* Age, and Intermarriage (Percentage)

	Intermarried Residential Concentration			Nonintermarried Residential Concentration		
	Low	Medium	High	Low	Medium	High
French Canadians						
25–44						
High	36.6	51.2	12.2	37.5	33.3	29.2
Medium	60.0	32.0	8.0	44.8	41.4	13.8
Low	—	—	—	—	—	—
45–64						
High	26.7	63.3	10.0	33.9	37.1	29.0
Medium	54.5	45.5	0.0	38.5	38.5	23.1
Low	—	—	—	—	—	—
Irish						
25–44						
High	78.6	21.4	0.0	—	—	—
Medium	80.0	20.0	0.0	76.9	23.1	0.0
Low	80.8	19.2	0.0	80.0	20.0	0.0
45–64						
High	75.0	25.0	0.0	80.0	20.0	0.0
Medium	100.0	0.0	0.0	90.0	10.0	0.0
Low	—	—	—	83.3	16.7	0.0
Italians						
25–44						
High	40.6	31.3	28.1	27.5	41.2	31.4
Medium	60.7	32.1	7.1	46.9	21.9	31.3
Low	56.5	30.4	13.0	45.8	33.3	20.8
45–64						
High	67.6	14.7	17.6	30.0	32.5	37.5
Medium	50.0	40.0	10.0	47.6	28.6	23.8
Low	—	—	—	66.7	16.7	16.7
Portuguese						
25–44						
High	37.5	40.0	50.0	36.4	27.3	36.4
Medium	33.3	8.3	58.3	—	—	—
Low	—	—	—	—	—	—
45–64						
High	30.0	0.0	70.0	50.0	15.0	35.0
Medium	—	—	—	—	—	—
Low	—	—	—	—	—	—

*High = at least some college; medium = completed high school; low = did not complete high school.

CONCLUSION

The data analyzed in this chapter point strongly in the direction of the persistence of ethnic residential concentration. Clearly, the concentration of ethnics is not limited to the older generation, the lower classes, least educated, homogamously married subpopulations. This is not to argue that there is no variation in ethnic residential concentration. To the contrary: systematic variation has emerged by cohort, class, and marriage patterns. The young, more educated middle classes and the intermarried are more likely to live in areas of lower ethnic density than the older, less educated, working classes who are married to wives with similar ethnic backgrounds. Nevertheless, ethnic residential integration does not tend toward very low levels but rather to less concentration at high levels of density.

It is not clear from the data available whether changes in ethnic residential concentration over time reflect a decline in ethnic identification or a decline in the way ethnicity is expressed among the young. Similarly, the increase in medium levels of residential concentration among some segments of young, middle class ethnics may reflect a real trend toward greater ethnic assertiveness expressed in residential choices.

It must be recalled that the data analyzed for ethnic concentration are cross-sectional and the dynamics of change have been inferred from cohort variations. Moreover, an analysis of the relative concentration and dispersal of religious subpopulations cannot be made because of the absence of census data on religion. The data analyzed are limited to one state (Rhode Island) and it is not clear whether the patterns on ethnic residential concentration are typical or exceptional. Scattered previous research, while not comparable directly, tend to strongly support the conclusions that have been reached for Rhode Island (cf. Kantrowitz, 1973). Finally, it should be noted again that census data on ethnic stock refer only to first and second generation immigrants and for some ethnics, particularly the Irish, the measure of ethnic concentration is a most conservative estimate.

Ethnic residential concentration and dispersal represent some of the clearest clues about the persistence of the ethnic factor as a major dimension of American social life. This theme will be pursued as the analysis of marriage and mobility processes proceeds. The implications of ethnic residential concentration for ethnic continuity will be investigated directly in subsequent analysis.

✻ *Part II*

Family Processes

When People Marry

The age at which people marry is of central importance for a wide range of social and demographic processes tied into the life cycle. The amount and timing of education, social and geographic mobility, and family formation and dissolution are among the many processes associated with when people marry. Ethnic variation and change in these broader social processes may be tied to patterns of age at marriage. In the United States, the pattern has been that women marry at younger ages than men, and socioeconomic status is positively related to age at marriage. Over time the trend has been toward marriage at younger ages. Several studies have concluded that age at marriage varies by ethnicity and that ethnic differences diminish among second and third generations (Greely, 1974, 1976; Carter and Glick, 1976). However, analytic issues associated with the ethnic factor in age at marriage have not been investigated systematically or comprehensively. The analysis of ethnic variation and change in the extent and stability of marriages in Chapter 3 raises a series of issues regarding the timing of marriage: What are the patterns of ethnic group variation in age at marriage for men and women? What have been the major changes in ethnic variation in age at marriage and is there a pattern of convergence over time in this ethnic differential? What are the variations in the timing of marriage by socioeconomic status within ethnic subpopulations? Do ethnic differences in age at marriage diminish when variation in socioeconomic status between ethnic groups is controlled?

The systematic analysis of these four issues allows for an evaluation of whether ethnic differences in the timing of marriage are temporary and transitional. To the extent that the ethnic differential in age at marriage is not limited to a particular cohort or socioeconomic stratum, the importance of examining ethnic differences is enhanced.

WHEN MEN MARRY

The data in Table 5-1 allow for an examination of ethnic variation in age at first marriage among ever-married males. Overall, Protestant and Catholic men have the same average age at marriage, with Jews marrying two years later. The overall Catholic pattern, however, masks important variation among ethnic Catholic subpopulations. Among Catholic ethnics, the average age at marriage of Irish males closely resembles the Jewish pattern while Italians, Portuguese, and French Canadians are similar to the overall Catholic-Protestant pattern. French Canadians have the youngest age at marriage of all ethnic groups—23.6.

Median age at marriage measures the mid-point of the distribution of ages at marriage. An examination of the upper and lower ends of the distribution reveals the importance of going beyond an analysis of averages. Data on the proportion marrying at younger and older ages show that only a very small proportion of Jewish males marry at ages 20 or younger compared to Protestants and Catholics, while 40 percent marry at age 27 or older. More importantly, the similarity in average age at marriage among Protestants and Catholics does not imply identical distributions. The proportions of Protestants marrying at older ages are significantly greater than for Catholics, yet Protestants are somewhat more likely to marry at younger ages, as well. Hence the distribution of age at marriage is more widely spread among Protestants than among Catholics: over half the Protestants marry at the younger or older ends of the distribution while almost six out of ten Catholic males marry between the ages 21 and 26.

The analysis of the proportion marrying at younger and older ages adds an important dimension to patterns of marriage among ethnic Catholics. The Irish pattern is not unexpected: a small proportion of Irish males marry at younger ages (but significantly higher than Jews) and over 40 percent marry at older ages. However, unlike the data on average age at marriage that show little variation among non-Irish Catholic ethnics, the distribution of age at marriage reveals important ethnic differences. The proportion of Italian men who marry at younger ages is significantly below the Portuguese and French Canadian level and the proportion of Italians marrying at

Table 5-1. Median Age at First Marriage and Proportion Marrying at Younger and Older Ages* by Ethnicity and Age: Ever-Married Men

	Total	Protestants	Jews	Catholics	French Canadians	Irish	Italians	Portuguese
All ages								
Median	24.4	24.4	26.3	24.4	23.6	26.2	24.2	24.0
Percent marrying young	14.2	16.3	2.9	14.3	20.0	8.0	12.7	18.8
Percent marrying old	30.1	34.0	40.0	28.4	21.3	40.5	30.2	25.0
Over age 45								
Median	26.1	26.4	26.7	26.0	24.7	27.7	25.3	24.0
Percent marrying young	8.7	9.2	0.0	9.4	14.0	4.5	9.6	15.7
Percent marrying old	42.8	47.1	41.2	41.7	33.1	58.2	38.4	40.7
Below age 45								
Median	23.0	22.5	24.0	23.2	22.6	24.5	22.9	23.7
Percent marrying young	20.4	26.7	5.6	19.5	26.9	11.9	16.3	21.9
Percent marrying old	15.1	16.9	39.0	14.2	7.7	20.4	20.2	9.3

*For males, young equals age 20 or below; old equals age 27 or above.

older ages is higher than for these Catholic subgroups. Thus, while only an Irish–non-Irish difference emerges from an analysis of average age at marriage, three distinct age-at-marriage patterns may be discerned from the distribution data: (1) late marriage patterns among Irish males; (2) early marriage patterns among Portuguese and French Canadian men; and (3) an Italian age at marriage pattern that is intermediate between these two.

These overall age-at-marriage patterns for ethnic subpopulations obscure important changes over time. Among older males, for example, median age at marriage was 26.1, three years later than among younger males; the proportion of males marrying for the first time at age 27 or above declined from 43 percent for older males to 15 percent among younger males; the proportion marrying young more than doubled when males over and under age 45 were compared.

Patterns of age at marriage of ethnic subpopulations may be examined for these two age cohorts. Among males age 45 and over, differences in age at marriage by religion are small. Catholics tend to marry at somewhat younger ages, on the average, when compared to Protestants, but the distributions of age at marriage are quite similar at the upper and lower ends. Average age at marriage among older Jews is somewhat later than Protestants or Catholics, with no older Jews in the sample marrying for the first time below age 21. The most significant variation in average age at marriage among older males is among Catholic ethnics: Irish males are conspicuous by their late average age at marriage (one year later than Jews) and almost six out of every ten older Irish males married for the first time at age 27 or over. In sharp contrast to this pattern are older Portuguese males who married over three-and-a-half years younger on average than the Irish and almost one-and-a-half years younger than the Italians. Older Italian males are clearly intermediate between the Irish, on the one hand, and the Portuguese and French Canadians, on the other.

A somewhat different pattern emerges for the younger cohort. Young Catholic males marry at later ages on the average than Protestants. However, this is not because a larger proportion of Catholics marry late: indeed, a smaller proportion of young Catholics marry at older ages when compared to Protestants. Rather, the later age at marriage among younger Catholics reflects the smaller proportion of Catholics marrying young when compared to Protestants and the greater concentration of marriage among young Catholics in the 21–26 age range. Among religious groups, young Jewish males stand out in the low proportion marrying before age 21 and in the high proportion marrying late.

For young Catholics, the Irish retain their pattern of late age at marriage mainly as a result of the low proportion marrying at young ages rather than because a large proportion marry at older ages. Indeed, the median age at marriage of young Irish males is slightly later than among young Jews despite the fact that almost twice as many Jews as Irish marry at older ages. Moreover, the proportion of young Irish and Italians who marry at age 27 or older is about the same, but over 16 percent of Italian males marry before age 21 compared to less than 12 percent of Irish males. Hence, the average age at marriage among young Irish males is over one-and-a-half years older than among young Italian males.

Therefore, the data show a much greater complexity in the timing of marriage among ethnic males when age is introduced. The only consistent pattern among religious subgroups by age is the Jewish-non-Jewish distinction, since older Catholics tend to marry at somewhat earlier ages and younger Catholics tend to marry at somewhat later ages than Protestants. The distribution data point to the narrower spread in age at marriage among Catholics than among Protestants with a larger proportion of Protestants in both age cohorts marrying at older ages.

The only consistent pattern for Catholic ethnic groups by cohort is the Irish-non-Irish distinction. Although not reflected in average age at marriage, distribution data show that a smaller proportion of Italians than Portuguese or French Canadians tend to marry at very young ages. Thus, there is some indication of a threefold rather than a dichotomous distinction among Catholic ethnic males when age is controlled.

In addition to examining these ethnic patterns within age cohorts, cross-sectional data by age provide the opportunity to infer patterns of change in age at marriage over time. The overall decline in average age at marriage does not uniformly characterize the ethnic subpopulations. The sharpest declines in average age at marriage have occurred for Protestants (from an average of 26.4 among older males to an average of 22.5 among younger males) and for the Irish (a decline of 3.2 years). Declines of about two years may be noted for other religious and Catholic ethnic subpopulations except for the Portuguese, where declines in age at marriage were insignificant.

The general decline in age at marriage and the different intensities of change for various ethnic subgroups imply an unmistakable convergence among Catholic ethnics in age at marriage: an age at marriage difference of almost four years among older Catholic ethnics has declined to less than two years among the younger cohort. This convergence is mainly the result of significant changes among the "exceptional" Irish, particularly the sharp decline in the proportion marrying late (from 58 to 20 percent). Nevertheless, despite the clear process of diminishing differences over time, the Irish remain later marrying males compared to other Catholic subpopulations.

The convergence pattern among Catholic ethnic males contrasts with the widening of age at marriage differences among the three religious subpopulations. Only a small range in average age at marriage was evident for the older cohort of Protestants, Catholics, and Jews: this difference more than doubles for the younger cohort. This reflects the sharper reduction in age at marriage among Protestants. Over one-fourth of the young Protestant males married at age 20 or younger while such young marriages characterized less than one out of ten for the older cohort. Hence, the sharp decrease in average age at marriage reflects this shift in the proportion marrying young.

The pattern of divergence in age at marriage among religious subpopulations and convergence in age at marriage among Catholic ethnic groups has resulted overall in a reduction of differences in the range of age at marriage. For the older cohort the range in average age at marriage was 3.7 years while for the younger cohort the range is only 2 years. It should be noted, however, that, in contrast, the ranges in the proportion marrying young and in the proportion marrying old have increased over time. This range is strongly affected by the extremes of the Jewish population. Changes in the distribution of age at marriage are modified considerably when the Jewish group is eliminated from the comparison of ranges in age at marriage. Most importantly, the intensity and direction of changes should not be confused with the remaining absolute level of differences. Despite diminished differences over time among Catholic ethnics and increased differences among religious subpopulations, *absolute* differences in the ages at which Catholic ethnic men marry are larger than the differences among Protestants, Catholics, and Jews.

Finally, the general reduction in the proportion marrying late and the increase in young marriages have resulted in a decline in the proportions of all subpopulations (except the Jews) at the two extremes of the age at marriage distribution. This means that there has been a significant increase over time in the proportion of males who marry within the limited range of ages 21-26. For the Irish these changes have been most dramatic: only about a third of the older Irish married for the first time between the ages 21-26; of the younger Irish males who marry, about two-thirds did so between those ages.

WHEN WOMEN MARRY

A comparison of Tables 5-1 and 5-2 reveals the lower age at marriage of women than men for each ethnic subpopulation. This is consistent with the general pattern in the United States. The question remains, however, whether ethnic variation and change noted in the pattern of male age at marriage characterizes women as well. Overall, the data on age at marriage among women strongly support the patterns noted for men and, with some minor qualifications, point to the importance of the ethnic factor in differentiating the timing of marriage.

An examination of the data in Table 5-2 shows that Protestant and Catholic women have the same average age at marriage and approximately the same distribution—about 30 percent marry as teenagers and about one out of four women marry after age 25. Jewish women have a distinctly later age at marriage with over one-third marrying for the first time at age 25 or later. As for males, Irish women resemble closely the average age at marriage of Jewish women with little variation among non-Irish Catholic ethnics. Again, the distribution data show that Italian women are at an intermediate level of age at marriage relative to Irish women, on the one hand, and Portuguese and French Canadian women, on the other.

Similarities between the patterns of age at marriage of men and women by ethnicity emerge within age cohorts. Jewish women marry at older ages on the average than Protestants or Catholics in both age cohorts; Catholic women over age 45 married at earlier ages than Protestants while the reverse pattern characterizes those below 45. About half the older Irish women married for the first time at later ages, with older Portuguese women marrying younger than other Catholic ethnics. Like the young male pattern, young Irish women retain their later age at marriage. However, the more than two-year difference between older Irish and Italian women in average age at marriage diminishes to less than one year for the younger age cohort.

Over time, there has been a decline of over two years in the average age women marry. As with men, the decline was sharpest for Protestants and the Irish. In general, there has been a convergence of Catholic ethnic differences in age at marriage among women similar to that for men. However, unlike the male pattern, differences in age at marriage among women of different religious subpopulations have diminished. Overall, therefore, there is much less of an ethnic difference in age at marriage for younger women than for older women.

Table 5-2.   Median Age at First Marriage and Proportion Marrying at Younger and Older Ages* by Ethnicity and Age: Ever-Married Women

	Total	Protestants	Jews	Catholics	French Canadians	Irish	Italians	Portuguese
All ages								
Median	21.8	21.8	23.4	21.8	21.6	23.5	21.8	21.4
Percent marrying young	28.7	30.9	17.9	28.9	30.4	15.5	23.1	33.0
Percent marrying old	24.0	25.4	35.9	23.1	21.8	35.3	20.2	22.0
Over age 45								
Median	23.3	23.8	24.9	23.0	22.8	24.9	22.7	22.2
Percent marrying young	21.4	21.6	21.7	22.3	23.8	13.2	23.2	24.3
Percent marrying old	37.0	40.1	47.8	35.1	30.1	49.5	28.4	32.4
Below age 45								
Median	21.0	20.7	22.3	21.0	20.6	22.3	21.5	20.8
Percent marrying young	36.3	41.9	12.6	35.4	38.7	18.3	23.0	38.1
Percent marrying old	10.3	8.1	18.9	11.2	10.9	18.3	10.9	15.9

*Young equals age 19 or below; old equals age 25 or above.

The data on the distribution of age at marriage among women of different ethnic backgrounds confirm these observations. Generally, there has been an increase in the proportion of women marrying in their teens: about one-fourth of the older women married before age 20 compared to more than one-third of the younger women. However, this increase in teenage marriage is not uniform for all ethnic groups. The increase among Protestant women is much stronger than among Catholics; the percentage of Jewish women marrying below age 20 actually declined from 22 to 13 percent.

A general convergence in the proportion of women marrying young has occurred among Catholic ethnics. This is the result of two distinct patterns: the relative stability over time in the proportion of Italian women marrying in their teens and the increase in the proportion of Irish women marrying young. However, for the older cohort, only Irish women have a distinctive age-at-marriage pattern; greater diversity and a distinct Italian intermediate level of age at marriage emerge in the younger cohort.

In general, between one-fourth and one-fifth of all women marry after age 25 with exceptions among Jewish and Irish women, where the proportion is more than one-third. Over time, there has been a clear reduction in the proportion of women marrying at later ages: for Protestants the reduction was from 40 percent to 8 percent; among Irish women the reduction was from 50 percent to 18 percent. Younger Portuguese women exhibit an interesting pattern of bimodality—a large proportion marry at young as well as at older ages. The overall similarity in the patterns of male and female age at marriage by ethnicity makes a convincing case for the importance of the ethnic factor in when people marry. The retention of ethnic differences despite processes of convergence suggests that at least under some conditions ethnic variation in marriage is neither transitory nor temporal. Although there are cohort and sex differences in age at marriage, ethnic differences in age at marriage are not solely a function of these differences and are retained when these factors are controlled.

SOCIAL CLASS AND THE TIMING OF MARRIAGE

The explanation most often suggested for ethnic differences in the timing of marriage is socioeconomic. The argument in its most simple form states that differences in age at marriage among ethnic groups reflect differential levels of education obtained, occupational status, or social class in general. Hence, the argument continues, it is not ethnicity per se that is related to the timing of marriage but variation in socioeconomic status characterizing ethnic groups. Ethnicity is thus an indicator of the more basic variables of social class. Although the argument seems reasonable and is consistent with the known facts about the socioeconomic composition of ethnic groups (see Chapter 2) few direct tests of its validity have been made.

Two general questions may be addressed with the data available: What are the socioeconomic differences in age at marriage within *ethnic* subpopulations? What are the ethnic differences in age at marriage within *socioeconomic* subgroupings? Two measures of socioeconomic status are available for both men and women: level of educational attainment and self-definition of current social class.

Social Class Variation in Age at Marriage

The basic pattern in age at marriage by education within ethnic subpopulations is that those with at least some college education tend to marry later on the average than those with less education. There appears to be no systematic difference in age at marriage between male high school graduates and those with lower education (Table 5-3). The only exception to this pattern of later age at marriage among the more educated is the Irish: the least educated Irish males have the highest average age at marriage. However, a more careful inspection of the Irish by cohort reveals that controlling for age the Irish conform to the general pattern. Hence, within both age cohorts, all ethnic groups without exception show the same pattern—college educated males marry later than less educated males.

A similar pattern emerges when subjective social class is used as an indicator of socioeconomic status. Generally, males who define themselves as upper or middle class marry later than males defining themselves as working or lower social class. French Canadians are the major exception to this pattern when age is controlled. Working class French Canadians tend to marry later than middle class French Canadians. It should be noted that this pattern is consistent with the data by education—among the two categories of educational attainment that are available for French Canadians of different age cohorts, those not completing high school married later than those completing high school.

The positive relationship between education and age at marriage (the higher the education, the later the age at marriage) is more consistent for females than males, since it holds for women with less education as well, although there are some exceptions among less educated Irish women and college educated Italian women (Table 5-4). Within age cohorts, the patterns are more consistent. In every case when age is controlled, college educated women marry later

Table 5-3. Median Age at First Marriage by Ethnicity, Age, Education, and Subjective Social Class: Ever-Married Men

Age and Socioeconomic Status	Total	Protestants	Jews	Catholics	French Canadians	Irish	Italians	Portuguese
Education*								
All ages								
High	25.2	25.5	26.0	25.3	24.5	26.4	24.7	—
Medium	23.5	23.6	25.0	23.5	22.7	25.4	22.9	24.1
Low	24.4	24.3	—	24.4	23.8	27.0	24.3	22.7
Over age 45								
High	27.1	27.5	—	27.4	—	28.0	27.5	—
Medium	25.1	26.5	—	25.8	24.0	27.5	25.4	—
Low	25.5	25.5	—	25.6	24.8	27.6	24.9	24.8
Below age 45								
High	24.2	23.9	23.8	24.6	—	24.9	24.3	—
Medium	22.6	22.2	—	22.7	22.3	24.3	22.3	23.5
Low	22.6	21.6	—	22.9	22.7	23.3	22.8	23.7
Social Class**								
All ages								
Middle	24.5	24.7	26.0	24.5	23.3	26.5	23.8	25.1
Working	24.2	23.8	—	24.2	24.0	25.6	24.5	23.8
Over age 45								
Middle	26.3	26.7	26.4	26.2	24.0	28.1	25.5	—
Working	25.6	25.5	—	25.8	25.9	26.7	25.2	24.5
Below age 45								
Middle	23.2	22.7	24.0	23.5	22.4	24.3	23.0	25.3
Working	22.7	21.9	—	22.9	22.7	24.8	22.7	23.4

*High = at least some college; medium = high school graduate; low = did not complete high school.
**Middle = middle or upper class; working = working or lower class.

Table 5-4. Median Age at First Marriage by Ethnicity, Age, Education, and Subjective Social Class: Ever-Married Women

Age and Socioeconomic Status	Total	Protestants	Jews	Catholics	French Canadians	Irish	Italians	Portuguese
Education*								
All ages								
High	23.5	23.9	22.9	23.3	—	24.3	21.2	—
Medium	22.0	22.0	23.5	21.9	21.6	23.0	22.2	22.1
Low	21.4	20.7	25.3	21.5	21.5	23.8	21.8	21.2
Over age 45								
High	25.8	25.6	—	26.5	—	—	—	—
Medium	24.3	24.6	—	24.2	23.0	24.4	24.5	—
Low	22.6	21.6	—	22.7	22.8	25.2	22.2	22.2
Below age 45								
High	22.5	22.5	—	22.7	—	23.6	—	—
Medium	20.2	20.9	—	21.3	21.3	22.0	21.8	21.8
Low	19.9	18.5	—	20.3	19.9	20.5	21.4	20.0
Social Class**								
All ages								
Middle	22.1	22.3	24.4	21.9	21.4	23.6	22.0	20.8
Working	21.5	21.0	—	21.7	21.9	23.1	21.7	21.9
Over age 45								
Middle	23.8	24.3	24.5	23.4	23.0	25.3	23.1	22.0
Working	22.8	22.9	—	22.7	22.7	24.3	21.8	22.3
Below age 45								
Middle	21.2	21.3	22.5	21.1	20.7	22.6	21.4	20.4
Working	20.5	19.0	—	20.8	20.6	21.5	21.7	21.6

*High = at least some college; medium = high school graduate; low = did not complete high school.
**Middle = middle or upper class; working = working or lower class.

than those who have completed high school and the latter tend to marry at older ages than women with lower education. The only exception to this relationship between education and age at marriage when age is controlled is among Irish women—Irish women who have graduated from high school tend to marry earlier than those with lower levels of educational attainment.

When social class is defined subjectively, women in higher social classes tend to have married at later ages than those in lower classes. This general pattern is consistent controlling for age and parallels the data on educational level and the findings for males. There are a few exceptions—particularly among Portuguese and younger Italian women. The weaker relationship between age at marriage and current subjective social class identification mainly reflects the timing differences between marriage and this measure of social status. Education, in contrast, is normally completed closer in time to the formation of families and may be expected to be a more sensitive measure of social class at the time of marriage.

Ethnic Variation Controlling for Social Class

More important than the confirmation of education and social class differences in age at marriage within ethnic subpopulations are comparisons among ethnic subpopulations within socioeconomic groupings. In this regard two interrelated issues may be analyzed. First, an examination can be made of the changing effects of ethnicity on age at marriage when social class is controlled; second, the question of increasing or decreasing ethnic differences in age at marriage over time can be investigated within social class categories.

Data in Table 5-3 suggest that after controlling for socioeconomic status and age, some important ethnic differences in age at marriage remain. Catholic men marry later than Protestants within all educational levels and social class categories for the younger cohort. Hence, the general finding that younger Catholics marry later than Protestants cannot be explained by educational, social class, or age differences between Catholic and Protestant subpopulations. For the older cohort, the pattern is not clear, reflecting in part the greater heterogeneity among older Catholics. The later age at marriage among Jewish men is reduced considerably when controls for age and education or social class are introduced. The small number of cases, however, prevents any firm conclusions on this point.

Furthermore, controls for socioeconomic status and age do not eliminate the Irish pattern of later age at marriage. This pattern, however, is much clearer in the older age cohort and diminishes for the younger age cohort. There is no clear pattern of differences in age at marriage among other Catholic ethnics when socioeconomic status is controlled. Data on the distribution of age at marriage not shown in the table reveal some tendency for Italians to retain their intermediate position but controls for socioeconomic status reduce considerably the consistency of this pattern. Hence, the overall differences in age at marriage among the non-Irish largely reflect differential social class composition.

These conclusions apply as well for age at marriage patterns among ethnic women. With some exceptions, Irish women tend to marry later than other Catholic ethnics, controlling for socioeconomic status and age; Italian women of higher socioeconomic status tend to have an intermediate age at marriage. Young Catholic women of all educational levels tend to marry later than Protestants and high socioeconomic status Jewish women marry later than non-Jewish women of comparable social class levels. Thus, controlling for age, sex, and two social class measures, the major patterns of ethnic variation in the timing of marriage are not eliminated.

There has been a reduction in age at marriage for all ethnic groups within socioeconomic categories. With some exceptions, this change has been more characteristic of Protestant and Irish men and women controlling for social class variables. Among both male and female Irish, the reduction in age at marriage is greater for the less educated and least for the more educated. In striking contrast is the pattern for Italian men and women: the reduction in average age at marriage among Italians is greater among the more educated and smaller among the less educated. However, this difference between Italians and Irish does not appear with the measure of subjective social class.

This finding raises the important general question of convergence or divergence over time in ethnic variation in the timing of marriage within social class groupings. The issue of convergence of divergence in age at marriage is complex and has to be considered separately for men and women, for religious and ethnic subpopulations and for education and subjective social class indicators. Two general conclusions may be drawn from these comparisons: first, a clear pattern of narrowing differences in age at marriage between Catholic ethnic groups emerges when socioeconomic status is controlled. This is true for both male and female patterns in age at marriage and with but minor exceptions for both education and subjective social class.

The second pattern that emerges relates to the trend in age at marriage for religious subpopulations controlling for socioeconomic status. This pattern is more complicated and ambiguous. With some exceptions, there seems to be an increased spread in religious differentials in male age at marriage that characterizes more recent cohorts for all socioeconomic categories. In contrast, age-at-marriage differences among Protestant, Catholic, and Jewish women appear to diminish over time at least for the more educated and middle class categories.

Although some convergence in ethnic variation in the timing of marriage may be evident, it is important to emphasize that absolute differences remain for the young and are certainly not confined to the lower socioeconomic strata. Clearly, from the evidence presented, there is no basis for concluding that differences in when ethnics marry are marginal or lower class phenomena that disappear in one or two generations. Indeed, the data point to the conclusion that for both sexes, for objective and subjective indicators of socioeconomic status for younger as well as older age cohorts, ethnic variation in the timing of marriage is an important continuing feature of contemporary American society. To the extent that the timing of marriage has implications for a wide variety of social processes, ethnic variation may have important consequences for ethnic differentials in these processes.

MARITAL AGE AND ETHNIC CONTINUITY

Up to this point, age at marriage has been analyzed from the perspective of ethnic change and variation in an attempt to isolate and identify differentials in when ethnics marry. In this section the focus is on the possible implications of these age at marriage patterns for selected indicators of ethnic continuity.[a] In particular, does the timing of marriage have consequences for marriage and residential choices that imply greater ethnic cohesiveness?

The first issue that may be examined relates to the effects of age at marriage on ethnic residential concentration. As was discussed earlier, differences in age at marriage are associated with complex processes related to ethnicity. Data in Table 5-5 show that age at marriage is related to ethnic residential concentration but in different ways for the various ethnic subpopulations. Two basic patterns emerge for males: there is a positive relationship between age at marriage and ethnic residential concentration for the Irish and

---

[a]Another more commonly analyzed consequence of age at marriage differentials is the timing and tempo of childbearing. This is examined in Bouvier and Rao, 1975. While the relationship between age at marriage and fertility is inverse, the authors suggest that differential age at marriage is the mechanism relating education and family size. A systematic analysis of the role of age at marriage in ethnic fertility differentials has not been made.

Italians—those who marry early are more likely to reside in areas of low ethnic concentration. The reverse pattern characterizes Portuguese and French Canadian males—those who marry late are more likely to live in areas of low ethnic concentration. These patterns hold for both cohorts and are consistent in large part with the socioeconomic characteristics of these ethnic subpopulations.

The relationship between the timing of marriage for women and residential concentration is much less pronounced than for men and with some exceptions tends to be positive—women who marry early are more likely to reside in areas of low ethnic concentration than women who marry late. Hence, for the Irish and Italians, late marriage and ethnic continuity as reflected in residential concentration are consistent with socioeconomic changes including higher levels of education. This is not true for either the French Canadians or Portuguese where the delay in marriage associated with higher education reduces the probability of ethnic residential concentration.

Another dimension of ethnic continuity is marital choice (for details, see Chapter 6). Do the processes associated with when people marry have consequences for ethnic homogamy? Data in Table 5-6 show the percentage intermarried for ethnics marrying early and late.[b] While there is no doubt that the timing of marriage has

Table 5-5. Percentage in Areas of Low Ethnic Residential Concentration by Age at Marriage,* Age, and Sex: Catholic Ethnic Groups

Age at marriage and Ethnicity	Males			Females		
	Total	Below Age 45	Age 45 and over	Total	Below Age 45	Age 45 and over
French Canadians						
Early	38	40	35	53	57	45
Late	43	43	43	47	59	43
Irish						
Early	86	80	100**	87	86	90
Late	77	75	78	84	90	81
Italians						
Early	55	62	44	48	54	39
Late	43	45	43	47	42	49
Portuguese						
Early	25	31	14**	47	44	57
Late	38	50**	36	29	43	21

*Early = below age 20 for females and below age 21 for males; late = above age 24 for females and above age 26 for males.
**Less than 10 cases.

[b]For religious intermarriage, these data refer to primary homogamy. See Chapter 6.

consequences for whom people marry, the relationship is far from uniform for ethnic subpopulations, for males and females, and over time. The complexity may be seen in examining Protestants. Overall, the proportion of Protestants who intermarry is about the same for men and women marrying early and late. However, when variations within cohorts are examined it appears that young Protestant men who marry late have a higher out-marriage rate than those marrying early; among Protestant men of the older cohort, marrying early is more associated with intermarriage. The reverse change characterizes Protestant women: young Protestant women who marry early have higher intermarriage rates, while older Protestant women who marry late are more likely to intermarry than those marrying early. This complexity suggests that the meaning of early and late marriage has changed over time for Protestants and differently for men and women. Moreover, given the general positive relationship between education and age at marriage examined earlier, it is clear that the influence of marriage age on homogamy is not solely a function

Table 5-6. Percentage Intermarried by Age at Marriage, Ethnicity, Age, and Sex

Age at marriage and Ethnicity	Males			Females		
	Total	Below age 45	Age 45 and over	Total	Below age 45	Age 45 and over
Protestants						
Early	56	50	68	60	62	66
Late	55	76	48	56	50	58
Jews						
Early*	21	23	20	39	44	31
Late	40	56	31	40	—	40
Catholics						
Early	8	10	4	16	18	10
Late	9	12	8	12	11	12
French Canadians						
Early	47	55	29	48	54	32
Late	46	48	45	49	74	40
Irish						
Early	72	77	57	82	85	73
Late	50	55	44	47	39	51
Italians						
Early	40	52	19	29	40	9
Late	9	34	27	36	36	36
Portuguese						
Early	57	71	29	52	71	—
Late	48	—	46	64	—	50

*Early = age 21–26 for Jewish men and age 20–24 for Jewish women.

of education differentials in either age at marriage or intermarriage for Protestants.

The relationship between age at marriage for Jews and Catholics follows a different pattern. For Jewish men and women of both cohorts, late marriage is associated with higher rates of intermarriage—a relationship that clearly reflects the effects of education. The number of Jewish cases available is too small for a statistical analysis of this interaction but this suggestion is consistent with some previous literature (cf. Goldstein and Goldscheider, 1968, Chapter 8).

The relationship between age at marriage and intermarriage for Catholics tends to follow the Jewish model for males (Catholic men who marry late, marry out), while Catholic women follow the reversals by cohort noted for Protestant women. The confusing Catholic pattern reflects in large part different trends for the four Catholic ethnic subpopulations that, in turn, are related to the different meaning of marriage age over time. For the Irish, for example, the pattern is clear: late marriage means homogamy. Over 80 percent of the Irish women and almost three-fourths of the Irish men who marry early are intermarried, while only about half the late marrying Irish men and women are intermarried. This is consistent with the general picture that emerges from an analysis of Irish age at marriage showing that late age at marriage is a continuing characteristic of Irish ethnics.

The Portuguese and French Canadian pattern is similar to that of the Jews (those who marry late, marry out) except for young, male French Canadians where the pattern reverses. Italian men and women in the older cohort who marry late have a higher rate of intermarriage while the reverse characterizes the younger cohort.

Taken together, these data present a complex picture of the relationship between age at marriage and intermarriage by ethnicity. It seems reasonable to argue that for those ethnics who have traditionally been characterized by late marriage, the relationship between age at marriage and intermarriage is inverse. However, intermarriage tends to be higher among those who marry late for groups traditionally characterized by early marriages. Undoubtedly, there is a strong cohort effect not only because of shifts in the timing of marriage but also because of changes in the levels of intermarriage and education. Nevertheless, it is clear that educational changes do not account for all of the effects of marital age on mate selection.

An attempt to isolate the effects of socioeconomic status on the relationship between age at marriage and interethnic marriage suggests two distinct patterns:[c] late age at marriage is associated with greater homogamy for the Irish, while later marriage is associated with higher rates of intermarriage for Italians, Portuguese, and French Canadians when socioeconomic status (measured by education and subjective social class) and cohort are controlled.

Ethnic residential concentration and intermarriage are not the direct consequences of variations in age at marriage. However, there seems to be a complex set of relationships that involves the effects of socioeconomic status and ethnic socio-cultural patterns on the relationship between the timing of marriage, on the one hand, and indicators of ethnic continuity (intermarriage and residential concentration), on the other. Differential age at marriage, therefore, may be viewed as a response to socioeconomic and ethnic socio-cultural patterns and may affect, in turn, elements of ethnic continuity. Illustrative of these relationships are the distinct patterns for Irish and non-Irish ethnics. Late age at marriage for the Irish is consistent with higher socioeconomic status and with elements of ethnic continuity. The relationship for non-Irish ethnics contrasts with this pattern. The relationship between higher socioeconomic status and age at marriage is inconsistent with homogamy and ethnic residential concentration for French Canadians, Portuguese, and, to a lesser extent, Italians. These patterns suggest that particular ethnic factors are important in the relationship between socioeconomic and marriage processes. Hence, in a society that emphasizes the attainment of higher levels of education, ethnic differences in the timing of marriage have consequences for group continuity.

---

[c]This is discussed more fully in Chapter 6.

Who Marries Whom:
Ethnic Intermarriage

The question of marriages which cross ethnic group boundaries is critical for an analysis of ethnic continuity. Intermarriage may reflect the dilution of ethnic cultural content and has implications for the maintenance of distinct ethnic communities. The central institution fostering ethnic identity is the family. The family continues to function as the major vehicle for the socialization of particularistic norms and provides the major link between the individual and the community. The rate of interethnic marriage is associated with structural and cultural assimilation, affecting the web of interpersonal relationships and the transmission of common parental values (Gordon, 1964). Thus, an analysis of ethnicity in contemporary America must focus on variation and change in ethnic intermarriage.

RELIGIOUS HOMOGAMY

Previous research at the national level suggests that rates of intermarriage are higher for Catholics than Protestants, and lower for Jews (Glick, 1960). However, other things being equal, the larger the community within which to select mates, the higher the probability of religious homogamy. The source of data for our study of religious homogamy is the state of Rhode Island where a majority of the population is Catholic. The question will be posed of how this demographic feature affects rates of religious intermarriage. In addition, the analysis may suggest which groups are considered to have higher status in mate selection when Catholics are in the majority.

The examination of religious intermarriages will be based on three categories relating to religious identification: (1) the religious up-bringing of both spouses; (2) current religious self-identification; and (3) conversion to current religious identification inferred from the difference between religious upbringing and current religious identification.[a] Data in Table 6-1 show the percentage in religiously homogamous marriages for those whose current religious identification is the same as the religious upbringing of the spouse (i.e., without conversion).[b] The Catholic rates of religious intermarriage in these data are clearly different from the national pattern. Fully 90 percent of all marriages for Catholic men and 86 percent for Catholic women age 25 or older were to persons brought up as Catholics. The Jews have the next highest level of religious homogamy, with about two-thirds of each sex having such marriages. Fewer than half of the Protestants (46 percent for males, 44 percent for females) married a Protestant.

This order—Catholics, Jews, Protestants—holds for each age group, but the patterns of change over time have differed by religion and sex. There has been a general decrease in the levels of religious homogamy that is consistent for men but is only clear for Protestant women. Evidence for a decline in homogamy by cohort for either Catholic or Jewish women is vague and inconsistent. As a result, there is a pattern of widening religious differences in homogamy for both men and women: For women, this has resulted from the decline of the group with the lowest level while the other two religious groups retained high levels of homogamy; for males the pattern of divergence results from the more rapid decline of homogamy among Protestants.

There is substantial variation, then, in religious homogamy, with Catholics being the most homogamous and Protestants the least. To what extent does the high Catholic level of religious homogamy characterize ethnic groups within the Catholic subpopulation? French Canadians, Irish, Italians, and Portuguese are Catholic sub-groups, and the data allow for the examination of whether their ethnic characteristics affect their marriage choices in terms of religion as much as they have been shown to do in terms of marriage age, extent, and stability. As can be seen in Table 6-1, the answer is clear: each of the four Catholic ethnic groups resemble each other and the total Catholic pattern in religious homogamy far more than they do the other religious groups; for both sexes, interethnic

---

[a]Specific questions are contained in Appendix A. Conversion in this chapter refers to changes in religious identification, informal as well as formal.

[b]This may be referred to as primary homogamy.

Table 6-1. Percentage in Religiously Homogamous Marriages Without Conversion of Spouse by Ethnicity, Age, and Sex

Sex and Age	Total	Protestants	Catholics	Jews	French Canadians	Irish	Italians	Portuguese
Males								
Total	77	46	90	68	89	82	91	88
25–44	76	41	88	61	87	75	89	84
45–64	79	49	91	78	90	87	92	91
65+	79	52	96	—	94	94	100	—
Females								
Total	77	44	86	64	87	78	91	89
25–44	73	42	85	62	84	82	89	86
45–64	77	44	90	62	90	76	92	92
65+	76	57	86	—	86	61	96	—

variation in religious homogamy is far less than the variation among Protestants, Catholics, and Jews.

Nevertheless, there are differences in religious homogamy among Catholic ethnics. For example, while French Canadians, Italians, and Portuguese are close to the overall Catholic level of religious homogamy of 90 percent, the Irish are markedly lower: 82 percent of the Irish men and 78 percent of Irish women are in religiously homogamous marriages. These levels are well above those of Jews and Protestants, but in every comparison, the Irish are consistently lower than non-Irish Catholics. By contrast, Italians of both sexes exhibit consistently higher levels of religious homogamy than the other Catholic ethnic groups, although differences are small.

For Catholic ethnic males, the same age pattern appears as for the religious subpopulations: a steady decline in religious homogamy is evident for all four groups. The extent of the decline varies, with the Irish showing the greatest declines in homogamy as well as the lowest overall levels. While nearly 95 percent of the Irish males aged 65 and older are homogamously married, only three-fourths of the youngest cohort are in homogamous unions. The patterns of change in religious homogamy for women are not so clear. While each cohort of Italian and Portuguese women has experienced a decline in religious homogamy, French Canadians have the highest levels of homogamy for the 45–64 age cohort, a pattern similar to that for all Catholics. The Irish, however, show a completely different pattern. There has been a steady increase in religious homogamy for Irish women over time, so that 61 percent of Irish women age 65 and older were in homogamous marriages, increasing to 76 percent for the 45–64 age cohort and to 82 percent of the 25–44 age cohort.

As a result of these different patterns by sex, the trend toward convergence differs over time for men and women. The rapid decrease in homogamy for Irish men has widened the range among the four groups in the youngest cohort, while the same cohort has the least range for ethnic Catholic women.

CONVERSION

An alternative process to religious homogamy based on marriage between persons of the same religion (primary homogamy) is conversion. Religious conversion, whether formally by rituals usually at marriage or informally through a change in self-identification, is a process whereby marriages are socially defined as homogamous in terms of the relationships between parents and children and between the family and the larger community.

The question of who converts in mixed marriages is complex, as data in Table 6-2 indicate. Although Catholics have traditionally emphasized conversion, in fact, Catholics marrying persons of other religions are much less likely to have their spouses convert than are Protestants or Jews. While all male non-Jewish spouses and three-fourths of the female non-Jewish spouses converted, only 34 percent and 45 percent of the male and female non-Catholic spouses converted. The Protestant levels are intermediate, with conversion rates of 70 percent and 62 percent for male and female non-Protestant spouses.

Sex differences in conversion rates are difficult to specify theoretically. On the one hand, it may be argued that religion is more important and meaningful for women than for men, and, therefore, the male would be more likely to convert. On the other hand, men normally have greater power within marriage and thus it would be women who are more likely to convert. The data show that there are no overall differences by sex: women are about as likely as men to have converted spouses. However, there are very sharp differences in conversion rates for women that are greater than appear for men, suggesting that it is more important for men than women to convert to the "higher status" religion. Whereas 62 percent of non-Protestant wives converted, 70 percent of non-Protestant husbands converted. Similarly, while 45 percent of non-Catholic wives converted to Catholicism, only 34 percent of non-Catholic husbands converted. None of the Jewish women are married to unconverted non-Jews, while more than 20 percent of Jewish men have non-Jewish wives who have not converted.

However, there has been some tendency toward convergence of these sex differences in the rate of conversion. Younger non-Catholic men are somewhat more likely to convert to Catholicism than are older non-Catholic men (34 percent for the husbands of women below age 45 compared to 28 percent for the husbands of women aged 65 and over) while younger non-Protestant husbands are less likely to convert (78 percent for the husbands of wives age 65 and over compared to 65 percent for younger husbands). These patterns of convergence may reflect a decline in the importance of the husband's conversion to a religious group that is characterized by higher socioeconomic status. However, data in Chapter 2 show that for the youngest cohort, the occupational ranking of Catholic males is higher than for Protestants, a reversal of the patterns for the older cohorts. Hence, this convergence appears to reflect real changes in the exchange patterns of religiously intermarried couples.

The trend toward convergence has accompanied an additional

Table 6-2.   Percentage of Religious Intermarriages in Which the Spouse Converts by Ethnicity, Age, and Sex

Sex and Age	Total	Protestants	Catholics	Jews	French Canadians	Irish	Italians	Portuguese
Males								
Total	58	62	45	78	51	54	53	54
25–44	51	55	41	67	44	58	43	56
45–64	65	68	55	83	67	50	69	50
65+	68	72	21	—	33	0	—	—
Females								
Total	56	70	34	100	45	30	38	42
25–44	53	65	34	100	53	35	23	33
45–64	62	75	34	100	41	31	63	67
65+	61	78	28	—	40	15	100	—

tendency among all three religious groups toward a decline in conversion rates with each younger cohort, suggesting a decrease in the social importance of religious homogamy. Thus, there has been a decline in religious homogamy from two processes: a decline in the proportion marrying spouses of similar religious upbringing (i.e., primary homogamy) and a decline in the proportion converting to the spouse's religion. The contrast is clearest between the two younger cohorts of male Catholics and of Protestants and Jews of both sexes. For Catholics of both sexes there was an increase in conversion between the oldest and the middle cohort, and Catholic women of the youngest cohort were the only group not to experience the most recent decline.

Among ethnic Catholics, relatively little variation in total conversion rate appears. The most consistent finding is that the overall level of conversion among these groups is higher than the all-Catholic level.[c] This is somewhat anomolous, since ethnics of both sexes were somewhat less likely than all Catholics to have married a Catholic. Irish women have a somewhat lower proportion of spouses converting than Irish males or other ethnic subpopulations.

Patterns of change over time are more pronounced and complex. The Portuguese have few cases and a pattern which is mixed by sex, as is the French Canadian pattern. However, the Irish and Italian pattern is clearer. Italians of both sexes have decreased their rates of conversion, while the Irish of both sexes have shown an increase with each cohort. These trends reinforce the tendencies observed earlier showing changes in religious homogamy for Italian men and women and for Irish women. Religious homogamy is increasing for Irish women from both processes: the growing tendency to marry Catholics and the increased probability of non-Catholic husbands converting. Similarly, younger Italian men and women have experienced a decline from both processes. Therefore, Irish and Italian women, as well as Italian men, are converging to the all-Catholic pattern.

In order to put together the patterns of primary homogamy and conversion, Table 6-3 presents the proportions in currently homogamous marriages (including conversions). The major patterns to be noted are the following: The high conversion rate for the non-Jewish husbands of Jewish women results in Jews having the most completely homogamous marriages. While male levels are lower for Jews than for Catholics, Catholic women have much lower proportions in homogamous marriages. Hence, if the sexes are combined, Jews would have the highest overall level. Furthermore, the higher

---

[c]This indicates that Catholics not in one of these four ethnic groups must have a lower level of conversion.

Table 6-3.   Percentage in Religiously Homogamous Marriages (with Conversion of Spouse) by Ethnicity, Age, and Sex

Sex and Age	Protestants	Catholics	Jews	French Canadians	Irish	Italians	Portuguese
Males							
Total	79	95	93	95	92	96	94
25–44	74	93	87	93	89	94	93
45–64	84	96	96	97	94	98	96
65+	87	97	—	96	94	100	—
Females							
Total	83	91	100	93	85	94	94
25–44	80	90	100	93	88	91	91
45–64	86	93	100	93	84	97	97
65+	91	90	—	92	67	100	—

conversion level of Protestants than Catholics reduces substantially the differences which existed in primary homogamy, but closes the gap completely only for the oldest cohort of women. Turning to the four Catholic ethnic groups, the combined trends have resulted in nearly complete convergence for Italians to the all-Catholic level, and dramatic, if not yet complete convergence for the youngest cohort of Irish women. Irish men, on the other hand, have paralleled the gradual decline in homogamy experienced by all male Catholics, at a slightly lower level.

RELIGIOUS INTERMARRIAGE AND SOCIAL STATUS

The relationship between socioeconomic status and homogamy raises a series of significant issues in terms of the changing structure of ethnic communities and the processes associated with ethnic continuity. The extent to which high status persons differentially marry out of their ethnic group has implications for socioeconomic composition, for mobilization of resources, and for the sociopolitical influence of ethnic communities. Moreover, differential intermarriage by socioeconomic status implies changes in the sources and content of ethnic cultural values.

The relationship between subjective social class identification and religious homogamy shows a different pattern for Protestants and Jews compared to Catholics (Table 6-4). In general, there is a positive relationship between social class and homogamy for Jews and Protestants: intermarriage is higher among the working and lower social classes. In contrast, the Catholic pattern is reversed, although differences are small. This implies that certain complex tradeoffs in mate selection may be operating: the higher group status of lower class persons (e.g., working class Protestants) may be exchanged for the higher status of persons from lower status groups (e.g., middle class Catholics). However, this class measure indicates current self-evaluation rather than status at the time of marriage. The relationship between education and homogamy, therefore, takes on particular importance. These data show that higher education is associated with *lower* levels of religious homogamy for the three religious subgroups of both sexes, except for Jewish men where the relationship is positive.

Turning to the effects of class on religious homogamy for Catholic ethnic groups, relatively little variation appears. The strongest relationships with perceived social class are for Irish and Portuguese men, but the directions are opposite: high status increases homogamy

Table 6-4.   Percentage in Religiously Homogamous Marriages Without Conversion of Spouse by Ethnicity, Subjective Social Class, Education, and Sex

Class	Total	Protestants	Catholics	Jews	French Canadians	Irish	Italians	Portuguese
				Males				
*Subjective Social Class**								
Middle	72	47	90	69	92	83	90	81
Working	80	44	91	60	88	78	93	93
*Education***								
High	69	46	84	77	82	80	84	82
Medium	73	39	90	47	84	83	92	82
Low	84	51	92	—	92	83	92	90
				Females				
*Subjective Social Class**								
Middle	73	45	88	63	87	82	90	92
Working	77	42	86	—	87	74	90	87
*Education***								
High	61	44	83	56	—	78	87	—
Medium	72	43	84	67	83	81	88	81
Low	80	46	89	—	89	74	93	91

*Middle = middle or upper class; working = working or lower class.
**High = at least some college; medium = completed high school; low = did not complete high school.

among Irish men; homogamy decreases sharply with status for Portuguese men. Since the Irish have the highest class standing among these groups, while the Portuguese have the lowest, higher status Portuguese and lower status Irish may well have difficulty finding a marriage partner who is appropriate on both religion and social class. Irish women show a similar pattern. The negative relationship between education and religious homogamy holds for men and women of all Catholic ethnic groups.

In part, these relationships between socioeconomic status and religious homogamy are reinforced by patterns of conversion. Data in Table 6-5 show that Protestant men and women have higher rates of conversion as perceived social class and education increase. For Catholic men and women, the more educated have lower rates of conversion. However, variation within the Catholic subpopulation is substantial. Socioeconomic status and conversion tends to be positively related for Irish and French Canadians while an inverse relationship characterizes Italians and Portuguese. There is some variation in all of these patterns of religious homogamy by cohort but the small number of cases and the complex relationships involved prevent more detailed analysis.

CATHOLIC INTERETHNIC MARRIAGE

An additional dimension of homogamy relates to marriages between ethnic group members within religious subpopulations. In the present context, the question of interethnic marriages among Catholic ethnic subgroups is of particular importance. Generally, the level of inter-religious marriages has been lower than the level of interethnic marriages. This finding has often been used to indicate that religious divisions within American society are primary, while ethnic variations within religious subpopulations are rapidly diminishing. This conclusion is perhaps premature for two reasons: first, it does not specify the changing extent of ethnic homogamy over time or in relationship to key socioeconomic variables. Moreover, high rates of interethnic marriages do not necessarily imply the absence of continued or newly created sources of ethnic solidarity. Indeed, scattered evidence from national surveys point in this direction for several Catholic ethnic subgroups (see, for example, Abramson, 1973; Alba, 1976; Greeley, 1974).

There are two methodological issues that need specification before analyzing interethnic marriages among French Canadians, Irish, Italians, and Portuguese. First, respondents were not asked how they identified themselves in terms of national origin. However,

Table 6-5. Percentage of Religious Intermarriages in Which the Spouse Converts by Ethnicity, Subjective Social Class, Education, and Sex

	Total	Protestants	Catholics	Jews	French Canadians	Irish	Italians	Portuguese
				Males				
*Subjective Social Class**								
Middle	62	68	44	80	55	57	57	67
Working	49	51	45	—	50	50	46	33
*Education***								
High	63	71	42	—	75	54	50	—
Medium	59	61	47	—	61	63	57	—
Low	52	53	47	—	41	50	53	—
				Females				
*Subjective Social Class**								
Middle	62	74	36	100	50	35	35	—
Working	48	62	33	—	43	28	41	22
*Education***								
High	62	68	28	100	0	29	0	—
Medium	60	78	36	100	60	35	33	33
Low	49	60	34	—	32	29	54	50

*Middle = middle or working class; working = working or lower class.
**High = at least some college; medium = completed high school; low = did not complete high school.

for both the respondent and spouse, questions were asked on what country their parents' "people came from originally". Hence, there is a single ethnic identification for parents' generation but not for the married couple. The second complication is that it is less clear what are the bases of ethnic identification, unlike religion, where ritual observance and religious practice are easier to measure.

The method of classification which has been followed is broadly inclusive. The respondents (and spouses) have been classified as members of one of the four Catholic ethnic groups if one parent is a member. In the case where each parent is a member of a different group among these four, ethnic identification was assigned on the basis of the father's nationality.[d] However, only one-third of the marriages of the parental generation which are not homogeneous ethnically are of this type. The effect of this procedure varies among the ethnic groups. If the requirement had been two parents rather than one, fully 89 percent of Italians would have been included. The other groups would have lost more: of those with at least one ethnic parent, 79 percent of Portuguese, 68 percent of French Canadians, and only 47 percent of the Irish have both parents identified as having the same national origin.

Marriages are ethnically homogamous in terms of national origins if two parents, one on each side, have the same national origin. This definition classes as homogamous many marriages others would classify as mixed (Alba, 1976) and yields relatively higher levels of homogamy than would more restrictive definitions. However, the expansion of the size of the ethnic groups reduces the probability of homogamy by including more persons of mixed backgrounds. For example, part of the difference between the proportion of Italian and Irish males marrying homogamously is due to the differing compositions of these two groups in terms of the homogamy of their parents. However, the relationships would be relatively unaffected by a different method of defining ethnic origin. Test calculations using a two-parent basis of identification show levels of

---

[d]This system differs from that used in other sections of this study in that persons with mothers who are identified as belonging to one of the four groups but whose fathers belong to none of them are classified with the mothers' groups. This expands the size of the groups somewhat. An examination of the data showed no evidence that gender of ethnic parent had an independent effect on whom their children married. Persons with one ethnic and one nonethnic parent were equally likely to marry within the ethnic group whether that parent was mother or father. There was some evidence that fathers were more important in mate selection for the Irish and French Canadians, and mothers for Italians and Portuguese, but it was slight.

homogamy for males aged 25 and older which are higher, but vary in the same direction.[e]

Variations in ethnic homogamy, by sex and cohort for each of the four Catholic ethnic groups are presented in Table 6-6. It is clear that ethnic homogamy based on national origins is much lower overall than religious homogamy even given the inclusive definition used. Intra-group marriage is a much less significant factor in the maintenance of ethnic identification for these groups. Variation among the four groups is also substantial. Italians of both sexes are most likely to have an Italian spouse (70 percent of males and 65 percent of females), while the Irish men and women are least likely to have married a person of Irish background. The French Canadians and Portuguese have intermediate levels of homogamy. As in religion, the differences are somewhat greater for women than for men. Irish women are somewhat less homogamous that Irish men, while Italian women have higher levels of ethnic homogamy than Italian men.

Furthermore, levels of homogamy have been falling rapidly: 95 percent of Italian males age 65 and over were in ethnically homogamous marriages compared to 56 percent age 25-44. Similarly, 75 percent of French Canadian women in the oldest cohort were married to French Canadians compared to only 42 percent of the youngest cohort. Each of the other groups experienced a similar decline. As with religious homogamy, some evidence of convergence for ethnic women appears due to the low level of homogamy for

Table 6-6. Percentage in Ethnically Homogamous Marriages by Ethnicity, Age, and Sex

Age and Sex	French Canadians	Irish	Italians	Portuguese
Males				
All Ages	56	42	65	45
25–44	50	36	56	32
45–64	58	44	70	57
65+	78	67	95	—
Females				
All ages	52	40	70	47
25–44	42	35	65	31
45–64	62	46	74	71
65+	75	44	89	—

[e]This procedure has the greatest effect on the Portuguese where only a very small proportion of persons with one Portuguese parent marry Portuguese. This suggests that the intermarried Portuguese are much less likely to identify with the Portuguese community compared to other ethnics.

older Irish women. Ethnic homogamy was higher for Irish women age 45-64 than for the older cohort. This may be the result of sex selectivity among Irish immigrants relative to other immigrant groups (cf. Kennedy, 1973). If this is the case, it would have important consequences not only for intermarriage but for marriage patterns (see Chapters 3 and 5). The Irish seem to have largely recovered from these sex ratio imbalances and differential homogamy for each of the four Catholic groups has narrowed considerably for the younger cohorts.

The relationships between ethnic homogamy and social class are very similar to those shown for religious homogamy (Table 6-7). Overall, higher levels of education and social class are associated with lower levels of homogamy for Portuguese, Italians, and French Canadians of both sexes. (The only exception is for Italian women when subjective social class is considered.) The clear exception to these patterns is the Irish. For both socioeconomic status measures, the higher the class, the higher the rate of homogamy. As a result of these different relationships, there is little difference in the rate of intermarriage between educated Irish and Italians, while French Canadians and Portuguese have much lower rates at similar high levels of education.

Table 6-7. Percentage in Ethnically Homogamous Marriages by Ethnicity, Subjective Social Class, Education, and Sex

	French Canadians	Irish	Italians	Portuguese
		Males		
Social Class*				
Middle	56	48	63	33
Working	55	30	67	54
Education**				
High	36	49	54	9
Medium	51	37	57	34
Low	59	41	70	54
		Females		
Social Class*				
Middle	48	44	73	44
Working	56	31	67	49
Education**				
High	47	53	56	—
Medium	39	38	63	24
Low	59	35	76	59

*Middle = middle or upper class; working = working or lower class.
**High = at least some college; medium = completed high school; low = did not complete high school.

It is important to recall that both higher education and homogamy are associated with later age at marriage for the Irish (see Chapter 5). It seems reasonable to argue that the traditionally high age at marriage for the Irish is compatible with the achievement of higher education without requiring out-marriage. This does not appear to be the case for educated non-Irish Catholic ethnics. The consistency among late marriage, homogamy, and education for the Irish may have facilitated their retention of ethnic identity without foregoing the attainment of high social status.

WHO MARRIES WHOM

An additional issue in the study of intermarriage relates to the marriage *choices* of those who marry outside their group—who marries whom. This analysis is restricted to the four Catholic ethnic subpopulations, to which a category of "other" has been added for completeness. Religious pairings are not examined since there are few Jews or persons of "other" or no religion. Two major questions are addressed in this section. The first focuses on specific ethnic group exchanges, i.e., whether there are specific combinations of ethnic group intermarriages that may be identified. Second, are there variations in specific marriage choices that are related to socioeconomic status. Social distance theory would suggest that such combinations would exist, since the cultural and geographic origins of these four ethnic groups differ substantially. On the other hand, it may be argued that the tendency of ethnic group members to marry within their group merely reflects preference for religious homogamy; hence, there would be few ethnic group preferences in intermarriage among the Catholic ethnic subpopulations. If patterns of preference exist and persist, this would have implications for the direction of ethnic group changes. There are many instances of ethnic group fusion (Horowitz, 1975) and the data available allow for an examination of this issue.

Some preliminary answers to the question of who marries whom in the form of relative marriage propensities may be drawn from data presented in Table 6-8. If each group of males who intermarry were to marry randomly among the women who married outside of their group, the expected relative marriage propensity would equal 1.00. For example, French Canadians are only 87 percent as likely to marry an Irish woman as would be expected by chance, and 11 percent more likely to marry a Portuguese woman. (These are presented as indexes of 0.87 and 1.11). The columns may also be read to indicate the ordering of relative preferences of out-marrying

Table 6-8. Relative Ethnic Marriage Propensities* by Education:** Males

Ethnicity and Education of Husband	Expected	Ethnicity of Wife				
		French Canadians	Irish	Italians	Portuguese	Others
All Educations						
French Canadians	1.00	—	.87	.89	1.11	1.12
Irish	1.00	.88	—	.98	.72	1.11
Italians	1.00	.93	.85	—	.87	1.22
Portuguese	1.00	1.15	.71	1.25	—	.95
Others	1.00	1.08	1.13	.83	.67	—
French Canadians						
High	1.00	—	1.24	.64	—	1.04
Medium	1.00	—	1.14	.96	.20	1.15
Low	1.00	—	.62	.93	1.42	1.14
Irish						
High	1.00	.94	—	.84	—	1.15
Medium	1.00	.85	—	1.09	1.02	1.06
Low	1.00	.90	—	.93	.60	1.26
Italians						
High	1.00	.46	1.04	—	—	1.39
Medium	1.00	.99	.49	—	1.51	1.33
Low	1.00	1.07	1.13	—	.54	1.04
Portuguese						
High	1.00	1.13	1.50	.87	—	.57
Medium	1.00	.64	.79	.76	—	1.69
Low	1.00	1.34	.30	1.68	—	.79
Others						
High	1.00	1.02	.90	1.10	—	—
Medium	1.00	1.05	1.17	.80	.73	—
Low	1.00	1.14	1.23	.71	.57	—

*Proportion of male ethnic out-marriers who marry a member of the given ethnic group relative to the size of that group of female out-marriers.

**High = at least some college; medium = completed high school; low = did not complete high school.

ethnic women, but here the expected proportion is not 1.00, but varies in each case. Out-marrying Portuguese women, for example, are most likely to marry French Canadian men, followed by Italians, Irish, and men of other ethnic backgrounds.

Several general conclusions may be drawn from these data. First, there is a general preference among each of the four Catholic ethnic groups to marry someone who is not a member of one of the other three groups. This is more true for men than for women. Second, while preference clearly exists, the intensity of preference does not seem to be great. Third, patterns of preference are not only weak but they are also inconsistent. There is a clear exchange between the Portuguese and French Canadians. For each sex, the other ethnic group is preferred by those who intermarry. There is another exchange that is more difficult to interpret. Italian males are the most likely of the four ethnic groups to marry wives from "other" ethnic backgrounds and are also the preferred husbands of such women. The clearest among the other exchange possibilities is the tendency for the Irish to avoid the Portuguese.

The most interesting feature of these data is the substantial variation in ethnic marriage exchanges by educational level. As was shown in Chapter 2, Catholic ethnic groups differ substantially in socio-economic status. In terms of education, the Irish have the highest levels, followed by the Italians, Portuguese, and French Canadians. Since studies have shown a preference for educational homogamy, it might be expected that level of education would affect the probability of marriage between ethnic groups. This is generally the case. The clearest examples occur when two groups differ substantially in education. For example, French Canadian men are less likely to marry an Irish woman than would be expected by chance (0.87). However, French Canadians who have not completed high school are much less likely to marry Irish women (0.62) and the probabilities increase for those who completed high school (1.14) and for those who have some college education (1.24). The same pattern holds even more strongly between Portuguese men and Irish women, where preferences range from 30 percent to 150 percent for the lowest and highest levels of education. Other ethnic combinations reflect a different relationship by education. The French Canadian preference for Portuguese women, for example, appears markedly to be associated with the least educated. While French Canadian men who have not completed high school are 42 percent *more* likely to marry a Portuguese wife than expected, this drops to being 80 percent *less* likely to choose a Portuguese wife for those completing high school. Italian men show a similar pattern with regard to French Canadian women: the relative probabilities drop from 1.07 to 0.99 to 0.46 with increases in education.

Examining these data further clarifies a more general issue which had not emerged earlier. Two combinations based on regional-cultural background appear. The two ethnic groups with southern European backgrounds—the Italians and Portuguese—tend to intermarry more than those with western European origins—Irish and French Canadians (and "others"). Since there are major class differences within each of these two groups, this "social distance" factor was obscured. For example, among men of "other" backgrounds who have not completed high school, the preference rank is Irish, French Canadian, Italian, Portuguese. The same order appears for those in this group who have completed high school, but the differences are not as sharp. French Canadians at the two higher levels of education clearly prefer Irish and persons of other backgrounds to Italians or Portuguese; the Portuguese with the least education prefer Italians. So there is some tendency for education to increase preference for a spouse with a western European background for all ethnic groups.

Very similar patterns appear when subjective social class is used instead of education as a control for socioeconomic status. (These data are not presented.) Tendencies toward class homogamy as well as homogamy of cultural background are evident, though the patterns are not as strong. Neither analysis, however, suggests a very strong preference pattern. One possible explanation for this is that convergence has occurred, so that over time and for recent generations, ethnicity has become relatively less important in the choice of a marriage partner. This inference is supported by a direct analysis of intergenerational changes in ethnic marriages. Ethnicity of all the parents of the respondent and his/her spouse is available to contrast with the ethnicity of the married couple (Table 6-9). It is clear that there has been a reduction in the relative preferences of specific ethnic groups. The marriages of the parental generation show much greater deviations from the pattern expected by chance. For almost every comparison, the change has been to reduce both positive and negative preferences. The exception to this trend is for husbands with "other" backgrounds. In addition to this tendency toward convergence, there are two striking patterns which emerge from an examination of these data. First, it is clear that the Portuguese–French Canadian exchange is a phenomenon of the current, not the past, generation. This current preference has replaced levels of marital avoidance that are among the strongest shown by the parental generation. French Canadian males of the parental generation were only 49 percent as likely to marry a Portuguese women as chance

Table 6-9.   Relative Ethnic Marriage Propensities of Two Generations: Males

Ethnicity and Generation of Male	Ethnicity of Wife					
	Expected	French Canadians	Irish	Italians	Portuguese	Others
French Canadians						
Parental	1.00	—	.56	.83	.49	1.38
Current	1.00	—	.87	.89	1.11	1.12
Irish						
Parental	1.00	.55	—	.75	.74	1.32
Current	1.00	.88	—	.98	.72	1.11
Italians						
Parental	1.00	.70	.77	—	1.41	1.31
Current	1.00	.93	.85	—	.87	1.22
Portuguese						
Parental	1.00	.56	.63	1.51	—	1.46
Current	1.00	1.15	.71	1.25	—	.95
Others						
Parental	1.00	1.05	1.05	.69	.70	—
Current	1.00	1.08	1.13	.83	.67	—

would expect, compared to 11 percent *more* likely for the current
generation. Similarly, Portuguese males in the older generation had a
probability 56 percent *less* than expected to marry French Canadians
while for the current generation there is 15 percent *positive* preference. The second finding, representing a shift of similar magnitude, is
the substantial decline generationally in the preference of Italian
men for marrying Portuguese women. This is shown by a reversal
of preference from 1.41 to 0.87.

What these broad patterns of convergence and reversals of preference suggest is that the ethnic factor has become much less important in marital preference between generations. The increasing
dissimilarities in class position between Italians and Portuguese seem
to have overcome the marital affinities based on common southern
European backgrounds. Similarly, the emergent Portuguese–French
Canadian pattern suggests that the effects of social class position
are stronger than differences in origin that had characterized these
groups in the past. Perhaps the boundaries separating these ethnic
groups have weakened considerably as social class differences have
taken on greater importance.

INTERMARRIAGE AND
EDUCATION EXCHANGES

As has been noted, the relationship between socioeconomic status
and intermarriage has important implications for the structure of
ethnic communities. Another dimension of this relationship is the
exchange patterns of who marry whom. In particular, what are the
educational exchanges between spouses who are intermarried or
nonintermarried? Two patterns are important in the present context: (1) exchanges of ethnic homogamy for educational homogamy,
implying the greater importance of educational relative to ethnic
similarities; (2) exchanges of higher education for the more "prestigious" ethnic group, defined in terms of aggregate socioeconomic
characteristics.

The proportions of ethnically homogamous and intermarried
couples with similar levels of education are presented in Table 6-10.
The first issue that may be resolved with these data is whether ethnic
homogamy is related to educational homogamy: are intermarried
persons more likely than nonintermarried persons to have levels of
education different from their spouses. The data show distinct
patterns of educational homogamy for Catholics and non-Catholics.
Intermarried Catholics are more likely to have different levels of
education than their spouses when compared to Catholics who marry

Table 6-10. Percentage of Spouses with the Same Education and an H/H* Index by Ethnicity, Ethnic Homogamy,** and Age

	Protestants		Jews		Catholics		French Canadians		Irish		Italians		Portuguese	
	Same	H/H*	Same	H/H*	Same	H/H*	Same	H/H*	Same	H/H*	Same	H/H*	Same	H/H*
Homogamous														
All ages	50	48	63	16	61	44	72	50	51	47	65	43	70	47
Below 45	50	48	60	0	57	44	60	60	55	29	60	43	63	57
45+	51	51	68	28	67	45	82	33	45	60	70	40	75	32
Intermarried														
Men														
All Ages	62	37	65	51	59	41	51	53	50	40	59	44	52	44
Below 45	62	32	—	—	61	44	48	50	49	41	53	34	53	43
45+	62	45	—	—	57	40	55	60	50	38	69	65	53	49
Women														
All ages	58	46	72	39	56	45	49	37	55	51	53	47	61	56
Below 45	55	40	60	50	52	40	40	37	59	39	49	45	56	61
45+	62	55	—	—	61	54	69	39	49	71	62	50	80	0

*The proportion of heterogamous marriages where the wife has higher education than her husband.
**Primary homogamy.

Catholics. In contrast, educational homogamy is higher for intermarried than nonintermarried Jews and Protestants. For example, 62 percent of the Protestant men have the same education as their non-Protestant wives, while 50 percent of the Protestant men have the same levels of education as their Protestant wives. In contrast, over 60 percent of the Catholic males marrying within their own religious group have the same educational level as their spouses compared to 56 percent of the intermarried Catholic women.

The overall Catholic pattern of greater educational differences between the intermarried and the homogamously married characterizes the French Canadian, Italian, and Portuguese ethnics. However, educational homogamy is higher for Irish women marrying non-Irish men than for Irish women marrying Irish men. Thus, Protestant, Jewish, and Irish (women only) who marry out of their ethnic communities are more likely to have spouses with levels of education similar to themselves than are those marrying within their ethnic communities. It may be argued, therefore, that intermarriage for these groups implies an exchange of ethnic homogamy for educational homogamy. The different Catholic pattern implies that Catholics are exchanging their educational achievements for a more "prestigious" ethnic status. Differences in the proportion of intermarried and nonintermarried couples with the same level of education are greatest for the two lower socioeconomic Catholic ethnic groups. About 70 percent of nonintermarried French Canadian and Portuguese couples have similar levels of education compared to about 50 percent for the intermarried couples. Since the better educated of both these groups are more likely to marry out, ethnic and educational differences between intermarried spouses are accentuated; educated French Canadians and Portuguese who marry out increase their chances of marrying someone with a different educational level. The high proportion of homogamously married French Canadians and Portuguese who have the same levels of education are concentrated at the very bottom of the educational scale. Thus, for intermarried Catholics, educational differences between spouses implies exchanges for the more "prestigious" ethnic group; for intermarried Jews and Protestants (and Irish women) the exchange is for educational homogamy (usually at high levels).

The cohort data indicate that there has been a general decline over time in educational homogamy for most ethnic groups, whether married homogamously or intermarried. The Irish are the major exception where educational homogamy has increased. It should be noted that this increase in educational homogamy parallels the general increase in ethnic homogamy for younger Irish that was demonstrated earlier in this chapter.

Most importantly, the cohort data reveal that intermarried Protestants and Jews have higher educational homogamy than the non-intermarried, controlling for cohort with some convergences over time. The lower level of educational homogamy for intermarried Protestants compared to intermarried Catholics only characterizes women. Intermarried Catholic men of both age cohorts are more likely to be in educationally homogamous marriages when compared to Catholic men marrying Catholic women. The lower educational homogamy for intermarried French Canadians, Portuguese, and Italians remains when cohort is controlled. The higher educational homogamy of intermarried Irish does not characterize Irish men of the younger cohort.

In addition to the question of the relationship between ethnic and educational homogamy, an examination of some specific educational-ethnic exchanges may be made. An index was constructed of the proportion of marriages where wives have higher education than husbands per 100 marriages where there are educational differences between husbands and wives. (This will be referred to as the H/H index, the proportion of educationally heterogamous marriages where the wife has higher education than the husband.) These data show clearly that the Protestants who intermarry are not exchanging ethnicity for higher education but for educational homogamy. This is true for intermarried Protestant men and women within both age cohorts. The sex difference for Jews is significant: Jewish men who marry out are more likely to exchange religion not only for educational homogamy but for more highly educated wives. The index for Jews who marry Jews is 16 percent; for intermarried Jewish men it is 51 percent. However, Jewish women who marry out are more likely than those not intermarrying to be in educationally homogamous marriages and also are more likely to marry men with somewhat less education than they have achieved. Therefore, exchange for intermarried Jewish women appears to be higher education for a non-Jewish husband of the majority ethnic groups. Catholic men and women follow the general pattern of exchanging education for more "prestigious" non-Catholic status. This is, however, more true for older than younger cohorts since there is a decline in the H/H index among Catholic intermarried women from 54 percent to 40 percent.

The exchanges for Catholic ethnic groups in terms of homogamy are more complex. Portuguese women who marry non-Portuguese men seem to be exchanging their higher education for moving out of a low "prestige" group. Similarly, French Canadian women who marry out (who generally have higher levels of education) not only receive lower educational homogamy but increase their probability of marrying a less educated husband. Italian and Irish women follow similar exchange patterns.

In short, the social forces that promote ethnic intermarriages are many and varied and the exchanges that intermarriage implies are complex. In the process of acculturation, ethnic intermarriages tend to increase and the salience of ethnic homogamy declines. As ethnic intermarriages become less marginal, ethnic groups may redefine the role of the intermarried within the larger ethnic community. Therefore, the implications of higher intermarriage rates may be less tied to the assimilation of ethnic communities and new forms of ethnic identification may evolve. The use of homogamy as an indicator of ethnic group boundaries may be changing as different forms of ethnicity emerge. The implications of who marries whom among ethnic groups will continue to represent an important aspect of the process of ethnic continuity.

❋ *Part III*

Social Mobility Processes

Chapter 7

Intergenerational Mobility

One of the major themes in American social life has been the dynamics of its opportunity structure. Whether the issue is educational attainment, occupational achievement, or social class fluidity, American society has been characterized or stereotyped as a "land of opportunity." Indeed, there are no better illustrations of this theme than the dramatic social changes that immigrant ethnic minorities have experienced over the last century. The "success" story of immigrants in America has been told and retold many times as confirmation of the American ideal of equality of opportunity. Within this context, intergenerational social mobility figures prominantly. The upward shifts of individuals and groups in the status hierarchy from one generation to another is the clearest indicator of the continuous process of socioeconomic integration and assimilation of America's heterogeneous subpopulations. And the nonmobility of groups out of (or downward mobility into) the lower strata is the surest sign of inequality, discrimination, and the persistent cycle of generational deprivation.

The centrality of the social mobility theme for America's ethnic minorities has not been matched by systematic empirical research to document and analyze the differential dynamics of this process. In particular, much of the research on national mobility patterns has rarely, if ever, focused on the ethnic dimension beyond race; national ethnic data have never incorporated sufficiently detailed data on social mobility patterns for more than a superficial analysis. Hence, much of what is known about ethnic intergenerational mobility is based on inferences from aggregate distribution changes over broad time periods for a few select subpopulations.

The challenge of this chapter is to confront the broad question of differential intergenerational social mobility of religious and Catholic ethnic subpopulations. The material presented on the stratification of ethnic groups in Chapter 2 has already revealed some of the broad outlines of change in educational levels, occupational rank, and social class identification inferred from cohort variation. These findings, however valuable, are based on macro group changes and aggregate distributional transformations. Beyond the question of the redistribution of the socioeconomic characteristics of groups over time are a series of complex analytic issues related to individual occupational and social class origins and individual mobility patterns from one generation to another.

This chapter focuses on ethnic variation and change in occupational and perceived social mobility between generations. Central to this focus are two general questions: What are the differential intergenerational social mobility processes of these ethnic subpopulations? Have patterns of occupational and class inheritance, recruitment, and mobility between generations resulted in a general convergence or divergence among ethnic groups?

OCCUPATIONAL ORIGINS OF
RELIGIOUS SUBPOPULATIONS

The analysis of intergenerational occupational mobility revolves around the interrelationships between the occupational rankings of fathers when their sons were growing up and the initial and current occupational rankings of those sons. The first issue to which our analysis is addressed is: What are the occupational origins of Protestants, Catholics, and Jews? Differential origins provides the first clues for understanding how the occupational rankings of these three religious subpopulations relate to where they have originated generationally.[a]

Data in Table 7-1 show the occupational rankings of the fathers of our sample by current religion of their sons. The occupational origins of the three religious subpopulations differ significantly:

---

[a]We clearly do not have an unbiased sample of fathers. Differential fertility, mortality, and migration of fathers and differential survivorship and migration of sons affect the resultant representativeness of data on fathers derived from a sample of families (cf. Blau and Duncan, 1967; Matras, 1975). Further, for some portion of the foreign-born sons (depending on their age at immigration), the occupation of the father when the son was growing up was not in the United States. However, since the rankings are based on American prestige norms, and since the ethnic groups are only differentially affected for sons over age 65, this should not be a problem in the analysis.

over one out of three Jewish fathers were in the top occupational rank compared to one out of four Protestant fathers and one out of ten Catholic fathers. At the bottom of the occupational hierarchy were 43 percent of the Catholic fathers compared to less than 30 percent of the Protestant fathers and only 3.4 percent of the Jewish fathers.

From the analysis of ethnic stratification presented earlier and from the general literature, cohort changes over time may be expected in the distribution of father's occupation. The overall pattern confirms these expectations with important exceptions among younger Protestants. For the three religious groups, improvements in occupational rank may be observed for the three oldest cohorts. While this pattern continues for younger Catholics, Protestant

Table 7-1. Occupational Rank* of Fathers, by Religion and Age of Son

Occupational Rank of Fathers	Total	Protestants	Jews	Catholics
All Ages of Sons				
I	14.3	24.1	34.5	9.7
II	21.9	22.7	34.5	20.7
III	25.9	24.7	27.6	26.3
IV	37.9	28.5	3.4	43.2
25-34				
I	15.8	19.1	—	12.4
II	23.9	25.0	—	23.7
III	29.6	27.9	—	30.8
IV	30.8	27.9	—	33.1
35-44				
I	15.8	30.6	—	11.4
II	25.3	24.2	—	25.1
III	24.9	24.2	—	24.6
IV	34.0	21.0	—	38.9
45-64				
I	12.3	23.8	23.1	7.3
II	20.8	23.0	46.2	18.2
III	25.4	23.8	30.8	25.8
IV	41.5	29.5	0.0	48.7
65+				
I	15.4	23.1	—	8.6
II	13.7	15.4	—	11.4
III	22.2	23.1	—	22.9
IV	48.7	38.5	—	57.1

*I = Duncan scale values 59 to 97; II = 34 to 58; III = 18 to 33; IV = 1 to 17.

fathers of the 25–34 cohort are more concentrated in the lower occupational ranks than the fathers of the previous cohort.

For the one age group where sufficient data are available (age 45–64) Jewish fathers maintain their exceptionally high occupational rank compared to Protestant and Catholic fathers. However, this distinctiveness is not in the concentration of Jewish fathers in the highest rank but in the absence of Jewish fathers in the lowest rank (compared to 49 percent of the Catholic fathers and 30 percent of Protestant fathers). There is a significantly higher proportion of Jewish fathers in the second ranked occupations compared to Protestant and Catholic fathers, but the higher concentration of Jewish fathers of all ages in the top ranked occupations must reflect the occupations of fathers of younger cohorts.

A general pattern of convergence or reduction of differences between the occupational ranks of fathers of Protestants and Catholics may be observed, with the retention among all age groups of the higher occupational ranking of Protestants. The top rank shows a greater concentration of Protestant than Catholic fathers for each age group, but the very large differences in the occupational concentration at this level of fathers of the older cohorts (3 to 1 in favor of Protestant fathers) have diminished to a small difference (19 to 12 percent) for the fathers of the youngest cohort. This convergence of occupational origins between Protestants and Catholics is as much a reflection of the *reduction* in the concentration of Protestant fathers in the highest occupational rank as it is an increase in the concentration of Catholic fathers in that rank.

Convergences may also be noted at the bottom rank: Catholic fathers of the 25–34 age cohort are more concentrated than Protestant fathers in the lowest occupational rank, but differences for this young cohort are much smaller than among the fathers of older age cohorts. Again, the pattern of convergence is a decline among Catholic fathers in the lowest occupational rank combined with an increase among Protestant fathers in that rank.

The deterioration of occupational rank for Protestant fathers of the youngest age cohort—the reduction in the highest rank and the increase in the lowest rank—may imply differential patterns of selective migration of Protestants and Catholics: upwardly mobile Protestants moving out of the state and lower origin Protestants moving into the state and selective mobility among Catholics. This theme will be examined in a subsequent chapter.

The fact that even among younger cohorts of Catholics, occupational origins tend to be lower than those of Protestants, combined with our earlier findings showing the higher occupational rank of younger Catholics compared to Protestants, implies a more vigorous intergenerational upward mobility among Catholics, particularly among the youngest age cohort. It is to this specific issue of differential occupational mobility of Protestants and Catholics that we turn.

THE INHERITANCE OF OCCUPATIONAL RANK

The first set of mobility issues that we need to examine revolves around where these differential occupational origins of Protestants and Catholics lead. For each occupational level of fathers we may follow the "outflows" or the occupational distribution of sons. The analysis of these outflows provides the basic for evaluating differential occupational inheritance of Protestants and Catholics. Outflow percentages for each of the four occupational ranks of fathers were computed to initial (occupation at age 25) as well as to current occupational rank of sons (Table 7-2).

The first major observation from these data relates to the importance of occupational origins for an analysis of occupational inheritance. Direct inheritance of occupational rank is clearly higher, the higher the occupational origins: inheritance of rank I occupations is 63 percent, rank II occupations is 38 percent, rank III occupations is 31 percent, and rank IV occupations is 28 percent. The same pattern holds for outflows to initial occupational rank of sons with an exception among the lowest ranked occupations.

The critical question relates to Protestant-Catholic differential inheritance of occupations. The data show clearly that Protestants are more likely than Catholics to enter and currently have occupations that are ranked at the top, if their fathers had top ranked occupations. Of all the Protestants whose fathers were in the highest ranked occupations, 43 percent entered and 69 percent are currently in the highest ranked occupations. These proportions compare to 38 percent and 55 percent, respectively, among Catholics. Moreover, a significantly greater proportion of Catholics than Protestants whose fathers had the highest ranked occupations enter and are currently in the lowest ranked occupations (8.3 percent compared to 2.4 percent initially and 5.5 percent to 1.4 percent currently) suggesting a stronger downward outflow for Catholics. For the lowest occupational origins, a larger proportion of Protestants than Catholics from the lowest ranked occupational origins enter and currently have the highest ranked occupations. Significantly, Catholics tend to have greater occupational inheritance of the lowest occupational

Table 7-2. Outflow Percentages, Intergenerational Mobility (Occupational Rank of Fathers to Initial and Current Occupational Rank), by Religion

Occupational Rank* Fathers	Sons	Total Initial	Total Current	Protestants Initial	Protestants Current	Catholics Initial	Catholics Current
I	I	41.2	63.1	42.9	68.6	37.5	54.8
	II	34.0	16.6	33.3	14.3	35.4	21.9
	III	18.6	16.6	21.4	15.7	18.8	17.8
	IV	6.2	3.8	2.4	1.4	8.3	5.5
II	I	23.9	29.2	29.3	31.8	22.5	26.9
	II	38.1	37.5	39.0	36.4	35.3	36.5
	III	20.6	19.2	17.1	22.7	23.5	18.6
	IV	17.4	14.2	14.6	9.1	18.6	17.9
III	I	17.2	27.5	11.1	30.6	18.5	23.7
	II	25.6	24.3	40.0	27.8	20.2	23.2
	III	31.7	31.0	28.9	36.1	33.1	30.8
	IV	25.6	17.3	20.0	5.6	28.2	22.2
IV	I	11.5	16.8	15.0	21.7	10.5	15.1
	II	18.8	22.6	16.7	20.5	19.0	23.7
	III	27.0	32.9	26.7	36.1	27.8	32.6
	IV	42.8	27.6	41.7	21.7	42.6	28.6

*I = Duncan scale values 59 to 97; II = 34 to 58; III = 18 to 33; IV = 1 to 17.

origins. Twenty-nine percent of the Catholics whose fathers were in the lowest ranked jobs are currently in similarly ranked jobs compared to 22 percent of the Protestants from similarly low occupational origins.

The outflows from fathers to initial and current occupational ranks of their sons suggest greater upward mobility for lower origin Protestants and greater stability for higher origin Protestants when compared to Catholics. Looking at the middle ranks a similar pattern emerges. Of those from occupational origins of the two middle ranks, more Protestants than Catholics enter and currently have occupations in the top two ranks. A significantly larger proportion of Catholics of all occupational origins end up at the bottom occupational rank. From origins higher than the lowest ranked fathers, Catholics are at least twice as likely as Protestants to end up (currently) in the lowest ranked occupations.

What do these outflow patterns suggest about intergenerational mobility for Protestants and Catholics? A consistent and clear picture seems to emerge from these data: at each level of occupational origin, Protestants are more likely than Catholics to be upwardly mobile and Catholics are more likely than Protestants to be downwardly mobile. With but minor exceptions, occupational inheritance is higher for Protestants in the top two occupational origin ranks while the reverse characterizes the lower two occupational origin levels.

How do these patterns of occupational inheritance vary by age cohort? Data in Table 7–3 show outflow percentages (father's occupational rank to son's current occupational rank) for three age cohorts (25–34, 35–44, and 45–64). Emerging from these data is a significant reversal for the youngest age cohort of the general pattern of occupational inheritance described above. For example, occupational inheritance of the highest ranked jobs is clearly higher for Protestants than Catholics for the 35–44 and 45–64 age cohorts. However, for the 25–34 age cohort, Catholics from the highest ranked occupational origins are more likely to have top rank occupations than are Protestants from similarly ranked occupational origins. (Data not presented show an identical pattern when initial occupations are examined.) Similarly, inheritance and/or mobility from second ranked occupational origins is greater for Protestants than Catholics for the two older age cohorts and reverses among those 25–34 years of age. For the two older cohorts, Catholic fathers who were in third ranked occupations were more downwardly mobile than Protestants while Protestants of the youngest cohort are more downwardly mobile from occupational level III than Catholics.

Table 7-3. Outflow Percentages, Intergenerational Mobility (Occupational Rank of Fathers to Current Occupational Rank), by Religion and Age

Occupational Rank*		25-34		35-44		45-64	
Fathers	Sons	Protestants	Catholics	Protestants	Catholics	Protestants	Catholics
I	I	46.2	61.9	78.9	66.7	79.3	31.8
	II	30.8	14.3	0.0	25.0	13.8	31.8
	III	15.4	19.0	21.1	8.3	6.9	27.3
	IV	7.7	4.8	0.0	0.0	0.0	9.1
II	I	17.6	35.0	40.0	32.1	35.7	18.2
	II	41.2	25.0	33.3	35.8	32.1	45.5
	III	29.4	27.5	20.0	13.2	25.0	18.2
	IV	11.8	12.5	6.7	18.9	7.1	18.2
III	I	21.1	40.4	40.0	21.2	37.9	19.2
	II	31.6	25.0	20.0	28.8	27.6	20.5
	III	36.8	28.8	40.0	32.7	31.0	28.2
	IV	10.5	5.8	0.0	17.3	3.4	32.1
IV	I	36.8	21.4	15.4	15.9	13.9	14.3
	II	21.1	30.4	15.4	25.6	16.7	24.5
	III	15.8	26.8	53.8	32.9	41.7	34.7
	IV	26.3	21.4	15.4	25.6	27.8	26.5

*I = Duncan scale values 59 to 97; II = 34 to 58; III = 18 to 33; IV = 1 to 17.

This same reversal by age occurs at the lowest ranked origins when the 25-34 age cohort is compared to the 35-44 age cohort—occupational inheritance at the bottom is greater for Catholics than Protestants for the 35-44 cohort and greater for Protestants than Catholics for the 25-34 cohort.

Hence, these outflow data by age show that the general pattern of greater upward mobility of Protestants, greater downward mobility of Catholics, and greater occupational inheritance at the top two ranks characterize only the older two age cohorts. The greater occupational inheritance among young Catholics at the highest rank and their greater upward mobility represent important qualifications to the general patterns noted when age was not considered. Moreover, this reversal by age fits the pattern observed in Chapter 2 for occupational stratification for age cohorts and in part reflects the changing occupational origins among the youngest cohort.

OCCUPATIONAL RECRUITMENT

An analysis of occupational inheritance provides one basis for examining patterns of continuity and mobility. A complementary strategy is to examine occupational recruitment. In lieu of following the *outflows* from father's occupational rank to initial or current rank, an examination can be made of the *inflows* to specific occupational ranks from the occupational ranks of fathers. In other words, we can examine the "recruitment" to occupational ranks from the range of occupational ranks of fathers. These data are presented by religion in Table 7-4.

Is there differential recruitment into occupational rankings for Protestants and Catholics? Protestants who entered or are currently in the top occupational rank are much more likely to be recruited from the highest ranked occupations than are Catholics. Indeed almost twice as many Catholics as Protestants who entered or are currently in the top occupational rank have been recruited from origins *below* the top rank. The spread of recruitment in the top Catholic occupational rank is about evenly divided by occupational origins while the recruitment for Protestants is significantly more concentrated at the upper end of the occupational hierarchy. In part this reflects the fact that Catholic origins are significantly lower than for Protestants and hence Catholic sons who are at the top are more likely to be from origins below the top.

The lowest ranked occupations have been recruited mainly from the lowest ranked occupational origins with few Protestant-Catholic differences in initial intergenerational recruitment patterns. In terms

Table 7-4. Inflow Percentages, Intergenerational Mobility (Initial and Current Occupational Rank from Father's Occupational Rank), by Religion

Occupational Rank* Sons / Fathers	Total		Protestants		Catholics	
	Initial	Current	Initial	Current	Initial	Current
I						
I	28.0	31.2	40.9	44.0	20.2	22.5
II	25.9	22.1	27.3	19.3	25.8	23.6
III	21.7	24.6	11.4	20.2	25.8	26.4
IV	24.5	22.1	20.5	16.5	28.1	27.5
II						
I	16.9	9.3	24.1	14.1	13.8	8.2
II	30.3	32.3	27.6	33.8	29.3	29.1
III	23.6	24.7	31.0	28.2	20.3	23.5
IV	29.2	33.7	17.2	23.9	36.6	39.3
III						
I	9.5	8.8	20.0	13.4	6.4	6.2
II	16.9	15.5	15.6	18.3	17.1	13.9
III	30.2	29.6	28.9	31.7	29.3	29.2
IV	43.4	46.1	35.6	36.6	47.1	50.7
IV						
I	2.9	2.9	2.4	3.4	2.5	2.4
II	12.9	16.7	14.6	20.7	11.9	16.6
III	22.0	24.0	22.0	13.8	22.0	26.0
IV	62.2	56.4	61.0	62.1	63.5	55.0

*I = Duncan scale values 59 to 97; II = 34 to 58; III = 18 to 33; IV = 1 to 17.

of current occupational level, Catholics in the lowest rank are more likely than Protestants to be downwardly mobile from occupational rank III. For Catholics, recruitment to the middle two ranks is more likely to come from the lowest ranked occupations while for Protestants recruitment to these middle two ranks is more likely from the top rank than for Catholics.

Thus, except for the lowest ranks, Catholic sons of the three highest occupational ranks have been recruited from lower ranks than they now occupy, implying greater upward mobility for Catholics than Protestants. Protestants are either recruited from occupational ranks similar to those or higher than they currently occupy. Even among those in the lowest occupational level, downward Catholic mobility is from the immediately adjacent higher ranked origins, while for Protestants downward mobility to the lowest rank is more likely from the top two occupational origins.

The results of these inflow data point to the generally *greater* upward mobility among Catholics than among Protestants and stand in marked contrast to the conclusion based on the outflow data. Thus, a paradox emerges: occupational inheritance data implied clearly greater intergenerational upward mobility among Protestants while occupational recruitment data point unmistakeably toward greater intergenerational upward mobility among Catholics.[b]

Do variations by cohort clarify these contradictory findings? Inflow data by age substantiate the overall pattern and do not resolve the paradox. For each age group, Catholics of the three highest occupational ranks have been recruited from lower occupational origins—i.e., Catholics show higher rates of upward mobility when compared to Protestants, controlling for occupational level and age (Table 7-5). (The same patterns emerge from inflow data on initial occupational rank not presented in tabular form.)

A more detailed examination of these data by age shows that greater Protestant recruitment from the highest level to the highest level characterizes each age group but differences have narrowed over time. Indeed, differential recruitment into the highest level from the two highest origins has narrowed from a Protestant-Catholic difference of 35 percentage points among the 45-64 age cohort to no Protestant-Catholic differences for the youngest age cohort. This also implies that recruitment into the highest rank from the

---

[b]It is interesting to note that Lenski using only outflow data on intergenerational occupational mobility presents findings that parallel our outflow data. He fails, however, to continue with inflow analysis and therefore comes to a distorted conclusion about Protestant-Catholic differences in intergenerational vertical mobility. (See Lenski, 1963, pp. 84-88.)

Table 7-5. Inflow Percentages, Intergenerational Mobility (Current Occupational Rank from Father's Occupational Rank), by Religion and Age

Current Occupational Rank* Fathers	25-34 Protestants	25-34 Catholics	35-44 Protestants	35-44 Catholics	45-64 Protestants	45-64 Catholics
I						
I	30.0	21.7	51.7	28.1	46.9	13.2
II	15.0	23.3	20.7	29.8	20.4	18.9
III	20.0	35.0	20.7	19.3	22.4	28.3
IV	35.0	20.0	6.9	22.8	10.2	39.6
II						
I	19.0	7.0	0.0	9.8	14.8	8.3
II	33.3	23.3	50.0	31.1	33.3	29.8
III	28.6	30.2	30.0	24.6	29.6	19.0
IV	19.0	39.5	20.0	34.4	22.2	42.9
III						
I	11.8	8.9	20.0	3.8	6.1	6.7
II	29.4	24.4	15.0	13.2	21.2	11.2
III	41.2	33.3	30.0	32.1	27.3	24.7
IV	17.6	33.3	35.0	50.9	45.5	57.3
IV						
I	10.0	4.8	—	0.0	0.0	2.6
II	20.0	23.8	—	25.0	15.4	13.2
III	20.0	14.3	—	22.5	7.7	32.9
IV	50.0	57.1	—	52.5	76.9	51.3

*I = Duncan scale values 59 to 97; II = 34 to 58; III = 18 to 33; IV = 1 to 17.

lowest two ranks has been higher for Catholics than Protestants with convergence over time.

Recruitment into the lowest occupational rank has been largely from the lowest rank—a pattern consistent with the data on occupational inheritance. But there appears to be a shift toward greater downward mobility among young Catholics while the reverse appears for the oldest cohort.

Recruitment to the middle two ranks shows a clear pattern of difference for Protestants and Catholics, with little variation by age. Recruitment that implies downward mobility (rank II from I and rank III from II and I) characterizes Protestants more than Catholics; recruitment that implies upward mobility (rank II from III and IV and rank III from IV) is more characteristic of Catholics than Protestants.

INTERGENERATIONAL MOBILITY OF PROTESTANTS AND CATHOLICS

In sum, the outflow analysis points to the fact that Catholics are more downwardly mobile than Protestants (i.e., of those whose fathers were of the same occupational rank, Catholics are more likely to end up lower than their fathers while Protestants are more likely to "inherit" or be higher than their father's occupational rank); the inflow analysis suggests that Catholics are more upwardly mobile than Protestants (i.e., Catholic sons are more likely than Protestant sons to be recruited from lower occupational origins). This paradox may be resolved by recalling the lower occupational origins of Catholics and the statistical necessity of upward mobility when Catholic sons are at the same occupational level as Protestant sons. Since inheritance of occupational rank is higher among Protestants and their occupational origins are higher, recruitment to initial or current occupational levels requires less occupational mobility. Therefore, Catholic sons at the same occupational level as Protestant sons will have different recruitment patterns—generally more upward mobility at higher ranks—than Protestants. Similarly, Protestants in the top ranked occupations are more likely to have attained a rank similar to their fathers, while Catholics in the higher ranked occupations are more likely to come from lower occupational origins. We may recall that only 10 percent of Catholic fathers were in the top ranked occupations (compared to 24 percent of the Protestant fathers) while 70 percent of Catholic fathers were in the two lowest ranks (compared to 52 percent of the Protestant fathers). Hence the pool of lower occupational origins is substantially greater for

Catholics—and there is no place to move except up from the bottom, just as there is no place to move from the top except down. It should be further noted that the younger cohorts of Catholics exhibit a somewhat reversed pattern, partly reflecting the changed origins of that cohort and the substantial upward mobility experienced by their fathers as evidenced by cohort changes.

This somewhat oversimplified explanation implies a number of contrasts between Protestants and Catholics in the relative distribution of occupations of fathers and sons by rank and age. First, we should expect that the differences between the occupational distribution of Catholic fathers and sons should be much larger than the differences between the occupational distribution of Protestant fathers and sons. In particular, we should expect much greater differences for Catholics than Protestants in the highest occupational rank (reflecting the larger gains among Catholic sons compared to Protestant sons) and in the lowest occupational rank (reflecting the greater declines in Catholic concentration in the lowest level compared to Protestants).

Data in Table 7–6 confirm these inferences. These data show the percentage point differences in the occupational distribution of fathers and sons and indicate the relative gains and losses in occupational concentration by religion and age. (A minus indicates that proportionately fewer sons were in the specific occupational rank than were their fathers.) For example, there was a gain of 14.6 percentage points in the current occupational concentration of all sons in the highest rank compared to fathers and a decline of 19.3 percentage points at the lowest rank. The data show larger differences between Catholic fathers and sons in the highest and lowest occupational ranks relative to differences between Protestant fathers and sons. Although the differences between fathers and sons in the lowest rank are impressive for both Protestants and Catholics, the declines for Catholics are larger. These patterns are consistent for the younger age cohorts while for those 65 and over differences in the occupational concentration of Protestant fathers and sons in the lowest rank are substantially greater than for Catholics. Contrasts between Protestants and Catholics are particularly sharp in the younger age cohort where Catholic sons have gained the most, relative to Catholic fathers in the highest rank, and have reduced their concentration in lower ranks.

It is interesting to examine the Jewish pattern since it differs considerably from Protestants and Catholics. There is much greater occupational concentration at the highest rank for sons (41.4 percentage point differences separate Jewish sons and fathers at that

Table 7-6. Percentage Point Difference Between Father's and Son's (Initial and Current) Occupational Rank, by Religion and Age

Occupational Rank* of Father	Total		Protestants		Jews		Catholics	
	Initial	Current	Initial	Current	Initial	Current	Initial	Current
All Ages								
I	6.2	14.6	1.1	13.4	11.1	41.4	8.0	14.0
II	5.4	3.5	9.1	1.7	11.1	-17.3	4.1	5.4
III	1.2	1.2	0.0	3.5	-22.2	-20.7	3.1	1.5
IV	-12.9	-19.3	-10.1	-18.5	—	-3.4	-15.3	-20.7
25-34								
I	16.7	19.0	4.7	10.3	—	—	23.0	23.1
II	1.3	2.4	9.6	5.9	—	—	-2.0	1.7
III	-4.7	-3.7	-4.7	-2.9	—	—	-4.0	-4.2
IV	-13.4	-17.8	-9.6	-13.2	—	—	-17.0	-20.7
35-44								
I	7.8	17.2	2.8	16.2	—	—	7.9	15.6
II	1.1	0.3	0.0	-8.1	—	—	1.3	3.8
III	5.2	1.4	-2.8	8.1	—	—	8.6	0.5
IV	-14.0	-18.9	0.0	-16.2	—	—	-17.9	-19.9
45-64								
I	2.6	13.1	-1.2	16.4	9.1	38.4	3.3	10.2
II	9.1	5.8	10.0	-0.9	9.0	-23.1	8.8	9.6
III	0.3	2.3	1.3	3.2	-18.2	-15.4	1.9	3.7
IV	-12.1	-21.2	-10.0	-18.8	—	—	-13.9	-23.5
65+								
I	-2.5	4.3	0.0	5.1	—	—	-2.3	2.8
II	9.0	5.1	16.6	17.9	—	—	-4.6	0.0
III	6.4	6.9	6.7	7.7	—	—	-6.8	8.5
IV	-12.8	-16.2	-23.3	-30.8	—	—	-9.1	-11.4

*I = Duncan scale values 59 to 97; II = 34 to 58; III = 18 to 33; IV = 1 to 17.

level) and each of the lower three ranks have declined in concentration for sons compared to fathers. This pattern undoubtedly varies by age, but the small number of Jews in the sample does not allow a detailed examination. Data for the one age group available suggest that Jewish patterns are substantially different from Protestants and Catholics in the very large formation of new positions at the top ranks and in the sharper declines in positions at the lower occupational ranks.

In addition, the analysis suggests that an examination of summary mobility measures will reveal that upward mobility across ranks should be higher for Catholics than Protestants and downward mobility greater for Protestants. This follows from the finding that Catholics are recruiting from lower ranks having had lower occupational origins, while Protestants have higher ranked occupational origins and higher rates of occupational inheritance. Moreover, the analyses of the different distributions of fathers' and sons' occupational ranks by religion suggest that structural mobility, i.e., the minimum proportion of a group that must change occupational categories in order for two distributions to be similar, should be higher among Catholics than Protestants. In short, we would expect that the amount of mobility generated by structural changes (shifts in the occupational distribution) should be higher among Catholics than Protestants.

These three inferences that (1) overall upward mobility is higher among Catholics; (2) downward mobility is higher among Protestants; and (3) structural mobility is higher among Catholics are clearly substantiated in the summary measures of intergenerational occupational mobility presented in Table 7-7. These data show that intergenerational upward mobility from father's occupational rank is higher for Catholics that Protestants. Protestants tend to be more downwardly mobile than Catholics in initial occupational rank but apparently "catch up" to Catholics in current occupational rank. (This is partly a function of differential cohort effects for Catholics and Protestants, as we shall see.) Structural mobility is higher among Catholics in initial and current occupation when compared to Protestants.

The Jewish rate of occupational stability is higher overall than for Protestants and Catholics reflecting their overall concentration in higher occupational ranks at all points—in origin, initially and currently. Thus, while rates of upward mobility among Jews are not conspicuously different from non-Jews, downward mobility is significantly lower among Jews. As we might expect, structural mobility among Jews is about twice as high compared to Protestants

Table 7-7. Intergenerational Mobility, Initial and Current Occupational Rank Compared to Father's Occupational Rank, by Religion (Summary Measures)

Intergenerational Mobility	Total		Protestants		Jews		Catholics	
	Initial Occupational Rank	Current Occupational Rank	Initial Occupational Rank	Current Occupational Rank	Initial Occupational Rank	Current Occupational Rank	Initial Occupational Rank	Current Occupational Rank
Upward	39.1	47.2	37.3	44.0	33.4	48.3	40.5	48.8
Downward	22.0	17.1	24.4	16.2	16.7	6.9	21.1	17.8
Nonmobility	38.8	35.7	38.3	33.9	50.0	44.8	38.3	33.4
Structural	12.9	19.3	10.2	18.5	22.2	41.4	15.3	20.8
Exchange	48.3	45.0	51.5	41.6	27.8	13.8	46.4	45.8

and Catholics. Exchange mobility among Jews is substantially lower since shifts in the occupational distributions of Jewish fathers and sons are so conspicuous.

The pattern of greater upward mobility for Catholics and greater downward mobility for Protestants is, however, not characteristic of all ages (Table 7-8). The summary mobility measures by age suggest that the higher upward mobility among Catholics is a pattern only for the two youngest cohorts while among the older two cohorts, Protestants had a higher rate of upward mobility. Similarly, Protestants are more downwardly mobile than Catholics for the two youngest cohorts, reversing the patterns for those age 45 and over. The greater stability of Protestants—reflected in occupational inheritance—is also limited to the cohorts below age 45, where Protestant stability reflects the inheritance of higher occupational rankings. The greater stability of older Catholics reflects the more recent

Table 7-8. Intergenerational Mobility, Initial and Current Occupational Rank Compared to Father's Occupational Rank, by Religion and Age (Summary Measures)

	Total		Protestants		Catholics	
	Initial	*Current*	*Initial*	*Current*	*Initial*	*Current*
25-34						
Upward	46.3	49.0	40.5	39.7	51.0	54.4
Downward	22.2	18.2	28.7	23.5	19.0	16.0
Nonmobile	31.5	32.8	30.9	36.8	30.0	29.6
Structural	17.1	21.5	14.3	16.1	23.0	24.9
Exchange	51.4	45.7	54.8	42.1	47.0	45.5
35-44						
Upward	37.3	48.1	25.0	41.9	39.7	49.3
Downward	19.2	14.7	22.2	12.9	18.4	16.1
Nonmobile	43.5	37.2	52.8	45.2	41.8	34.6
Structural	14.1	18.9	2.8	24.3	18.0	19.9
Exchange	42.4	43.9	44.4	30.5	40.2	45.5
45-64						
Upward	38.9	48.2	40.0	45.1	38.8	49.3
Downward	22.7	17.6	22.5	13.1	23.2	19.9
Nonmobile	38.3	34.2	37.5	41.8	40.0	30.8
Structural	12.1	21.2	11.3	19.7	14.0	23.5
Exchange	49.6	44.6	51.2	38.5	46.0	45.7
65+						
Upward	30.8	37.6	40.0	51.3	27.3	31.4
Downward	25.7	18.0	26.7	18.0	25.0	18.6
Nonmobile	43.5	44.4	33.3	30.8	45.7	50.0
Structural	15.4	16.2	23.3	30.8	11.4	11.4
Exchange	41.1	39.4	43.4	38.4	40.9	38.6

timing of occupational upward mobility and the greater inheritance of lower ranked occupations of the older generations of Catholics. This may be clearly seen in the greater structural shifts in occupations that characterize the younger cohorts of Catholics and the greater structural mobility among Protestants in the oldest cohort. The few exceptions to these patterns for current in contrast to initial occupational rank suggest a greater intragenerational mobility among Catholics for the middle-age cohorts—a pattern that will be examined in detail in the next chapter.

Hence, examining the Catholic mobility pattern over time reveals a steady increase in the rate of upward mobility and a trend toward decline in downward mobility for both initial and current occupational rank. There is also a trend toward a general decline in stability among Catholics and an increase in structural mobility—more for initial than for current occupational rank. Protestants exhibit a somewhat less clear pattern of changes over time, but there is a tendency toward a decline in the rate of upward mobility over time (for current occupational rank) and an increase in downward mobility, particularly for the youngest age cohort. These tendencies among Protestants are the reverse of the Catholic pattern.

There are too few Jewish cases in our sample for a detailed analysis of changes in occupational mobility by age. Data available for one age group (age 45-64) show that the overall pattern noted earlier holds: Jews have higher rates of upward mobility (54 percent), lower rates of downward mobility (15 percent), and higher rates of structural mobility (38 percent) when compared to Protestants and Catholics of the same age cohort.

PERCEIVED INTERGENERATIONAL MOBILITY OF RELIGIOUS SUBPOPULATIONS

In addition to occupational changes that reflect social mobility, there is the subjective dimension of perceived mobility. We have already examined self-identification of current social class as one aspect of social stratification. Data were also collected on how the respondents characterize the social class of their parental household when they were growing up. These data may be compared to provide an indicator of perceived intergenerational mobility.[c]

Protestants place their parents in higher social classes than Catholics while Jews perceive their social class origins as higher than do the

---

[c]No direct comparison was requested from the respondent and we compare the responses to these two separate questions. The questions are listed in Appendix A.

Protestants. These differential patterns of subjective origins parallel the findings on father's occupational rank by religion. Identical rankings characterize the three age cohorts over age 35, while a larger proportion of Catholics of the youngest cohort place their parents in the upper or middle class when compared to Protestants. (These data are not presented in tabular form.) Of all those who defined their parents as upper or middle class, a larger proportion of Protestants than Catholics defined themselves in that same social class. The reverse pattern characterizes outflows from the working and lower classes: a larger proportion of Catholics than Protestants who define their parents as working or lower class define themselves as lower or working class. Thus, subjective social class inheritance is higher among Protestants in the upper two social classes while the reverse characterizes the lower two social classes. These patterns persist for age except for the youngest cohort. Upward mobility from the lower classes is higher among younger Catholics than younger Protestants and lower social class inheritance is higher among Protestants than Catholics. Jews have a distinctive pattern of perceived origins and social class placement when compared to Protestants and Catholics, and Jewish–non-Jewish differences tend to be larger than Protestant-Catholic differences. All the Jews from middle class origins define themselves as middle class; more Jews from working class origins define themselves as middle class than Protestants and Catholics from the same origins. Hence, the implied upward mobility of Jews from working class origins is greater than for non-Jews. All of these outflow patterns by religion and age parallel data on occupational mobility.

Findings based on an analysis of inflows to perceived social class point to higher upward mobility among Catholics than Protestants of middle class identification, reflecting, as with intergenerational occupational mobility, the lower class origins of Catholics and the greater social class inheritance among middle class Protestants. There are few systematic differences between Catholics and Protestants in the inflows to the working class with only a slightly larger proportion of working class Catholics placing their parents in the lower classes. The exception to the overall pattern is for young middle class Catholics, who are more likely to come from middle class origins than are Protestants. In general, middle class Jews are relatively more stable than Protestants and Catholics in their perceived middle class origins and this pattern holds controlling for age.

The summary subjective intergenerational mobility data (Table 7-9) reflect these inflow and outflow patterns for the three religious subpopulations. Several major points emerge clearly: first, a high proportion (six out of ten) of each group define themselves as being in the same social class as their parents. For Protestants and Jews this means higher perceived occupational inheritance at the middle and upper classes, while occupational continuity is higher at the lower and working classes for Catholics. Second, over three times as many perceive their origins as lower rather than higher than themselves; hence, perceived upward mobility for all groups is significantly greater than perceived downward mobility.

Upward mobility is somewhat higher among Catholics reflecting both their lower perceived origins and the stability of middle class Protestants and Jews. Indeed, indexes of dissimilarity that were computed (reflecting the differences between the distributions of social class self-identification and perceptions of the social class of parents) show significant increases in middle class concentration among all three groups, with the greatest increases among Jews, followed by Protestants and Catholics. Declines in intergenerational working class identification are most characteristic of Jews and least characteristic of Catholics, but the intergenerational decline in lower class identification is high among Catholics than Protestants. These

Table 7-9. Subjective Intergenerational Mobility, by Religion and Age (Summary Measures)

	Protestants	*Jews*	*Catholics*
All Ages			
Same	65.9	69.2	60.8
Downward	7.3	7.7	8.6
Upward	26.7	23.1	30.6
25-34			
Same	64.2	63.6	65.3
Downward	5.0	9.1	8.7
Upward	30.9	27.3	26.0
35-44			
Same	68.9	62.6	55.7
Downward	6.1	6.3	9.1
Upward	25.1	31.3	35.3
45-64			
Same	63.5	81.0	59.7
Downward	8.6	4.8	7.7
Upward	27.8	14.3	52.6
65+			
Same	70.5	—	67.6
Downward	10.3	—	11.5
Upward	19.2	—	21.0

Protestant-Catholic patterns, with some exceptions, characterize the three older age cohorts over age 35 but reverse somewhat among the youngest cohort.

Finally, there is a remarkable consistency between the patterns that emerge from an analysis of perceived intergenerational social mobility and those that characterize occupational mobility of fathers and sons. Thus, the data on subjective mobility between generations reinforce the conclusions based on occupational mobility and suggest that mobility patterns have been sufficiently clear to the various religious subpopulations to be perceived accurately—at least on an aggregate basis.

Occupational Origins, Inheritence, and Recruitment of Catholic Ethnic Groups

Patterns of occupational origins, inheritance, and recruitment vary substantially among French Canadian, Irish, Italian, and Portuguese ethnic groups. The data on the occupational rank of the fathers of these Catholic ethnic subgroups (Table 7-10) show patterns consistent with those presented earlier for occupational rank of sons (Chapter 2). Irish fathers are more concentrated in the top occupational ranks—14 percent are in the highest rank and 52 percent are in the top two ranks. Next follow Italian fathers (11 percent in the top and 28 percent in the top two ranks), French Canadian fathers (8 percent and 25 percent, respectively) and the lowest occupational origins characterizes the Portuguese fathers (3 percent and 14 percent, respectively). The reverse ranking characterizes, as expected, the bottom occupational rank: 59 percent of Portuguese fathers are in the bottom rank compared to 46 percent, 43 percent and 30 percent of the French Canadian, Italian, and Irish fathers, respectively. It should be noted that the variations in father's occupational rank within the Catholic subpopulation are significantly greater than variation between Protestant and Catholic fathers. Nevertheless, Protestants have higher occupational origins than any of the Catholic ethnics, including the Irish.

This ranking among the fathers of Catholic ethnic groups holds for most comparisons by age. For the older two cohorts, distinctions between the occupational origins of French Canadians and Italians are not clearly marked nor are there clear differences between the occupational origins of young French Canadians and Portuguese. However, Irish fathers in general tend to be in the top occupational ranks and Portuguese fathers in the lowest ranks. Among those age 25-34, occupational origins tend to be dichotomous (Irish-Italian versus Portuguese-French Canadian) rather than a clear fourfold differentiation. The concentration of French-Canadian and Portuguese fathers in the lowest two occupational ranks (over seven out of ten of the fathers of the youngest cohort are from these ranks) and the small proportion found in the top two ranks (including Italian fathers) stand in marked contrast to the Irish pattern. Over time, Irish origins have improved considerably from the bottom two ranks, Italian fathers have moved from the lowest rank, while French Canadian fathers have changed the least by cohort. Slower changes over time characterize Portuguese fathers—mainly declines in the

Table 7-10. Occupational Rank of Fathers, by Catholic Ethnic Groups and Age

Occupational Rank* of Fathers	French Canadians	Irish	Italians	Portuguese
All Ages				
I	8.3	14.4	10.9	3.2
II	16.7	37.6	17.0	11.1
III	28.9	17.6	29.3	27.0
IV	46.1	30.4	42.8	58.7
25-34				
I	7.1	16.7	18.9	5.9
II	21.4	40.9	9.4	23.5
III	26.2	13.3	43.4	23.5
IV	45.2	30.0	28.3	47.1
35-44				
I	7.7	25.0	11.1	7.1
II	15.4	52.8	27.0	0.0
III	32.7	8.3	25.4	35.7
IV	44.2	13.9	36.5	57.1
45-64				
I	8.3	8.3	6.4	0.0
II	17.9	33.3	17.0	6.9
III	31.0	27.1	24.5	27.6
IV	42.9	31.3	52.1	65.5
65+				
I	11.5	—	10.5	—
II	7.7	—	5.3	—
III	19.2	—	26.3	—
IV	61.5	—	57.9	—

*I = Duncan scale values 59 to 97; II = 34 to 58; III = 18 to 33; IV = 1 to 17.

lowest ranks—with a significant shift to the second rank among
fathers of the youngest cohort. This is exactly the same process that
was observed by cohort in the occupational changes among sons
(Chapter 2).

Unlike the convergence over time observed for the differences
between Protestant and Catholic occupational origins, there is no
consistent pattern of convergence among Catholic ethnic groups.
Much sharper differences, for example, characterize the occupational
origins of young Irish and Italian cohorts (particularly in the middle
two occupational ranks) than older cohorts. In contrast, the origins
of young French Canadians and Portuguese are quite similar to each
other relative to older cohorts but are clearly different from Irish or
Italian patterns. To the extent that such differences in origins persist—and the current stratification of ethnic Catholics supports this
assumption—ethnic differences in inheritance, recruitment, and social
mobility will continue to exhibit differential patterns. If the convergence in the occupational origins of Protestants and Catholics
implies a convergence in mobility and stability patterns between
generations, the persistence of ethnic Catholic differences in occupational origins implies continuity in differential patterns of social
mobility and stability.

The outflows from these occupational origins follow a fairly
consistent pattern (Table 7-11): Irish sons are most likely among
Catholic ethnics to move from lower origins to higher occupational
ranks, followed more or less by Italians and French Canadians;
Portuguese are most likely to remain at the bottom. However,
occupational inheritance is higher for Irish from high ranked occupational origins, followed by Italians and French Canadians. Thus, of
all Catholic ethnics from the lowest occupational origins, 65 percent
of the Portuguese enter the labor force in the lowest rank (46 percent are currently in that rank) and fewer move to top ranked
occupations when compared to other Catholic ethnics of the same
origins. In sharp contrast, only 19 percent of the Irish whose fathers
were in the lowest rank entered the labor force at that rank (10 percent currently) and over 50 percent entered the labor force in the
two highest occupational ranks. Italians tend to be more stable at
the lowest occupational rank than French Canadians but those who
are mobile are more likely to move to higher ranks than are French
Canadians—42 percent of the Italians of the lowest occupational
origins are currently in the top two ranks compared to 22 percent
of the French Canadians from the same origins. This pattern does
not characterize initial occupational rank of Italians and French
Canadians suggesting a more vigorous intragenerational mobility
pattern for Italians than French Canadians.

Table 7-11. Outflow Percentages, Intergenerational Mobility (Occupational Rank of Fathers to Initial and Current Occupational Rank): Catholic Ethnic Groups

Occupational Rank*		French Canadians		Irish		Italians		Portuguese	
Father	Son	Initial	Current	Initial	Current	Initial	Current	Initial	Current
I	I	7.7	35.3	58.3	61.1	41.2	56.0	—	—
	II	46.2	23.5	25.0	22.2	35.3	20.0	—	—
	III	38.5	29.4	16.7	16.7	11.8	24.0	—	—
	IV	7.7	11.8	0.0	0.0	11.8	0.0	—	—
II	I	13.6	20.6	37.1	44.7	4.5	15.4	—	—
	II	22.7	50.0	51.4	36.2	27.3	30.8	—	—
	III	40.9	26.5	8.6	12.8	27.3	15.4	—	—
	IV	22.7	2.9	2.9	6.4	40.9	38.5	—	—
III	I	11.1	16.9	28.6	22.7	23.8	34.3	—	17.6
	II	11.1	25.4	28.6	22.7	26.2	23.9	—	5.9
	III	38.9	33.9	14.3	13.6	31.0	29.9	—	47.1
	IV	38.9	23.7	28.6	40.9	19.0	11.9	—	29.4
IV	I	9.9	13.8	3.7	7.9	6.8	14.3	11.5	8.1
	II	15.5	8.5	48.1	36.8	17.8	27.6	3.8	10.8
	III	35.2	47.9	29.6	44.7	21.9	20.4	19.2	35.1
	IV	39.4	29.8	18.5	10.5	53.4	37.8	65.4	45.9

*I = Duncan scale values 59 to 97; II = 34 to 58; III = 18 to 33; IV = 1 to 17.

An examination of occupational inheritance at the highest occupational rank suggests that higher rates characterize the Irish (61 percent). This compares to 56 percent for the Italians and 35 percent for the French Canadians. The same pattern characterizes initial labor force entrance, although the French Canadians are much less likely to enter initially into the top occupational rank held by their fathers (only 7 percent compared to 41 percent of the Italians and 58 percent of the Irish). The pattern for the middle two ranks is less clear. Some of these inconsistent patterns, particularly for current occupational rank, are a function of the differential cohort effects for the Catholic ethnic groups.

How do recruitment patterns vary among Catholic ethnics? Data in Table 7-12 show that recruitment to the highest occupational rank (initial and current) from the highest occupational rank of fathers is significantly lower among French Canadians than either for Irish or Italians. The upward mobility of Irish sons to the highest ranked occupations is largely from the second ranked occupations of fathers while recruitment to the top occupational rank for Italians is from the lower two ranks. In large part, these differential sources of recruitment reflect the larger pool of Irish fathers in the second rank and the concentration of Italian origins in lower occupational ranks. Clearly, the recruitment of French Canadians to the top ranked occupations reflects much greater occupational mobility than that of other Catholic ethnics and is affected by the much larger pool of fathers in lower ranked occupational origins. Recruitment to the lowest occupational rank varies significantly by ethnicity. The overwhelming majority of Portuguese in the lowest occupational rank have been recruited from the lowest occupational origins (81 percent), while recruitment among the Irish to the lowest rank is least likely to be from fathers in the lowest rank. Italians entering the labor force in the lowest occupational ranks are more likely than French Canadians to be recruited from the lowest occupational origins but this reverses itself for current occupation. Again, these inflow differences are related to the sharp ethnic differences in occupational origins.

Irish in the second occupational rank are most stable while Italians are most likely to be upwardly mobile to the second occupational rank. Indeed, 72 percent of Italians in the second rank are from occupational origins ranked III or IV compared to 51 percent of the French Canadians and 48 percent of the Irish. However, the Irish who enter or are currently in occupations ranked III are more likely to be upwardly mobile (53 percent and 59 percent, respectively) followed by French Canadians and Italians. Irish in this

Table 7-12. Inflow Percentages, Intergenerational Mobility (Initial and Current Occupational Rank from Father's Occupational Rank): Catholic Ethnic Groups

Occupational Rank*		French Canadians		Irish		Italians		Portuguese	
Sons	Fathers	Initial	Current	Initial	Current	Initial	Current	Initial	Current
I	I	6.7	16.7	28.0	27.5	30.4	24.6	—	—
	II	20.0	19.4	52.0	52.5	4.3	10.5	—	—
	III	26.7	27.8	16.0	12.5	43.5	40.4	—	—
	IV	46.7	36.1	4.0	7.5	21.7	24.6	—	—
II	I	23.1	9.1	7.9	10.0	16.7	8.3	—	—
	II	19.2	38.6	47.4	42.5	16.7	20.0	—	—
	III	15.4	34.1	10.5	12.5	30.6	26.7	—	—
	IV	42.3	18.2	34.2	35.0	36.1	45.0	—	—
III	I	9.4	6.3	13.3	10.3	5.4	11.5	0.0	0.0
	II	17.0	11.4	20.0	20.7	16.2	11.5	33.3	12.5
	III	26.4	25.3	13.3	10.3	35.1	38.5	25.0	33.3
	IV	47.2	57.0	53.3	58.6	43.2	38.5	41.7	54.2
IV	I	2.1	4.4	0.0	0.0	3.4	0.0	0.0	0.0
	II	10.4	2.2	10.0	18.8	15.5	25.0	0.0	4.3
	III	29.2	31.1	40.0	56.3	13.8	13.3	19.0	21.7
	IV	58.3	62.2	50.0	25.0	67.2	61.7	81.0	73.9

*I = Duncan scale values 59 to 97; II = 34 to 58; III = 18 to 33; IV = 1 to 17.

occupational rank are least likely to be recruited from similar origins while Italians are most likely. Portuguese sons in the third ranked occupation are the least likely to be upwardly mobile of all Catholic ethnics. With but minor exceptions, these patterns hold by age where comparisons are possible.

In summary, the data show extensive and complex Catholic ethnic variations in occupational origins, inheritance and recruitment. Such variations are significantly larger among Catholic ethnics than between Protestants and Catholics. An examination of summary occupational mobility measures suggests the following general patterns (Table 7–13).

1. The Irish have been more upwardly mobile than non-Irish Catholic ethnics and this also holds for most comparisons by age for initial occupation. Most importantly, Irish have been most upwardly mobile out of the lowest ranks and most stable in the higher ranks. As the composition of occupational origins has changed for the Irish toward higher occupational levels, there is a smaller pool of lower level origins and therefore reduced probabilities of upward mobility. The Irish have the highest proportion of structural mobility among Catholic ethnics for initial occupational rank, reflecting the larger distributional shifts between Irish fathers and sons.

2. The Portuguese tend to be the least upwardly mobile of all Catholic ethnics and this holds for initial and current occupation, controlling for age. Moreover, they are the most stable of all ethnics. The combined proportion of downward mobility and nonmobility is highest among Portuguese and is particularly significant when their low occupational origins and current rank are taken into consideration.

3. Italians are less likely than French Canadians to be upwardly mobile but are also more likely to be stable. French Canadians have a somewhat higher amount of structural mobility than Italians, but differences between these two subpopulations are relatively small. Moreover, differences between initial and current occupational rank reflect in part the different cohort effects for Italian and French Canadian subpopulations.

4. A comparison of the distribution of occupational ranks of fathers and sons shows the importance of taking the flows between specific ranks into account. The major changes between generations of Irish Catholics has been at the two extreme occupational ranks: declines at the lowest rank and gains in the highest rank. For the Portuguese and French Canadians the reduction in occupational concentration among sons relative to fathers at the lowest rank has resulted in major gains in third ranked occupations but less conspicuous

Table 7-13. Intergenerational Mobility, Initial and Current Occupational Rank Compared to Father's Occupational Rank, Catholic Ethnic Groups, by Age (Summary Measures)

	French Canadians		Irish		Italians		Portuguese	
	Initial	Current	Initial	Current	Initial	Current	Initial	Current
All Ages								
Upward	37.9	48.0	48.8	52.0	36.4	46.3	30.0	39.7
Downward	28.1	17.2	14.7	20.0	21.4	17.5	20.0	15.9
Nonmobility	33.8	34.8	36.5	28.0	42.2	36.2	50.0	44.4
Structural	16.2	24.0	19.3	23.2	13.0	23.2	17.5	22.2
Exchange	50.0	41.2	44.2	48.8	44.8	40.6	32.5	33.4
25–34								
Upward	42.3	57.1	61.9	53.3	50.0	50.9	30.0	41.2
Downward	23.1	14.3	14.3	16.7	16.7	13.2	40.0	17.7
Nonmobility	34.6	28.6	23.8	30.0	33.3	35.9	40.0	41.2
Structural	30.9	30.0	33.4	33.4	33.3	39.6	50.0	41.2
Exchange	34.9	40.5	42.8	36.6	33.3	24.5	20.0	17.6
35–44								
Upward	47.5	48.1	37.0	47.2	30.9	49.2	27.3	35.7
Downward	25.0	17.3	18.5	13.9	19.0	19.1	18.2	0.0
Nonmobility	27.5	34.6	44.4	38.9	50.0	31.8	54.6	64.7
Structural	22.5	25.0	18.6	30.6	14.3	19.1	9.1	21.4
Exchange	50.0	40.4	37.0	30.5	35.7	49.1	36.3	13.9
45–64								
Upward	30.0	47.6	51.5	50.0	38.8	46.8	33.3	44.8
Downward	35.0	20.2	12.1	27.1	25.4	20.2	5.6	17.2
Nonmobility	35.0	32.1	36.3	22.9	35.8	33.0	61.1	37.9
Structural	6.7	20.3	30.3	16.7	10.5	21.2	16.7	20.7
Exchange	58.3	47.6	33.3	60.4	53.7	45.8	22.2	41.4
65+								
Upward	37.5	34.6	—	72.7	13.3	21.1	—	—
Downward	18.8	11.5	—	18.2	20.0	10.5	—	—
Nonmobility	43.8	53.9	—	9.1	66.7	68.4	—	—
Structural	43.8	26.9	—	54.6	13.4	5.2	—	—
Exchange	12.4	19.2	—	36.3	19.9	24.4	—	—

changes in the top two ranks. Italian sons, in contrast, have gained most relative to fathers in the second ranked occupations. Hence the mobility pattern of Catholic ethnic subpopulations has resulted in the greater concentration of the Irish at the top of the occupational hierarchy, the Italians in the second ranked occupations, the French Canadians in the third, and the Portuguese in the lower occupational ranks.

PERCEIVED INTERGENERATIONAL MOBILITY OF CATHOLIC ETHNICS

The final dimension of our analysis of intergenerational social mobility revolves around the subjective social class origins and perceived mobility of Catholic ethnics. Irish sons are more likely to identify their social class origins as middle or upper class, followed by Italians, French Canadians and Portuguese. Differences between Irish and Portuguese in perceived social class origins are substantial while Italian–French Canadian differences are slight overall. However, the social class origins of Italians and French Canadians by age show that for the two younger age cohorts, a larger proportion of Italians identify their origins as middle or upper class, while the reverse pattern characterizes the two older cohorts. (These data are not presented in tabular form.)

The Irish of middle class origins are more likely than other Catholic ethnics to identify themselves as middle class and are the least downwardly mobile. Italians are ranked next in the proportion who perceive themselves as "inheriting" the social class origins of their parents with little difference between the patterns of middle class inheritance of French Canadians and Portuguese. It is significant to note that a larger proportion of middle class Irish tend to identify their origins as middle class—a pattern that does not characterize other Catholic ethnics. Hence, the contrasts between Protestant and Catholic middle class inheritance noted earlier is mainly a Protestant-non-Irish Catholic difference.

Working class inheritance is highest for Portuguese and lowest for Irish and somewhat greater for French Canadians than Italians. These patterns fit consistently with those of perceived social class recruitment. The Irish middle class are most likely relative to other Catholic ethnics to identify themselves in terms of middle class origins and least likely to identify themselves from lower class origins. Relative to Protestants, the Irish are less recruited from the middle classes and more likely to be upwardly mobile. Middle class Portuguese are the least likely to identify their origins as middle class and recruit from the larger pool of lower and working classes. Only a slightly higher proportion of middle class Italians perceive their origins as lower or working class when compared to French Canadians. The Irish and Portuguese patterns of perceived recruitment persist when age is controlled while the Italian-French Canadian difference in upward mobility to the middle class characterizes only the two older cohorts. There is a very high perceived recruitment to the working class from working class origins among all Catholic ethnics.

A summary profile of Catholic ethnic perceived mobility suggests the following major patterns (Table 7-14):

1. Overall, a large proportion of Portuguese identify themselves in the same social class as their origins and that generally means of the lower and working classes. This pattern is consistent by age. Younger Portuguese ethnics have a somewhat higher proportion upwardly mobile, mainly out of lower and working class origins.

2. The Irish have the lowest rate of downward mobility and a combination of higher mobility from lower and working class origins and stability from middle class origins. Among two of the three older

Table 7-14. Subjective Intergenerational Mobility, Catholic Ethnic Groups, by Age (Summary Measures)

	French Canadians	Irish	Italians	Portuguese
All Ages				
Same	61.5	61.8	59.4	64.8
Downward	10.2	6.9	8.7	7.2
Upward	28.2	31.4	32.1	27.9
25-34				
Same	67.6	72.4	62.6	71.5
Downward	9.1	5.1	12.0	0.0
Upward	23.4	22.3	25.3	28.6
35-44				
Same	53.0	53.7	59.8	61.3
Downward	8.4	5.6	10.8	9.7
Upward	38.5	40.8	29.5	29.0
45-64				
Same	60.2	60.3	57.5	62.5
Downward	11.4	8.9	4.8	10.0
Upward	28.4	30.7	37.9	27.5
65+				
Same	71.8	57.1	59.4	—
Downward	12.8	7.1	12.5	—
Upward	15.5	35.7	28.2	—

cohorts upward mobility is highest among the Irish, while stability is highest for Irish of the youngest age cohort. These changes by age reflect the changing distributions of Irish origins over time from lower and working to middle and upper classes.

3. Italians tend to be more upwardly and less downwardly mobile than French Canadians. This upward mobility pattern characterizes three of the four age cohorts, while the pattern of lower Italian downward mobility only characterizes the older two age cohorts. Older Italians tend to be more mobile than French Canadians, who remain at lower social class levels. More recent cohorts show the reverse pattern: French Canadians exhibit a more vigorous mobility out of the lower social classes, while Italians are more stable at higher social class levels.

CONCLUSION

Taken together, the data analyzed in this chapter have presented a complex picture of a variety of elementary issues focusing on inter-generational social mobility. Simplistic questions about whether Protestants are more mobile intergenerationally than Catholics, whether Italians have closed the mobility gap with the Irish, whether perceived mobility between generations is an adequate substitute for occupational mobility patterns cannot be answered simply. We have demonstrated that the process of social mobility is exceedingly complex, particularly when faced with a variety of changing occupational origins and social class levels, when generational-age dynamics confound the dynamics, when variations within and between ethnic mobility experiences are so large and have varied over time, and when structural changes in occupational and social class distributions have been transformed over the last half-century. The complex reality of intergenerational social mobility for ethnic populations precludes simple generalizations. The recognition of the dimensions of that complexity is an indispensable step in grappling with the un-answered questions posed by this analysis of intergenerational social mobility.

Nevertheless, one overriding conclusion is inescapable: differences in social mobility continue to characterize ethnic subpopulations and are the consequences of a set of structural processes associated with wide variations in social class origins and opportunity structures. These intergenerational mobility patterns, whatever their sources, not only have implications for social structure and processes but are persistent features differentiating ethnic communities.

Chapter 8

Intragenerational Mobility

The analysis of changes in occupation and social class from one generation to another has provided one basis for evaluating the changing social structure of ethnic communities. The differential importance of social origins for subsequent occupational and social class attainment has been a major theme in the analysis of intergenerational mobility. An additional perspective on ethnic social structure relates to the impact of individual rather than parental origins on subsequent occupational attainment. This chapter focuses on intragenerational mobility of religious and Catholic ethnic groups in order to examine one central issue: Are members of ethnic subpopulations characterized by differential changes in occupational achievement in their life cycle? Differential social mobility reflects differential access to the broader opportunity structure and changes in ethnic occupational concentration. Implications for the changing structure of ethnic communities are therefore related to whether an ethnic subpopulation has experienced uniform or differential patterns of career mobility and whether all groups have shared similar patterns of occupational change.

CAREER MOBILITY

Do ethnics with similar occupational rankings when they enter the labor force follow different occupational careers? The analysis of career mobility begins with an examination of outflows from initial (i.e., occupation at age 25) to current occupational rank. In general, the data in Table 8-1 show that career occupational continuity is

Table 8-1. Outflow Percentages, Career Mobility (Occupational Rank at Age 25 to Current Occupational Rank), by Ethnicity

Occupational Rank* Age 25	Current	Total	Protestants	Jews	Catholics	French Canadians	Irish	Italians	Portuguese
I	I	75.2	73.0	75.0	75.8	41.7	91.4	90.6	—
	II	15.6	15.9	25.0	14.4	37.5	5.7	9.4	—
	III	8.3	11.1	0.0	8.3	16.7	2.9	0.0	—
	IV	0.9	0.0	0.0	1.5	4.2	0.0	0.0	—
II	I	28.5	39.8	35.7	22.7	25.0	13.5	24.1	—
	II	43.7	37.6	57.1	45.9	39.6	59.6	43.1	—
	III	18.6	19.4	7.1	19.3	25.0	17.3	24.1	—
	IV	9.3	3.2	0.0	12.1	10.4	9.6	8.6	—
III	I	9.7	13.2	—	8.5	10.4	4.2	10.0	10.5
	II	20.8	25.0	—	19.8	13.4	29.2	15.0	21.1
	III	52.2	50.0	—	52.8	58.2	58.3	51.7	52.6
	IV	17.3	11.8	—	18.9	17.9	8.3	23.3	15.8
IV	I	6.4	5.4	—	6.2	6.2	9.1	2.1	13.5
	II	19.2	18.9	—	19.0	21.0	9.1	21.1	10.8
	III	31.2	35.1	—	31.5	30.9	31.8	26.3	43.2
	IV	43.2	40.5	—	43.2	42.0	50.0	50.5	32.4

*I = Duncan scale values 59 to 97; II = 34 to 58; III = 18 to 33; IV = 1 to 17.

significantly higher in the highest occupational rank compared to lower ranks: Those who entered the labor force in the highest occupational rank are more likely to be in the same rank currently when compared to those whose initial occupational rank was lower. Not unexpectedly, career mobility is more likely to occur to the next highest occupational rank and a larger proportion of those mobile are upwardly rather than downwardly mobile. These overall patterns are similar to those of intergenerational mobility.

An examination of religious differences in career outflows shows that Catholics exhibit greater career stability than Protestants from all four initial occupational ranks. Conversely, Protestants whose occupational rank at age 25 was at either the highest or lowest level are more likely to be mobile when compared to Catholics from the same occupational rank—more mobile downward from the highest initial occupational rank and more mobile upward from the lowest initial occupational rank. However, career mobility differences between Protestants and Catholics from these extreme occupational ranks, while consistent, are relatively small.

The most substantial career mobility changes occur from the middle two ranks. Protestant and Catholic mobility outflows are more pronounced from both middle level occupational ranks: Protestants whose careers begin in occupations ranked second or third in the occupational hierarchy are more likely than Catholics of similar initial occupational levels to have current occupations ranked higher than initial occupations. About 40 percent of the Protestants whose initial occupations were ranked in the second category are currently in the highest occupational rank compared to 23 percent of the Catholics; 38 percent of the Protestants entering occupations ranked in the third category have moved up currently to the top two occupational ranks compared to 28 percent of the Catholics. Moreover, downward career mobility is more characteristic of Catholics than Protestants from both middle occupational ranks: 31 percent of the Catholics entering occupations ranked II and 19 percent of the Catholics entering occupations ranked III are currently in occupations *lower* than their initial occupational rank. This compares to 23 percent and 12 percent, respectively, for Protestants.[a]

The Jewish pattern of career mobility differs significantly from the Protestant-Catholic pattern. A high proportion of Jews entering

---

[a]These intragenerational mobilities are similar to the results obtained from the data on intergenerational mobility based on the outflow analysis (see Chapter 7).

the labor force in the highest occupational rank are currently in the highest or next to the highest rank. Jews are somewhat less up-wardly mobile than Protestants from initial occupational rank II and there is a higher rate of stability in Jewish career patterns. Fully 93 percent of the Jews who enter the labor force in second ranked occupations either remain in that rank or are currently in the highest rank. This compares to 77 percent of the Protestants and 68 percent of the Catholics. The greater stability of Jews and their lower rate of downward mobility is consistent with their concentration in high occupational ranks, initially and currently (see Chapter 2).

Data by age show that the patterns of religious differences in career mobility cannot be explained by differential cohort effects for these subpopulations (Table 8-2). For each age group without exception, Protestants entering the two middle occupational ranks are more upwardly mobile to current occupational rank than are Catholics. With but one exception (the youngest age cohort entering occupational level III) Catholics are more downwardly mobile from the two middle occupational ranks. Catholic career stability is generally higher than Protestant in ten out of fifteen age comparisons for all ranks. Two exceptions are noteworthy: (1) among those entering the labor force in the highest occupational rank, Protestants are more downwardly mobile for the two youngest age cohorts; (2) among those whose initial occupational rank is at the bottom of the occupational hierarchy, young Catholics are more upwardly mobile than Protestants, a reversal from the pattern characterizing the 35-44 age cohort. The first pattern may be related to the selec-tive outmigration of Protestants that will be examined in a subse-quent chapter. The exception among younger Catholics is reflected in their current stratification patterns noted earlier (Chapter 2).

The overall Catholic pattern of career mobility and the small differences between Protestants and Catholics at the two ends of the occupational hierarchy are clearly affected by major ethnic variations within the Catholic subgroup. The treatment of Catholics as a homogeneous group obscures the very wide differences in career mobility characteristic of Catholic ethnic groups that are signifi-cantly greater than those between Protestants and Catholics. Data in Table 8-1 show the very high proportion (over 90 percent) of Irish and Italian Catholics who remain in the top occupational rank having initially entered the labor force in that rank. This greater occupation-al career stability of Irish and Italians contrasts with non-Catholics and the Catholic average. It also stands in marked contrast to the French Canadian pattern. Only 42 percent of the French Canadians whose initial occupation was in the highest rank are currently in

Table 8-2. Outflow Percentages, Career Mobility (Occupational Rank at Age 25 to Current Occupational Rank), by Religion and Age

Occupational Rank*		25-34		35-44		45-64		65+	
Age 25	Current	Protestants	Catholics	Protestants	Catholics	Protestants	Catholics	Protestants	Catholics
I	I	71.4	73.7	75.0	83.3	76.0	74.3	—	—
	II	21.4	17.5	0.0	5.6	20.0	17.1	—	—
	III	7.1	5.3	25.0	11.1	4.0	8.6	—	—
	IV	0.0	3.5	0.0	0.0	0.0	0.0	—	—
II	I	35.3	18.6	35.3	26.7	45.2	21.7	35.3	25.0
	II	47.1	58.1	41.2	46.7	35.7	41.3	29.4	33.3
	III	17.6	16.3	23.5	10.0	16.7	25.0	23.5	33.3
	IV	0.0	7.0	0.0	16.7	2.4	12.0	11.8	8.3
III	I	12.5	12.2	10.0	9.9	16.7	6.3	8.3	5.0
	II	25.0	12.2	20.0	16.9	23.3	26.3	33.3	20.0
	III	50.0	68.3	70.0	52.1	40.0	46.3	58.3	50.0
	IV	12.5	7.3	0.0	21.1	20.0	21.3	0.0	25.0
IV	I	7.1	9.7	14.3	9.7	0.0	4.3	7.1	4.8
	II	14.3	16.1	28.6	22.6	12.5	20.3	28.6	11.9
	III	21.4	29.0	28.6	29.0	43.8	32.6	35.7	33.3
	IV	57.1	45.2	28.6	38.7	43.8	42.8	28.6	50.0

*I = Duncan scale values 59 to 97; II = 34 to 58; III = 18 to 33; IV = 1 to 17.

that rank and therefore exhibit high rates of downward mobility.

Examining the bottom occupational rank reveals less sharp differences among Catholic ethnics but differences are still greater within the Catholic subpopulation than between Protestants and Catholics. Irish and Italian Catholics are most stable from the lowest initial occupational rank while high rates of upward career mobility characterize Portuguese and French Canadians whose initial entry into the labor force was in the lowest ranked occupations. Two out of three Portuguese whose initial occupations were at the lowest level are currently in higher occupational ranks compared to 58 percent of the French Canadians and half of the Italians and Irish. Perhaps, Irish and Italians who enter at the lowest occupational level represent the occupationally unsuccessful remnants who, unlike other members of their ethnic groups, have not been able to take advantage of their longer standing access to career occupational mobility. There is a larger proportion of Portuguese and French Canadians entering low level occupations and therefore many more respond to what appears to be a new opportunity structure for them.

Career outflows from the middle ranks are more complex among Catholic ethnics. Of those entering occupations ranked in the second level, Irish are most stable and least downwardly mobile in their occupational careers, with more vigorous upward mobility characterizing French Canadians and Italians. From initial occupational level III, the Irish are most upwardly mobile while Italians are most downwardly mobile. There are similarities in the career mobility patterns of French Canadians and Italians from initial occupational level III.

Emerging from these outflow data (initial to current occupational ranks) are the following major patterns: Irish and Italians tend to have high rates of career stability from the highest and lowest initial occupational ranks and follow the general Catholic model in this respect. The Irish, similar to Jews, also have stable career patterns from second ranked occupations. Higher rates of upward career mobility characterize the Irish whose initial occupational rank is at the third level and the Italians from initial occupational rank II. Portuguese and French Canadians have high rates of upward career mobility from the lower ranked occupations; French Canadians also show a pattern of downward mobility from the highest initial occupational rank. With but minor exceptions these patterns hold for all age cohorts. (Data by age have not been presented in tabular form.) Overall, the data point to the importance of ethnicity as a differentiator of occupational career patterns with greater variation within the Catholic population than between Protestants and

Catholics. Moreover, career mobility patterns vary significantly by initial occupational rank, but show no major patterns by cohort that are differential for ethnic groups.

An additional perspective on career mobility patterns focuses on differential inflows to current occupational levels. The question we now ask is, What are the initial occupational rankings of those in each of the four current occupational rankings? Data in Table 8-3 show these career mobility inflows for each of the ethnic groups. Of all those who are currently in the highest occupational rank, Jews are more likely than non-Jews and Catholics more likely than Protestants to have entered the highest occupational rank at age 25. The greater career stability of Catholics compared to Protestants and the higher upward career mobility of Protestants are demonstrated with these data and are identical with the outflow patterns. At the lowest occupational level, Protestants exhibit greater career stability and Catholics are more downwardly mobile, again a pattern consistent with the greater downward mobility characterizing the outflows from the two middle occupational levels. The greater inflows to the middle occupational levels from lower occupational levels among Catholics reflect the larger pool of Catholics at lower occupational levels (see Chapter 2). This is further reinforced when inflow data by age are examined. We may recall that major shifts in occupational concentration characterize the youngest cohort of Catholics, so much so that younger Catholics are more concentrated in the higher occupational ranks than Protestants. The career mobility inflow data by age show that for the older Catholics inflows to the two middle occupational ranks are from lower initial occupational levels when compared to Protestants; the reverse characterizes the younger cohorts. Hence, as the pool of Catholics in lower occupational levels shrinks absolutely and relative to Protestants, the pattern of upward mobility inflows to the middle occupational ranks shifts as well.

A similar pattern accounts for the inflows to current from initial occupational levels among Catholic ethnics. Overall, Irish exhibit very high rates of career stability (higher than Jews) for the two highest current occupational ranks. Portuguese and French Canadians draw to the highest current occupational rank from the lower occupational levels reflecting again their greater occupational concentration at the lower levels. Indeed, the Portuguese of the three highest ranks exhibit the most upward mobility compared to all ethnic subpopulations. Upward mobility is more characteristic of Italians than French Canadians currently in the two middle ranks. These patterns hold for most comparisons by age.

A detailed examination of changes in the occupational distributions

Table 8-3. Inflow Percentages, Career Mobility (Current Occupational Rank from Occupational Rank at Age 25, by Ethnicity

Occupational Rank* Current / Age 25	Total	Protestants	Jews	Catholics	French Canadians	Irish	Italians	Portuguese
I								
I	53.4	47.9	71.4	54.9	29.4	76.2	56.9	27.3
II	30.0	38.5	23.8	25.8	35.3	16.7	27.5	9.1
III	9.1	9.4	4.8	9.9	20.6	2.4	11.8	18.2
IV	7.5	4.2	0.0	9.3	14.7	4.8	2.9	45.5
II								
I	11.2	13.2	38.5	9.1	16.7	4.8	5.3	8.3
II	46.4	46.1	61.5	45.7	35.2	73.8	43.9	25.0
III	19.7	22.4	0.0	20.2	16.7	16.7	15.8	33.3
IV	22.7	18.4	0.0	25.0	31.5	4.8	35.1	33.3
III								
I	5.3	8.2	—	4.4	5.0	3.2	0.0	3.7
II	17.6	21.2	—	16.1	15.0	29.0	20.0	0.0
III	44.3	40.0	—	45.0	48.8	45.2	44.3	37.0
IV	32.8	30.6	—	34.5	31.3	22.6	35.7	59.3
IV								
I	0.8	0.0	—	1.1	1.9	0.0	0.0	0.0
II	12.7	7.3	—	13.5	9.6	27.8	7.5	25.0
III	21.1	19.5	—	21.6	23.1	11.1	20.9	15.0
IV	65.4	73.2	—	63.8	65.4	61.1	71.6	60.0

*I = Duncan scale values 59 to 97; II = 34 to 58; III = 18 to 33; IV = 1 to 17.

from initial to current occupational rank clarifies these outflow and inflow patterns of career occupational change. Data in Table 8-4 show the actual percentage point differences between initial and current occupation by ethnicity and age. Overall, the most important shifts for Protestants are the declines from the lowest and second occupational ranks while for Catholics there are declines only in the proportion at the lowest occupational level. The sharper gains in the concentration of Protestants in the highest occupational rank result from declines in the second ranked occupations. Jews exhibit a unique pattern, reflecting their heavy concentration in the higher ranked occupations, initially and currently. Distributional changes among Jews are small and generally are from the second to the highest occupational rank.

With minor exceptions the Protestants and Catholic patterns hold by age, but the Catholic ethnic pattern is much less consistent when age is controlled. For example, among the older Irish (and to a lesser extent among older Italians) redistribution of occupations from initial to current levels is heavily out of the lowest occupational rank with major gains in the next highest occupational level. This movement out of the lowest rank characterizes the Portuguese (age 35-44 and age 45-64) and French Canadians (age 25-34 and 45-64). However, for the age cohort 35-44, declines from initial to current occupational rank characterize the lower three occupational levels of Irish, Italians and French Canadians. In the youngest cohort, distributional shifts out of the lowest rank characterize the non-Irish ethnics. Part of these cohort changes may be attributed to the changing occupational concentrations of Catholic ethnics over time and therefore the changing pool of persons in lower and middle level occupations. Hence, career upward mobility among the Irish is largely confined to the older cohort, many of whom entered at the lowest occupational level. For the youngest age cohort, in contrast, so few Irish entered the lowest occupational level that no distributional changes out of the lowest rank are observed. The Portuguese pattern shows declines in the lowest occupational rank for the two middle age cohorts, reflecting the very heavy concentration of initial occupations in this occupational rank.

It should be noted that career mobility patterns for the youngest cohort are problematic for analysis since for some, initial (age 25) and current (age 25-34) occupation are identical. Thus, small distributional changes characterize this cohort when compared to the older age cohorts. This does not necessarily reflect changes in career mobility patterns over time but the shorter time span relative to older cohorts that has been available to those age 25-34 to change their occupational ranking.

Table 8-4. Percentage Point Difference Between Initial and Current Occupational Rank, by Ethnicity and Age

Age and Occupational Rank*	Protestants	Jews	Catholics	French Canadians	Irish	Italians	Portuguese
All Ages							
I	11.1	2.7	6.1	4.6	5.3	7.7	8.6
II	- 5.7	- 2.7	0.1	2.7	- 7.5	- 0.4	4.2
III	5.7	0.0	4.5	5.9	5.3	4.1	11.5
IV	-11.1	—	-10.6	-13.2	- 3.0	-11.5	-24.3
25-34							
I	8.2	—	0.6	0.0	3.4	2.2	10.5
II	0.0	—	1.2	4.4	0.0	0.0	-10.5
III	- 1.6	—	3.5	4.4	3.4	4.4	5.3
IV	- 6.6	—	5.2	- 8.8	0.0	- 6.7	- 5.3
35-44							
I	8.7	—	10.1	6.4	13.6	12.4	22.2
II	- 7.0	—	- 1.7	- 1.6	- 8.1	- 3.1	5.5
III	15.8	—	- 2.6	1.7	2.7	- 6.2	5.5
IV	-17.6	—	5.7	- 3.3	- 2.7	- 3.1	-33.4
45-64							
I	13.9	5.0	6.4	4.7	0.0	8.0	0.0
II	- 8.6	- 5.0	0.3	8.2	-14.5	0.9	13.8
III	3.1	0.0	8.1	11.8	10.9	8.1	20.7
IV	- 8.5	—	-14.8	-24.7	3.6	-16.9	-34.5
65+							
I	9.8	—	5.2	6.9	8.4	4.3	—
II	- 3.9	—	2.5	- 6.9	8.4	0.0	—
III	9.8	—	11.6	6.9	25.0	13.1	—
IV	-15.7	—	-19.2	- 6.9	-41.6	-17.4	—

*I = Duncan scale values 59 to 97; II = 34 to 58; III = 18 to 33; IV = 1 to 17.

The outflow and inflow patterns of occupational change from initial to current occupational rank and the distributional changes within occupational ranks help place into context the summary measures of career mobility (Table 8-5). In general, these data show that Protestants are slightly more upwardly mobile and less downwardly mobile. Structural mobility, i.e., changes in the distributions of occupational ranking from initial to current levels, is higher among Protestants while exchange mobility, i.e., mobility among positions, is higher among Catholics. Consistent with the more detailed data are the relatively small differences between Protestants and Catholics in these summary career mobility data. Jews show a high degree of stability with lower rates of upward mobility and lower rates of structural career mobility.

The Portuguese show the highest rates of upward mobility reflecting their low occupational rankings initially, followed by French Canadians and Italians. The Irish, like the Jews, have high rates of career stability overall and the lowest rates of upward mobility of all Catholic ethnics. French Canadians have the highest rates of downward mobility among Catholic ethnics, reflecting their greater downward mobility from the highest occupational rank. Consistent with these patterns is the much higher level of structural mobility among the Portuguese not only in contrast to other Catholic ethnics but to Protestants as well.

Career mobility differentials between Protestants and Catholics (higher Protestant upward mobility, lower Protestant downward mobility and higher Protestant structural mobility) hold generally for each of the four age cohorts. However, there is some variation by age in career mobility for Catholic ethnic subpopulations, particularly among the Irish. For the oldest age cohort, the Irish have the highest rate of upward mobility (higher than Protestants and non-Irish Catholics) and conspicuously high structural mobility— reflecting the heavy concentration of older Irish in the lower initial occupational ranks and their upward career mobility from that rank. In contrast, the younger Irish (below age 65) are characterized by relatively lower levels of upward career mobility, higher rates of career continuity, and, hence, low levels of structural mobility. The Portuguese patterns vary much less by age and show higher rates of upward mobility, lower rates of stability and higher rates of structural mobility than non-Portuguese Catholic ethnics, with but minor exceptions in the youngest age cohort. Career patterns by age for Italians and French Canadians tend to fall between these Irish and Portuguese extremes. Italians have somewhat higher rates of career stability compared to French Canadians while French Canadians

Table 8-5.   Career Mobility, by Ethnicity and Age (Summary Measures)

	Total	Protestants	Catholics	French Canadians	Irish	Italians	Portuguese
All Ages							
Upward	32.2	35.8	31.8	34.2	19.6	31.0	45.7
Downward	16.3	15.4	16.6	19.7	14.3	14.6	14.2
Nonmobile	51.4	48.6	51.5	46.3	66.2	54.3	40.0
Structural	11.9	16.8	10.7	13.2	10.6	11.9	24.3
Exchange	36.7	34.6	37.8	40.5	23.2	33.8	35.7
25–34							
Upward	22.2	29.5	20.3	26.7	6.9	22.1	26.3
Downward	14.9	14.7	16.2	17.7	6.9	15.6	15.8
Nonmobile	62.8	55.7	63.4	55.5	86.2	62.3	57.9
Structural	5.1	8.2	5.3	8.9	3.4	6.7	10.6
Exchange	32.1	36.1	31.3	35.6	10.4	30.0	31.5
35–44							
Upward	31.7	33.3	31.9	36.1	21.6	29.3	55.6
Downward	16.3	14.0	16.2	27.9	2.7	13.9	11.1
Nonmobile	52.2	52.7	52.0	36.1	75.7	56.8	33.3
Structural	10.3	24.6	10.1	6.5	13.6	12.4	33.4
Exchange	37.5	22.7	37.9	57.4	10.7	30.8	33.3
45–64							
Upward	36.2	38.0	36.1	37.6	16.4	35.8	55.2
Downward	17.0	15.6	17.4	14.1	27.2	15.2	13.8
Nonmobile	46.9	46.5	46.3	48.3	56.4	49.1	31.0
Structural	14.7	17.1	14.8	24.7	14.5	17.0	34.5
Exchange	38.4	36.4	38.9	27.0	29.1	33.9	34.5
65+							
Upward	37.8	41.2	37.1	30.9	58.3	30.4	—
Downward	16.3	17.6	15.4	20.6	8.3	13.0	—
Nonmobile	45.9	41.1	47.4	48.3	33.3	56.5	—
Structural	17.1	19.6	19.3	13.8	41.7	17.4	—
Exchange	37.0	39.3	33.3	37.9	25.0	26.1	—

have slightly higher rates of upward mobility compared to Italians of all age cohorts. No clear pattern of difference between French Canadians and Italians in structural mobility and downward mobility emerges by age. Generally, differences in career mobility by age are small between French Canadian and Italian ethnics except for the higher rates of downward career mobility among French Canadians in the oldest and 35–44 age cohorts.

SHORT-TERM OCCUPATIONAL MOBILITY

Intragenerational mobility can be measured not only for career occupational changes—initial to current occupational rank—but also for shorter term occupational changes (changes in occupational rank over a five-year period). Comparing occupational rank five years ago to current occupational rank is most meaningful for the youngest age cohort, where such short-term mobility tends to be more conspicuous, and least meaningful for cohorts above the age of 45. Hence, the examination of short-term mobility departs somewhat from the previous analyses in that data for all ages and for the two older cohorts have been eliminated.

Do ethnics of these two younger cohorts experience changes in occupational rank over a short period of time? Outflow data on short-term occupational change for the two younger age cohorts are presented in Table 8–6. In general, these data point in the direction of differential patterns by age for Protestants and Catholics. Among those who were in the highest occupational rank five years ago, more Protestants than Catholics are currently in the highest occupations for the youngest cohort, while the reverse characterizes the older cohort. Similar reversals by age characterize the second occupational rank: among the 35–44 age cohort significantly more Protestants than Catholics experience short-term upward mobility from rank II occupations, while among the 25–34 age cohort more Catholics than Protestants experience upward mobility. Short-term downward mobility from rank II occupations is higher among Catholics in the older cohort and among Protestants in the younger cohort; short-term mobility from the lowest occupational rank is less among older Catholics and more among younger Catholics. These reversals do not characterize the third occupational level where Protestants of both age cohorts experience slightly higher rates of short-term upward mobility and stability and Catholics have higher rates of downward mobility. These reversals suggest that patterns of short-term mobility among Protestants and Catholics may have changed over time, partly reflecting the changing concentration of young Catholics in higher occupational ranks.

Table 8-6. Outflow Percentages, Short-Term Mobility (Occupational Rank 5 Years Ago to Current Occupational Rank), by Ethnicity and Age

Occupational Rank*							
Five Years Ago	Current	Total	Protestants	Catholics	French Canadians	Irish	Italians
				25–34			
I	I	65.7	72.7	62.0	54.5	100.0	64.3
	II	20.9	9.1	24.0	36.4	0.0	28.6
	III	9.0	9.1	10.0	0.0	0.0	7.1
	IV	4.5	9.1	4.0	9.1	0.0	0.0
II	I	28.7	23.1	29.8	21.4	27.3	42.9
	II	41.4	38.5	42.1	35.7	54.5	28.6
	III	25.3	34.6	22.8	35.7	18.2	28.6
	IV	4.6	3.8	5.3	7.1	0.0	0.0
III	I	16.4	12.5	18.4	33.3	—	18.2
	II	19.4	25.0	18.4	13.3	—	36.4
	III	55.2	56.3	53.1	53.3	—	27.3
	IV	9.0	6.3	10.2	0.0	—	18.2
IV	I	8.7	0.0	8.6	0.0	—	9.1
	II	21.7	0.0	28.6	20.0	—	45.5
	III	26.1	44.4	22.9	40.0	—	9.1
	IV	43.5	55.6	40.0	40.0	—	36.4
				35–44			
I	I	88.0	79.2	90.7	—	100.0	100.0
	II	5.3	8.3	4.7	—	0.0	0.0
	III	6.7	12.5	4.7	—	0.0	0.0
	IV	0.0	0.0	0.0	—	0.0	0.0
II	I	17.9	45.0	8.6	0.0	0.0	0.0
	II	61.9	45.0	67.2	66.7	91.7	62.5
	III	10.7	10.0	10.2	16.7	0.0	18.8
	IV	9.5	0.0	13.8	16.7	8.3	1.4
III	I	3.9	7.1	3.3	0.0	—	9.1
	II	9.2	7.1	9.8	5.6	—	9.1
	III	72.4	78.6	70.5	77.8	—	63.6
	IV	14.5	7.1	16.4	16.7	—	18.2
IV	I	4.2	0.0	5.0	0.0	—	5.6
	II	19.4	30.0	18.3	18.2	—	16.7
	III	23.6	30.0	23.3	27.3	—	11.1
	IV	52.8	40.0	53.3	54.5	—	66.7

*I = Duncan scale values 59 to 97; II = 34 to 58; III = 18 to 33; IV = 1 to 17.

However, these reversals by age do not characterize short-term mobility among Catholic ethnics. The patterns that emerge from the outflow data are fairly consistent where comparisons are possible by age. The Irish show higher levels of short-term stability when compared to non-Irish Catholics and Protestants. Greater short-term stability characterizes French Canadians than Italians for both age cohorts and all ranks, while Italians tend to have higher rates of upward mobility than French Canadians in the lower three occupational ranks. Too few Portuguese are available in our sample for an outflow analysis of short-term mobility of these age groups.

Inflow data also show some reversals by age in short-term mobility for Protestants and Catholics (Table 8-7). Catholics of both age cohorts who are currently in second ranked occupations are more likely than Protestants to have been in lower occupational ranks five years earlier. Protestants currently in the highest ranked occupations are more likely than Catholics to have been in lower occupational levels five years ago. For those currently in third ranked occupations, a clear reversal by age appears in the inflow data for Protestants and Catholics: younger Catholics are less upwardly mobile than Protestants; older Catholics are more upwardly mobile than Protestants. Greater downward mobility characterizes young Catholics in current occupations ranked second, a reversal of the pattern characterizing the 35-44 age cohort. No particular pattern emerges from the inflow data on short-term mobility among Catholic ethnics that was not described by the outflow data.

As an aid in clarifying these short-term inflow and outflow patterns, a brief examination of the changing occupational distribution of religious and Catholic ethnic groups is instructive (Table 8-8). First, the extent of short-term change in occupational distribution is significantly greater among Protestants than Catholics. Perhaps of more importance is the consistency among Protestants of short-term changes for both age cohorts and the changing pattern by age among Catholics. For Protestants of both age groups, five-year changes in occupational distribution reflect decreases in the occupational concentration at the bottom and second ranks. For older Catholics, shifts in the occupational distribution over a five-year period show declines only in the lowest occupational rank, while for younger Catholics declines in short-term occupational distribution may be noted in the lowest and second ranked occupations. Short-term shifts in occupational distribution for younger Catholics follow the Protestant pattern, but at lower levels. Hence, the short-term mobility reversals noted in the outflow and inflow data reflect these distributional shifts among Catholics.

Table 8-7.   Inflow Percentages, Short-Term Mobility (Current Occupational Rank from Occupational Rank 5 Years Ago), by Ethnicity and Age

Occupational Rank*							
Five Years Ago	Current	Total	Protestants	Catholics	French Canadians	Irish	Italians
25–34							
I	I	52.4	50.0	51.7	42.9	72.7	50.0
	II	29.8	37.5	28.3	21.4	27.3	33.3
	III	13.1	12.5	15.0	35.7	0.0	11.1
	IV	4.8	0.0	5.0	0.0	0.0	5.6
II	I	19.2	6.7	21.8	28.6	—	23.5
	II	49.3	66.7	43.6	35.7	—	23.5
	III	17.8	26.7	16.4	14.3	—	23.5
	IV	13.7	0.0	18.2	21.4	—	29.4
III	I	7.8	4.3	9.6	0.0	—	—
	II	28.6	39.1	25.0	26.3	—	—
	III	48.1	39.1	50.0	42.1	—	—
	IV	15.6	17.4	15.4	31.6	—	—
IV	I	9.1	12.5	8.3	—	—	—
	II	12.1	12.5	12.5	—	—	—
	III	18.2	12.5	20.8	—	—	—
	IV	60.6	62.5	58.3	—	—	—
35–44							
I	I	75.9	65.5	79.6	—	100.0	73.7
	II	17.2	31.0	10.2	—	100.0	10.5
	III	3.4	3.4	4.1	—	—	10.5
	IV	3.4	0.0	6.1	—	—	5.3
II	I	5.2	13.3	3.4	0.0	0.0	0.0
	II	67.5	60.0	67.2	61.5	84.6	66.7
	III	9.1	6.7	10.3	7.7	7.7	13.3
	IV	18.2	20.0	19.0	30.8	7.7	20.0
III	I	5.8	15.8	3.1	8.3	—	0.0
	II	10.5	10.5	9.2	8.3	—	15.8
	III	64.0	57.9	66.2	58.3	—	73.7
	IV	19.0	15.8	21.5	25.0	—	10.5
IV	I	0.0	—	0.0	0.0	—	0.0
	II	14.0	—	16.0	11.8	—	5.9
	III	19.3	—	20.0	17.6	—	23.5
	IV	66.7	—	64.0	70.6	—	70.6

*I = Duncan scale values 59 to 97; II = 34 to 58; III = 18 to 33; IV = 1 to 17.

Table 8-8. Percentage Point Differences between Occupational Rank 5 Years Ago and Current Occupational Rank, by Ethnicity and Age

Age and Occupational Rank*	Protestants	Catholics	French Canadians	Irish	Italians	Portuguese
25-34						
I	8.1	5.4	5.5	11.5	8.0	5.2
II	-17.7	-1.0	0.0	-11.5	6.0	-15.8
III	11.3	1.5	7.2	0.0	-4.0	10.5
IV	-1.6	-5.7	-12.8	0.0	-10.0	0.0
35-44						
I	7.3	2.7	-3.3	0.0	7.1	21.4
II	-7.3	0.0	1.6	2.8	-1.5	-21.5
III	7.3	1.8	9.8	0.0	-4.3	7.1
IV	-7.3	-4.5	-8.2	-2.8	-1.4	-7.2

*I = Duncan scale values 59 to 97; II = 34 to 58; III = 18 to 33; IV = 1 to 17.

Irish short-term mobility patterns are clearly toward the top ranked occupations from the next lower occupational rank among the young and to the second ranked occupations from the lowest occupational rank among those age 35–44. For French Canadians, short-term declines in the concentration at the highest occupational level characterize the older age cohort (i.e., downward mobility), while declines among the younger cohort are from the bottom (i.e., upward mobility). Italian shifts in short-term occupational distribution are from the bottom three occupational levels for the older cohort and from the bottom two occupational levels for the younger cohort. The Portuguese occupational changes represent still another pattern. In short, these data show differential patterns by ethnicity as well as by age for short-term occupational changes.

These differential patterns of occupational change emerge from an examination of summary measures of short-term mobility (Table 8–9). The pattern of short-term mobility clearly varies by religion and age: For the younger cohort, Catholics are more upwardly mobile in the five-year period, Protestants are more stable and more downwardly mobile. This pattern respresents a complete reversal of short-term occupational changes characterizing older Protestants and Catholics. However, for both age cohorts, structural mobility is higher for Protestants than Catholics pointing clearly to the differential cohort effects on the Catholic pattern of short-term mobility. This reversal in short-term mobility patterns by age reflects a complex interaction of five related factors: (1) generational effects, i.e., young Catholics clearly exhibit a different pattern of short-term mobility relative to older Catholics and relative to the overall pattern of Protestant short-term occupational changes; (2) career, life cycle effects, i.e., Protestants may tend to be more upwardly mobile at later points in their careers or life cycles compared to Catholics; (3) changing occupational concentration of younger Catholics relative to Protestants; (4) changing ethnic heterogeneity within the Catholic subpopulation with respect to short-term mobility; (5) migration selectivity that alters the composition of the populations that remain in the area.[b]

While Protestant-Catholic differences in short-term mobility are relatively small, ethnic Catholic differences are quite pronounced. For example, the range of short-term stability among younger Catholic ethnics varies from a high of almost 70 percent among the Irish to 40 percent among Italians. This contrasts to a difference of 52 percent and 50 percent between young Protestants and Catholics.

---

[b]The issue of differential migration will be examined in Chapters 9 and 10.

Table 8-9. Short-Term Mobility (Current Occupational Rank by Occupational Rank 5 Years Ago), by Ethnicity and Age (Summary Measures)

	Total	Protestants	Catholics	French Canadians	Irish	Italians	Portuguese
25–34							
Upward	28.1	25.8	29.3	34.6	19.2	38.0	21.1
Downward	20.6	22.5	20.9	20.0	11.5	32.0	26.3
Nonmobile	51.3	51.6	49.7	45.5	69.2	40.0	52.6
Structural	10.1	19.4	6.8	12.8	11.5	14.0	15.8
Exchange	38.6	29.0	43.5	41.7	19.3	46.0	31.6
35–44							
Upward	19.2	25.0	18.5	18.0	11.1	17.1	35.7
Downward	12.1	11.8	12.6	14.8	5.6	11.4	14.3
Nonmobile	68.7	63.2	68.9	67.2	83.3	71.4	50.0
Structural	7.2	14.6	4.5	11.5	2.8	7.2	28.6
Exchange	24.1	22.2	26.6	21.3	13.9	21.4	21.4

The Irish have the lowest rates of upward and structural mobility for both age cohorts. The older Portuguese have high rates of short-term upward and structural mobility. However, for the younger cohort, Portuguese experience high rates of short-term downward mobility—higher in fact than their level of upward mobility. The pattern of short-term occupational change of Italians and French Canadians falls intermediate between the Irish and Portuguese patterns and no major differences between Italians and French Canadians emerge.

PATHS TO OCCUPATIONAL ACHIEVEMENT

The complex patterns of intergenerational mobility that emerged from our analysis in Chapter 7 and the patterns of career and short-term mobility presented in this chapter require synthesis. The importance of occupational origins and initial occupational rank on subsequent mobility patterns and on current occupational level have been clearly demonstrated. It has also been suggested that the inter-relationships of these factors differ for the various ethnic subpopulations and, hence, the process of occupational achievement varies for religious and Catholic ethnic groups. In the previous chapter, contrasts and comparisons were made between occupational and subjective social class intergenerational mobility, and the stratification of ethnic groups by education and occupation was described in Chapter 2. The challenge remaining is to see how these various elements fit together systematically.[c] In particular, we need to investigate for each of the ethnic groups the interaction of the following elements: (1) occupational origins (i.e., occupational rank of fathers); (2) subjective social class identification of parents; (3) educational attainment; (4) initial occupational rank; (5) current occupational rank. For recent cohorts occupational rank five years ago may be included. The analysis of the interdependence of these variables should shed light not only on the relationship between intergenerational and intragenerational mobility but should provide important clues to the understanding of ethnic differentials in occupational achievement.

The data have been organized to allow for an examination of the relative effects of initial occupation, education, father's occupation, and parents' social class on current occupation; the relative effects of education, father's occupation, and parents' social class on initial

---

[c]One model that looks at ethnic differentials in occupational achievement using census-type data is Duncan and Duncan, 1968.

occupation; and the relative effects of father's occupation and parents' social class on education. Standardized regression coefficients were calculated for these effects that show the strength of relationship of each variable controlling for the other variables. These coefficients are presented for the seven ethnic groups in Table 8-10.

Examining first the direct effects on current occupation, several distinct patterns by ethnicity emerge. For Protestants, initial occupation is about twice as important as education for current occupational achievement and there is a small but significant effect of parents' social class. The only significant direct effects on the current occupation of Catholics are initial occupation and education. However, education has a relatively greater impact on current occupation among Catholics than Protestants. Therefore, for both Protestants and Catholics, initial occupation and education have important effects. However, initial occupation contributes more to current occupation for Protestants than for Catholics, while education is relatively more important for Catholics than for Protestants. The Jewish pattern shows the importance of both initial and father's occupation for current occupation, reflecting greater occupational inheritance intergenerationally and intragenerationally.

If initial occupation has greater effect than any other variable in the model as a determinant of current occupational status, what are the relative effects of education, father's occupation, and parents' social class on initial occupation? The data show the greater importance of educational attainment relative to occupational and social class origins for the three religious groups. However, education is a somewhat more powerful influence in the initial occupational attainment of Catholics. While father's occupation has little relationship to initial occupation for any group (independent of the effects of social class and education) it has relatively greater importance for Protestants. Parental social class has a significant relationship to the initial occupational status of Jews that does not characterize non-Jews.

The paths to educational attainment also vary by religion. Father's occupation contributes more than parental social class in the education of Protestants, while the reverse characterizes Catholics. Occupational origins are clearly more significant for the educational attainment of Jews than for either Protestants or Catholics. In sum, the path to the current occupational achievements of Protestants is through the effects of father's occupation on education and through education to initial occupational status. For Catholics, the process tends to be through parental social class to education, and from education directly to current occupation and through the effects

Table 8-10. Standardized Regression Coefficients for a Model of the Process of Current Occupational Achievement by Ethnicity

	Protestants	Jews	Catholics	French Canadians	Irish	Italians	Portuguese
Current Occupation (R^2)	(.48)	(.48)	(.48)	(.38)	(.61)	(.51)	(.40)
Initial Occupation	.51*	.40*	.41*	.30*	.48*	.49*	.19
Education	.24*	.18	.37*	.35*	.40*	.32*	.55*
Father's Occupation	-.04	.31*	-.02	.13*	-.05	-.02	-.22*
Parents' Social Class	.11*	-.03	.01	.07	.01	.03	.03
Initial Occupation (R^2)	(.30)	(.36)	(.36)	(.22)	(.36)	(.34)	(.05)
Education	.44*	.52*	.56*	.45*	.56*	.54*	.22
Father's Occupation	.13	-.07	.08	-.01	-.03	.18*	-.02
Parents' Social Class	.11	.26*	.04	.05	.11	-.05	-.03
Education (R^2)	(.13)	(.28)	(.10)	(.12)	(.17)	(.06)	(.07)
Father's Occupation	.26*	.50*	.16*	.02	.30*	.11	.19
Parents' Social Class	.17*	.06	.25*	.34*	.21*	.20*	.20

*Significant at least at the 0.05 level.

of education on initial occupation. For Jews, the path is from father's occupation directly to current occupation and from father's occupation (and parental social class) to current occupation through education and initial occupational status.

The paths to current occupational status also vary for Catholic ethnic subpopulations. Initial occupation contributes more to the current occupational status of Irish and Italians relative to French Canadians and Portuguese. In contrast, education has greater impact on current occupational achievement for French Canadians and Portuguese. Overall, education is more valuable for Catholic ethnics than for Protestants or Jews and is particularly significant for Portuguese and Irish (at different educational levels). The relative impact of education is stronger in affecting initial occupation. While the absolute contribution of education to the initial occupational attainment of Irish and Italians is greater (based on unstandardized regression coefficients), education is relatively more important than origins for the two lower socioeconomic Catholic ethnic groups. It is interesting to note the important effects of father's occupation on the initial occupation of Italians (controlling out the effects of education) that do not appear for any other ethnic group. The determinants of education among Catholic ethnics vary, and show the relative importance of class and occupational origins. For French Canadians, social class origins are most important for education; occupational origins are more important than class for Irish and the reverse characterizes the Italians; Portuguese education is about equally affected by social class and occupational origins.

It is clear from these data that ethnic differences in the paths to current occupation are varied and complex; a conclusion that is consistent with the analysis of detailed intergenerational and intragenerational mobility. The relative influence of origins, education, and initial occupation combine in a myriad of ways to produce the differential occupational structure of ethnic communities. Hence, any argument that proposes a "melting pot" theory of ethnic occupational assimilation distorts the complex processes associated with continuing occupational differentiation among ethnics and oversimplifies the differential paths to occupational success.

A final element in the analysis of paths to occupational attainment relates to cohort effects. As the detailed data revealed, there are complex patterns of cohort changes in occupation (initial and current), education, and origins (occupation and social class). The regressions show complex patterns as well. For example, there are very strong direct effects of origins (social class and occupation) on current occupation of older Catholics, implying much greater direct occupational inheritance than for older Protestants or younger cohorts of both subpopulations. For younger cohorts, the educational factor has become more important as a determinant of initial and current occupational status for Catholics and relatively less important for Protestants. For each cohort except the oldest, parental social class contributes more than occupational origins to the educational attainment of Catholics; the reverse characterizes the Protestants.

As an illustration of these complexities, Table 8-11 presents standardized regression coefficients for the youngest age cohort (ages 25-34) that include an additional variable—occupation five years ago. The main points that emerge from these data are:

1. Only for Protestants is there any significant effect of occupation five years ago on current occupation (independent of other effects). This is consistent with our earlier finding that short-term mobility is higher for Catholics than Protestants of the youngest cohort. While for both Protestants and Catholics, education has significant effects on initial occupation, two patterns differentiate young Protestants from Catholics. First, education has an independent direct effect on current occupational status of Catholics, while for Protestants the effect of education on current occupational status is through its effects on initial occupation. Second, father's occupation is an important factor in the educational attainment of Protestants, while parental social class has relatively greater impact on the educational attainment of Catholics.

2. The effect of initial occupation on current occupation is very strong for Irish, Italians, and Portuguese. Initial occupation has less effect on the current occupation of French Canadians relative to other Catholic ethnics, while education has effects equivalent to initial occupation. The relatively weaker impact of initial on current occupation for French Canadians may reflect the somewhat greater short-term downward mobility of French Canadians noted earlier at high occupational levels.

3. The relative effects of education and father's occupation on the initial occupations of young Irish and Italians are similar. Comparing these patterns for older cohorts and for totals in Table 8-10 suggests a strong convergence over time for those two groups and contrasts with the French Canadian and Portuguese pattern. However, while the paths to initial occupation are similar for young Irish and Italian ethnics, the effects of origins on education differ significantly. For the Irish, both father's occupation and parents' social class have an important impact on education, with somewhat stronger effects produced by parents' social class. In contrast,

Table 8-11. Standardized Regression Coefficients for a Model of the Process of Current Occupational Achievement, by Ethnicity: Age 25-34

	Protestants	Catholics	French Canadians	Irish	Italians	Portuguese
Current Occupation (R²)	(.77)	(.57)	(.50)	(.92)	(.69)	(.97)
Occupation 5 Years Ago	.42*	.03	-.08	-.03	-.13	.11
Initial Occupation	.47*	.55*	.49*	.92*	.87*	1.01
Education	.02	.28*	.42*	.10	.18	.05
Father's Occupation	-.00	-.09	.05	.11	-.28	-.08
Parents' Social Class	-.04	.02	.08	-.17*	-.09	-.05
Occupation 5 Years Ago (R²)	(.80)	(.78)	(.81)	(.99)	(.73)	(.86)
Initial Occupation	.89*	.84*	.94*	1.00*	.69*	.84*
Education	.03	.09	-.03	.03	.24*	.12
Father's Occupation	-.09	-.03	-.14	.04	-.21*	-.02
Parents' Social Class	-.01	-.93	.02	-.02	.10	-.07
Initial Occupation (R²)	(.33)	(.36)	(.13)	(.55)	(.45)	(.46)
Education	.53*	.54*	.38*	.59*	.58*	.48*
Father's Occupation	.11	.15	.09	.22	.25*	-.38
Parents' Social Class	-.01	.05	-.17	.06	.15	-.17
Education (R²)	(.113)	(.13)	(.14)	(.40)	(.02)	(.07)
Father's Occupation	.37*	.14	-.05	.34*	.00	.23
Parents' Social Class	-.17	.31	.38*	.46*	.13	.20

*Significant at the 0.05 level.

origins have a minimal impact on the education of young Italians.

The continuing diversity of the paths to the occupational achievements of Catholic ethnics, even among the young, combined with the distinctive patterns for Protestants and Catholics, suggest pluralism among ethnics in the processes associated with status attainment, as well as in the resultant levels of occupational achievement. Despite the convergences that characterize recent cohorts, it is clear that multidimensional processes are operating that have different consequences for ethnic groups. To the extent that origins, education, and initial occupational status continue to have distinctive effects on the current occupational achievements of ethnic groups, the resultant stratification mosaic will continue to differentiate ethnic groups in the next generation.

Part IV

Processes of Geographic Mobility

Chapter 9

Migration, Ethnic Continuity, and the Life Cycle

Ethnic migration patterns are tied to the central question of ethnic continuity. Ethnic identification is reinforced at both the family and community levels by residential stability. The more ethnics change their place of residence, the weaker their ties not only to the local community and its institutions but also to the multiplicity of ethnic family relationships. The vitality of ethnic community institutions is dependent on a large core of permanent and stable residents. Residential stability implies greater ethnic continuity since there is more potential for ethnic family and social interaction. On the other hand, extensive migration tends to break ethnic cohesiveness in the community and may reduce the importance of ethnicity for migrants.

The analysis of ethnic migration patterns is complicated by the effects of life cycle processes. In general, migration and residential mobility are closely linked to life cycle and family building patterns. Marriage and family formation have been found to be the most consistent determinants of geographic mobility (Speare et al., 1974; Goldscheider, 1971). However, the relationship between life cycle events and residential change has never been examined systematically for ethnic communities. Any analysis of ethnic migration must first examine the effects of life cycle variations. In turn, these life cycle effects must be controlled in order to isolate the ethnic factor in residential mobility.

The data collected provide the unique opportunity to relate ethnicity to extensive migration histories.[a] Residential changes were

---

[a]General migration patterns have been analyzed extensively using these data for a variety of processes in Speare et al., 1975, and a preliminary analysis of religious differences suggested the richness of the possibilities for more detailed examination (Toney, 1971).

reconstructed for each family that relate to periods within the life cycle determined by the age of the male head of household and by family events (marriage and the birth of children). Three measures that reflect different aspects of residential change have been constructed: (1) the proportion stable; (2) the average number of moves for movers; and (3) the proportion of movers who ever migrate (across a county boundary). Each measure will be related to life cycle intervals and refers to behavior during a given interval. The proportion stable, the velocity of residential changes (repeat mobility), and the proportion migrant among movers relate to different dimensions of continuity in ethnic communities.

LIFE CYCLE AND MIGRATION

Are there ethnic differences in migration that relate to life cycle changes and that remain when life cycle effects are controlled? Data in Table 9-1 allow an examination of the question for the three measures of residential change. Overall, residential change for each reconstructed age interval is greater for those who have experienced some family formation event. The impact of age at marriage can be clearly seen: about half of those who did not marry between the ages 18 and 24 (almost none married earlier) are stable compared to 10 percent or less for those who married. These family building events continue to affect stability up to age 45, as a result of increases in family size associated with the birth of children, but with diminishing impact. For example, the proportion of Italians who were stable in the 18-24 interval is six times higher for those without events compared to those with events (62 percent and 10 percent). Italians in the 35-44 interval who had no events are more stable than those with some events, but the difference is only 58 percent compared to 45 percent. Consistent with the general literature, stability increases with age.[b]

Variation in age at marriage by ethnicity noted earlier (Chapter 5) has an important impact on patterns of residential stability. A comparison of the overall proportion stable among the three religious groups for the first life cycle interval (18-24) shows that the Jews are the most stable (35 percent) followed by Catholics and Protestants (31 percent and 30 percent, respectively). The higher Jewish

_____

[b]The high levels of stability for those who did not marry between age 18 and 24 reflect in part the shorter length of the period examined. The 25-34 life cycle stage is three years longer, so that the proportion stable is less for those with no family building events. However, stability is greater for the next ten-year segment—35-44—and similar proportions stable are observable for the twenty-year interval between ages 45 and 64.

stability, however, is an artifact of their higher age at marriage. Neither married nor nonmarried Jews are more stable than Protestants or Catholics, and for those who marry, the differences are substantially greater. For the second life cycle interval, Catholics are more likely to be stable than Protestants, similar to the patterns in the first interval, but differences are greater. For the older age intervals, there is some tendency for lower stability among Catholics: 47 percent of Catholics were stable in the interval 45-64 compared to 55 percent of the Protestants.

Of those who move, Catholics make the fewest residential changes, averaging about two moves during each life cycle interval compared to Protestants and Jews, whose average number of moves is closer to three. For all three groups, a greater number of moves occur among those having life cycle events than those with none. The only exception is young Jews, who average more moves before marriage than after, which may be related to geographic mobility associated with higher education.

The sharpest contrasts in mobility patterns among these religious groups appear for the proportion of movers who ever migrate. Moves involving crossing a county boundary (i.e., migration) are much less characteristic of Catholics than of the other two religious groups. The Jews are the most migratory at the younger ages, but appear to be the least at the oldest ages. The probability of migration declines with age, but more rapidly for Jews than for Catholics, while for Protestants migration probabilities change very little with age. These patterns by life cycle imply greater attachment to community for Catholics than for Protestants. A significantly lower proportion of Jews than non-Jews migrate in the 35-44 interval, suggesting that community ties are established later in the life cycle of Jews compared to Catholics but may, by that stage, be more intense.

Variation in these three measures of residential change appears to be greater for Catholic ethnic subpopulations. The most distinctive overall pattern is for Italians, who are most stable, move the fewest times, and are least likely to migrate, indicating a high level of cohesiveness for the Italian community. The Irish tend to be less stable, moving more often and across more geographic boundaries, although differences are less marked and consistent than for Italians. French Canadians are intermediate, resembling the all-Catholic pattern, while the Portuguese show rather complex relationships among the indicators.

The pattern of low Italian residential mobility is very marked. Fully 62 percent of Italians who have not yet married are stable in the 18-24 life cycle interval, the highest level for all life cycle

Table 9-1.   Percentage Stable, Migrant Velocity, and Percentage Ever Migrate by Life Cycle and Ethnicity

Reconstructed Life Cycle Interval*	Protestants	Jews	Catholics	French Canadians	Irish	Italians	Portuguese
			Proportion Stable				
18–24	30	36	31	26	36	34	21
No Events	53	53	56	58	56	62	42
Some Events	8	0	8	6	9	10	8
25–34	16	18	20	20	16	20	28
No Events	27	—	43	40	36	53	—
Some Events	13	10	16	17	11	17	26
35–44	45	46	44	51	31	52	23
No Events	51	53	51	58	54	58	23
Some Events	37	33	36	42	16	45	23
45–64							
Total	55	—	47	41	44	55	—
			*Average Number of Moves**				
18–24	2.8	2.7	2.0	2.4	2.4	2.1	2.1
No Events	2.0	3.1	1.8	1.7	2.3	1.8	1.5
Some Events	3.2	2.3	2.4	2.6	2.6	2.2	2.4
25–34	2.9	2.8	2.4	2.4	2.5	2.1	2.5
No Events	2.6	—	2.1	2.2	2.2	1.7	—
Some Events	3.0	2.8	2.4	2.4	2.6	2.1	2.7
35–44	2.0	1.8	1.7	1.9	1.8	1.4	1.5
No Events	2.0	—	1.5	2.0	1.7	1.2	1.4
Some Events	2.0	—	1.9	1.8	1.9	1.5	1.7
45–64							
Total	1.9	—	1.7	1.8	—	1.4	—

Table 9-1. continued

Reconstructed Life Cycle Interval*	Protestants	Jews	Catholics	French Canadians**	Irish	Italians	Portuguese
			Percent Ever Migrate**				
18-24	57	59	34	37	38	26	40
No Events	52	64	40	30	53	39	32
Some Events	58	53	32	39	28	21	43
25-34	55	57	32	35	41	19	41
No Events	55	—	32	39	44	13	—
Some Events	56	57	32	34	41	19	44
35-44	52	15	25	35	26	16	20
No Events	48	—	24	44	40	8	20
Some Events	55	—	26	26	21	23	20
45-64							
Total	42	—	20	28	—	21	—

*Reconstructed life cycle combines age intervals with the occurence of one or more family formation events (marriage and/or the birth of children) during the interval.

**For movers only.

intervals and for all ethnic groups. Although the proportion stable drops to 53 percent for Italians with no family building events in the 25-34 interval, this contrasts with 40 percent for French Canadians and 36 percent for the Irish. Only 45 percent of Italians age 65 and older moved at all during the twenty years between the interval 45-64, compared to 56 percent of Irish and 59 percent of French Canadians. Portuguese tend to have low proportions stable, particularly for those with no family building events.

Relatively few clear patterns emerge for the velocity of moving other than the small number of moves made by Italians. Portuguese move relatively less than other Catholic ethnics in the oldest life cycle interval as do Portuguese who neither marry nor have children in the first two life cycle intervals. Few differences in the patterns of repeat mobility emerge between French Canadians and Irish.

Major differences among Catholic ethnics appear in the proportion of movers who migrate. Italians have the lowest and the Irish the highest proportions who ever migrate. The French Canadians and Portuguese show different relationships over the life cycle; Portuguese are much more migratory when young than later in their lives, while French Canadians seem to have the same probability of migrating at all life cycle stages. Since the general pattern for non-French Canadian Catholics is a decrease in migration over the life cycle, the proportion of French Canadians who migrate is particularly high at the later life cycle intervals.

Several of these ethnic patterns of residential change are the result of cohort variations. Table 9-2 presents cohort data on the proportions stable for each of these subpopulations controlling for life cycle stage. Two important cohort patterns are noteworthy. The oldest cohort of Protestants and Catholics had lower proportions stable when they were young and unmarried compared to more recent cohorts. This may be related to events during the 1920s when these moves occurred. Economic growth and the continued opening of opportunities in Rhode Island up to this period resulted in the migration of young persons, both from elsewhere in the country and from abroad. The expansion of population in the area led to further changes in patterns of ethnic residential distribution (Mayer and Goldstein, 1958). Hence, over 55 percent of the two middle cohorts of Protestants and Catholics who had not yet married in the interval 18-24 were residentially stable while only 48 percent of the oldest cohort were stable in that life cycle stage. Similarly, data not presented in the table (because of small numbers) show this same pattern for French Canadians and Italians: 58 percent of the

Table 9-2.   Percentage Stable, by Ethnicity, Life Cycle, and Age

Life Cycle Interval and Current Age	Protestants		Catholics		French Canadians	Irish	Italians	Portuguese
	None	Some	None	Some	Some Events*			
18-24								
25-34	44	5	58	3	4	3	2	0
35-44	58	5	56	8	4	4	12	6
45-64	56	13	58	13	10	16	15	15
65+	48	12	48	20	15	—	21	—
25-34								
35-44	17	8	35	17	20	6	18	29
45-64	19	15	46	16	15	12	16	28
65+	47	17	44	13	15	27	9	—
35-44								
45-64	55	40	49	36	45	14	41	23
65+	42	27	55	38	33	25	70	—
45-64								
65+	55	—	47	—	41	44	55	—

*Marriage or the birth of children during the interval. Includes both "some" and "none" for the life cycle interval 45 to 64.

Italians and 69 percent of the French Canadians (unmarried in the first life cycle interval) were stable for the middle two cohorts, while only 46 percent of the oldest French Canadians and 41 percent of the oldest Italians were stable during that early part of their lives. The Irish, who immigrated earlier, and the Portuguese, many of whom arrived later, do not show this pattern. Interestingly, those of the older cohort who had already married in the interval 18-24 do not show high rates of mobility, except for French Canadians. This suggests that for some, migration may have resulted in a pattern of deferred marriage.

The second major cohort difference is the marked decline in stability at the youngest life cycle stage for those who have already married. This intercohort decline is sharper for Catholics than Protestants, and is pronounced among all Catholic ethnic groups (with the exception of the oldest French Canadians mentioned earlier). The proportion stable in this life cycle category dropped from 20 percent for the oldest Catholic cohort to 3 percent for the youngest. The Protestant decline was less dramatic, with levels of 12-13 percent for the two older cohorts compared to 5 percent for the two younger cohorts. This pattern also characterizes unmarried Protestants (44 percent stable for the youngest cohort compared to 56-58 percent for the next two older cohorts) but not unmarried Catholics. Among the Catholic ethnics, such decreases in stability for the unmarried at 18-24 appear only for the Irish.

For the second life cycle interval (25-34), Protestants, whether or not they experienced any family formation events, also show declines in the proportion residentially stable. For the oldest cohort, 47 percent of those with no events and 17 percent with some events were stable, compared to 17 percent and 8 percent for the youngest cohort. Catholics, on the other hand, seem to have increased their residential stability somewhat for each category, except for the youngest cohort with no family building events.

Among the Catholic ethnic groups, relatively few cases are available for those having no family building events, but for those who have, each group but one experienced the increase in stability. The exception again is the Irish, whose pattern of residential stability in this interval shows rapid convergence to the *Protestant* pattern: while 27 percent of Irish in the oldest cohort were stable during the 25 to 34 interval (if they experienced some family event) compared to 17 percent for Protestants, for both younger cohorts the Irish proportion residentially stable was lower than that for Protestants— 12 and 16 percent for each younger cohort compared to 15 and 8 percent for Protestants. Hence, the Irish pattern of decline follows the Protestant model, while the non-Irish Catholic ethnics follow the Catholic pattern of increase in stability between cohorts.

This overall cohort pattern showing proportions residentially stable (high residential mobility rates for the older cohorts when they were young, followed by stability that is decreasing for more recent cohorts of Protestants and Irish and increasing for all non-Irish Catholics) does not appear when intercohort changes in migration velocities are considered. Table 9–3 presents these data. The most consistent pattern is a general increase in the number of moves made in an interval. But the magnitude of the change is small and the patterns variable. The most important feature in these data is the fact that within each cohort, Protestants move more than Catholics, controlling for life cycle. There appears to be a tendency toward convergence in repeat mobility for the most recent cohort of Catholic ethnics when compared to older cohorts.

The data on the proportion who migrate reinforce the patterns that were shown for the proportion residentially stable (Table 9–4). High rates of migration for the oldest cohort early in their lives appear for all comparisons that can be presented. In addition, cohort increases in proportion migrating in each interval appear which are not restricted to Protestants and Irish, but as in average moves per mover, characterize most Catholic and Catholic ethnic comparisons as well. Again, it should be emphasized that Protestants have a significantly higher level of migration than Catholics, holding cohort and life cycle constant. For the youngest cohort who have not married, for example, 61 percent of the Protestants who have moved, migrated at least once compared to 52 percent of the Catholics. Of those who have married, over half the Protestants migrated compared to one-third of the Catholics. During the second life cycle interval for the 45–64 age cohort, three times as many Protestant as Catholic movers migrate when there are no family formation events and twice as many Protestant as Catholic movers migrate when there is at least one family formation event. Italians migrate less than other Catholic ethnics when all of these factors are controlled (except in the younger cohort at the earliest life cycle interval).

ETHNIC CONTINUITY AND MIGRATION

Inferences about ethnic continuity may be made from the patterns of residential stability, repeat mobility, and migration of ethnic subpopulations. These inferences are reinforced when life cycle and cohort effects on mobility are taken into account. A more concrete

Table 9-3. Average Number of Moves, by Life Cycle, Ethnicity, and Age

Life Cycle Interval and Current Age	Protestants		Catholics		French Canadians	Irish	Italians	Portuguese
	None	Some	None	Some	Some Events*			
18–24								
25–34	3.1	3.2	2.3	2.6	2.6	2.4	2.6	2.7
35–44	2.0	3.5	1.8	2.2	2.3	2.7	2.0	2.2
45–64	1.9	3.1	1.7	2.3	2.8	2.8	1.8	2.2
65+	1.5	2.5	1.7	2.4	2.7	—	2.1	—
25–34								
35–44	1.9	3.2	3.4	2.5	2.4	2.9	2.3	2.7
45–64	3.2	3.0	1.6	2.3	2.3	2.5	2.1	2.7
65+	—	2.7	2.1	2.1	2.5	1.5	—	—
35–44								
45–64	1.8	2.0	1.5	1.8	1.9	1.9	1.4	1.7
65+	2.2	2.1	1.8	1.9	1.7	—	—	—
45–64								
65+	1.9	—	1.7	—	1.8	—	1.4	—

*Marriage and/or the birth of children during the interval. Includes both "some" and "none" for the life cycle interval 45 to 64.

Table 9-4. Percentage of Movers Who Ever Migrate, by Ethnicity, Life Cycle, and Age

Life Cycle Interval and Current Age	Protestants		Catholics		French Canadians	Irish	Italians	Portuguese
	None	Some	None	Some	Some Events*			
18–24								
25–34	61	54	52	34	31	27	32	37
35–44	40	64	42	32	36	32	14	44
45–64	57	56	30	27	42	25	13	45
65+	45	71	57	43	58	—	36	—
25–34								
35–44	60	53	53	37	39	46	21	40
45–64	62	55	19	27	29	36	18	43
65+	—	65	40	36	38	—	19	—
35–44								
45–64	49	57	23	27	29	25	22	20
65+	48	50	27	20	20	—	—	—
45–64								
65+	42	—	20	—	28	—	21	—

*Marriage and/or the birth of children during the interval. Includes both "some" and "none" for the life cycle interval 45 to 64.

way of examining the issue of ethnic continuity with data on migration histories is to analyze the relationship between patterns of residential stability and direct measures of the intensity of ethnicity. The data available allow for the investigation of two such measures: (1) intermarriage and (2) ethnic residential concentration.

It may be hypothesized that ethnic continuity as measured by marital homogamy and high ethnic residential concentration will be associated with lower levels of residential change, repeat mobility, and migration. More specifically, the intermarried have been shown to have less distinctive ethnic patterns and probably have fewer ethnic ties. Therefore, there should be fewer constraints on migration for the intermarried. One consequence of these hypothesized migration implications of intermarriage is that those who marry out of the ethnic community are more likely to live in areas of lower ethnic concentration. These patterns have already been demonstrated (Chapter 4) but the migration mechanism has only been inferred. Hence, this section focuses first on the patterns of residential change among homogamous and intermarried families and second on the relationship between these changes of residence and current ethnic residential concentration.

Data in Table 9-5 show the proportion stable for intermarried and nonintermarried families by ethnicity, controlling for life cycle. The relationship between homogamy and residential stability is different for Protestants and Catholics. The Catholic pattern is consistent with the hypotheses: intermarried Catholics are more likely to be residentially mobile than are Catholics in homogamous marriages. Intermarried Protestants, on the other hand, are more residentially stable. These different patterns characterize each life cycle interval, whether or not there are life cycle events.[c]

The finding demonstrated earlier that Protestants are less stable residentially than Catholics is true only for the homogamously married. Intermarried Catholics have higher levels of residential mobility than intermarried Protestants so that religious intermarriage is associated with greater residential change for Catholics than Protestants. These patterns reflect the different selectivity of Protestants and Catholics who intermarry (see Chapter 6), the greater cohesiveness of Catholic community structure, and the fewer ethnic ties that intermarried Catholics are likely to have.

---

[c]These relationships hold generally for all cohorts (data not shown), but the higher mobility of the oldest cohort in the first two life cycle intervals (which is the cohort which is the most homogamous) made it necessary to standardize for these cohort effects in these intervals.

Table 9-5. Percentage Stable, by Ethnicity, Life Cycle, and Homogamy*

Life Cycle Interval and Homogamy	Protestants		Catholics		French Canadians	Irish	Italians	Portuguese
	None	Some	None	Some	Some Events**			
*18–24****								
Homogamous	51	7	57	10	4	0	14	20
Intermarried	55	10	45	9	7	13	8	0
*25–34****								
Homogamous	20	13	43	16	24	7	18	43
Intermarried	22	14	37	9	16	12	13	32
35–44								
Homogamous	46	32	52	36	50	15	50	—
Intermarried	56	42	39	36	32	17	30	—
45–64								
Homogamous	53	—	46	—	39	62	45	—
Intermarried	57	—	—	—	—	—	—	—

*For religion, primary homogamy.
**Marriage and/or the birth of children during the interval. Includes both "some" and "none" for the life cycle interval 45 to 64.
***Standardized for age.

Patterns of repeat mobility and migration are generally consistent with and reinforce these findings on proportions stable (Tables 9-6 and 9-7). Intermarried Catholics are more likely to be repeat movers than are those homogamously married. While this is somewhat the case for Protestants, differences are small and there is greater variation by life cycle stage. Protestant-Catholic differences in repeat mobility persist but are weakened considerably for the intermarried.

There is a clear pattern of greater migration for Protestants than Catholics for both homogamously and intermarried families. Catholics who intermarry are more likely to migrate than Catholics married to other Catholics, while intermarried Protestants are less likely to migrate than homogamously married Protestants, except in the youngest life cycle interval.

Examining the patterns of mobility for Catholic ethnic subpopulations, the following patterns emerge (Tables 9-5, 9-6, 9-7):

1. Italians and Portuguese in homogamous marriages are more stable residentially than are the intermarried. In contrast, the Irish are less stable when married homogamously than when intermarried. Thus, the Italian and Portuguese relationship between intermarriage and residential mobility is similar to the overall Catholic pattern, while the Irish follow the Protestant model. The French Canadians are similar to the Italians and Portuguese, except for the earliest life cycle interval. These relationships hold for all cohorts (data not shown).

2. Italian and Irish intermarried families lose their distinctive ethnic residential mobility patterns: Italians are *more* mobile than the homogamously married Italians and the intermarried Irish are *less* mobile than Irish who marry other Irish. Therefore, intermarriage does not have the same meaning for community and ethnic continuity for the Irish as it does for Italians, Portuguese, and French Canadians. Ethnic community boundaries appear much weaker for the Irish and, hence, residential constraints are less intense for the intermarried as well as for the homogamously married. Where ethnic boundaries are clearer and communities more cohesive residentially, intermarriage loosens the constraints on residential mobility. The non-Irish Catholic ethnics who intermarry are therefore more likely to be residentially mobile. A similar argument may be made for the overall Protestant-Catholic difference in residential stability.

3. Convergences in residential stability among ethnics characterize the intermarried. Intermarried Italians, for example, do not have the high rates of stability of nonintermarried Italians while intermarried Irish are not as mobile as the Irish who marry within their group. Therefore, the distinctive patterns of residential mobility for Catholic

Table 9-6. Number of Moves per Mover, by Life Cycle, Homogamy,* and Ethnicity

Life Cycle Interval and Homogamy	Protestants		Catholics		French Canadians	Irish	Italians	Portuguese
	None	Some	None	Some	Some Events**			
18–24								
Homogamous	1.7	3.0	1.8	2.3	2.2	2.5	2.1	1.7
Intermarried	2.2	3.3	1.9	2.6	3.0	2.6	2.4	2.8
25–34								
Homogamous	2.3	2.9	2.0	2.3	2.3	2.5	1.9	2.6
Intermarried	3.1	3.0	—	2.9	2.5	2.7	2.5	2.7
35–44								
Homogamous	2.0	2.2	1.5	1.8	1.9	2.2	1.6	—
Intermarried	1.9	1.7	2.0	2.1	1.7	1.6	1.3	—
45–64								
Homogamous	2.1	—	1.6	—	—	—	—	—
Intermarried	1.7	—	—	—	—	—	—	—

*For religion, primary homogamy.
**Marriage and/or the birth of children during the interval. Includes both "some" and "none" for the life cycle interval 45 to 64.

Table 9-7. Percentage of Movers Who Ever Migrate, by Ethnicity, Life Cycle, and Homogamy*

Life Cycle Interval and Homogamy	Protestants		Catholics		French Canadians	Irish	Italians	Portuguese
						Some Events**		
	None	Some	None	Some				
*18-24****								
Homogamous	54	57	39	31	33	17	16	27
Intermarried	56	61	57	38	46	33	31	51
*25-34****								
Homogamous	62	56	32	30	32	41	12	46
Intermarried	44	55	29	45	36	40	32	38
35-44								
Homogamous	57	66	22	24	26	17	21	—
Intermarried	39	42	43	36	26	26	29	—
45-64								
Homogamous	50	—	21	—	—	—	—	—
Intermarried	33	—	—	—	—	—	—	—

*For religion, primary homogamy.
**Marriage and/or the birth of children during the interval. Includes both "some" and "none" for the life cycle interval 45 to 64.
***Standardized for age.

ethnics are weakened considerably for those who intermarry.

4. For all intermarried ethnics the proportion who are repeat movers and migrants is higher than for ethnics marrying within their own group. Convergence patterns among ethnic groups in both of these measures of residential change are clearer for the earlier life cycle intervals, with minor exceptions when cohort and life cycle events are controlled.

An additional dimension of the ethnic continuity issue may be seen in the relationship between residential change and current ethnic residential concentration. Data in Table 9-8 show the proportion stable, average number of moves, and the proportion who migrate for three levels of current ethnic residential concentration.[d] (For definitions and limitations of this measures see Chapter 4.) These data reveal a clear pattern of association between high ethnic residential concentration and measures of prior residential stability. This relationship is particularly consistent for that stage of the life cycle where initial residential mobility following marriage and childbearing has been completed (i.e., age 35–44 with no life cycle events). This life cycle stage is of critical importance for the development of strong community attachments.

For French Canadians the relationship holds for all life cycle intervals and is particularly strong for those who have experienced some life cycle events. For example, 24 percent of the French Canadians who currently reside in areas of high ethnic concentration did not move in the 25–34 interval (some events) compared to 14 percent of those currently in areas of low French Canadian concentration. Moreover, the average number of moves and the extent of migration are inversely related to current ethnic concentration. Those living in areas of low ethnic concentration moved much more often in this life cycle interval than those in areas of high ethnic concentration. Almost half of the French Canadians in areas of low ethnic concentration who moved in this life cycle interval migrated, compared to 15 percent of those currently in areas of high ethnic concentration.

The extent of residential concentration for the Irish is much lower than other ethnics (Chapter 4). Nevertheless, the pattern is consistent for proportion moving and average number of moves for critical life cycle intervals. For example, significantly fewer Irish with some or no life cycle events in the 35–44 interval who are in

---

[d]These data have been presented for only three of the four Catholic ethnic subpopulations because of the small number of cases and the problems of measuring Portuguese ethnic concentration with census data.

Table 9-8. Percentage Stable, Migrant Velocity, and Percentage Ever Migrate, by Ethnicity, Life Cycle, and Ethnic Concentration

Ethnic Concentration and Life Cycle Interval	Percent Stable						Average Moves			Percent Migrate		
	French Canadians		Irish		Italians		French Canadians	Irish	Italians	French Canadians	Irish	Italians
	Some	None	Some	None	Some	None	Some	Some	Some	Some	Some	Some
18-24												
High	5	68	—	—	12	73	1.9	—	2.0	33	—	19
Medium	8	59	7	53	7	59	3.0	2.3	2.6	39	92	23
Low	2	52	10	57	12	60	2.4	2.6	2.0	41	68	21
25-34												
High	24	{40	—	—	21	{63	1.6	—	1.9	15	—	12
Medium	16		0	—	18		2.4	1.9	2.0	30	28	15
Low	14	40	13	39	12	38	2.8	2.8	2.3	47	44	24
35-44												
High	67	50	—	—	29	83	1.2	—	1.3	{20	{25	{9
Medium	36	57	27	67	59	54	1.9	1.6	1.2			
Low	38	61	13	52	40	49	1.9	2.0	1.8	38	21	38
45-64*												
Medium**	46		—		56		—	—	—	23	—	—
Low	33		53		54		1.8	—	—	33	—	—

*Includes both those who did and did not have a life cycle event during this life cycle interval.
**Includes high.

areas of low ethnic concentration were stable compared to those in areas of higher ethnic concentration.

The clearest relationship between residential change and ethnic concentration characterizes Italians. Examining the 35-44 interval for Italians with no life cycle events shows that about half in areas of low ethnic concentration are stable compared to over 80 percent in areas of high concentration. The extent of repeat mobility is also higher for those in areas of low Italian concentration and the proportion of movers who migrate is over four times as high when compared to Italians in areas of higher concentration. These patterns characterize as well the 25-34 interval, but differences, while substantial, are less pronounced.

Underlining the importance of the 35-44 life cycle interval are the substantial differences for the Portuguese in the proportion not moving by ethnic concentration. Two-thirds of the Portuguese in this life cycle interval who are in areas of high concentration changed their residence compared to all of those currently in areas of low concentration areas (data not presented).

These patterns, with but minor exceptions, characterize each of the four cohorts and most of the life cycle stages within them. It should be noted that stability is much higher for ethnics with no life cycle event and increases in stability occur over the life cycle. Nevertheless, ethnic patterns remain and the relationship beween residential change and ethnic continuity as measured by ethnic residential concentration goes beyond cohort and life cycle effects.

CONCLUSION

The importance of migration for ethnic groups has often focused on issues of immigration and on residential segregation. Rarely have data been available to analyze in detail patterns of ethnic residential changes that include, on the one hand, the extent of mobility, repeat mobility, and migration and, on the other hand, take into consideration life cycle stages (intervals and events) as well as cohort. The data analyzed in this chapter suggest that ethnic differentials in residential mobility are substantial and are related in significant ways to ethnic continuity. While it is clear that family life cycle and cohort effects are relatively more important in determining residential changes, ethnicity is an important differentiator within these processes. When the general effects are taken into account, ethnic variation remains as an important factor.

The important implications of ethnic differentials in residential mobility for the continuity of ethnic communities emerge when relationships between mobility and ethnic intermarriage and residential concentration are examined. For example, ethnic variations in residential mobility are eliminated for intermarried ethnics; current ethnic residential concentration and residential mobility patterns are closely related. Supporting evidence for the role of migration in ethnic continuity may be observed by examining an interesting sidelight from the survey data available. For each surviving birth to all women in the survey, data were obtained on the current residence of children no longer living at home. These data allow for the determination of the proportion of children who have migrated from Rhode Island for each ethnic group. Ethnic differences are striking. Over 70 percent of Jewish children have migrated compared to less than half of the Protestant and about one-third of the Catholic children. Italians are the most stable generationally with 70 percent of their children remaining in the state. This contrasts with 60 percent of the Irish and about two-thirds of the French Canadians and Portuguese.[e] Hence, the continuity of ethnic communities is not only tied to mobility processes within generations but to intergenerational community stability.

---

[e]This issue will be further examined in relationship to stratification in the following chapter.

Chapter 10

Stratification, Social Mobility, and Residential Change

Changes in ethnic community structure and ethnic continuity may be inferred from the analysis of family and mobility processes. The dramatic changes over time in socioeconomic status and family patterns have resulted clearly in changes in the structure of ethnic communities. Furthermore, residential change, intermarriage, and ethnic residential concentration—individually and in combination—have contributed significantly to differential ethnic continuity. These two themes—changes in ethnic community structure and differential ethnic continuity—may be investigated more directly through an analysis of the relationship between ethnic stratification and residential change, on the one hand, and social and geographic mobility, on the other. Undoubtedly, selective residential mobility among socioeconomic subgroups involves major structural consequences for the community. The two mobility processes—social and geographic—have often been assumed to be strongly related. The argument has been made that moving up socially requires movement away from the community of origin. Hence, low rates of geographic and repeat mobility, as well as migration, should be associated with socioeconomic continuity between and within generations.

Previous research has shown that geographic mobility is related to socioeconomic status in different ways over the life cycle. Generally, for the younger adult ages, the higher the social status, the higher the probability of residential change. The reverse characterizes the middle and older ages. But even this oversimplified empirical generalization is not universal for all geographic mobility processes under all conditions (Speare et al., 1975; Goldscheider, 1971). Moreover, there has been little systematic empirical research on the relationship between social mobility and residential change and only inferential evidence on this relationship for ethnic subpopulations.

This chapter focuses on two analytic questions: (1) How do residential change patterns vary by socioeconomic status and social mobility for ethnic groups? (2) Do differences in residential change among ethnic groups reflect differential socioeconomic and social mobility patterns? Several indicators of socioeconomic status will be examined in this analysis: husband's education, initial and current occupation, and subjective social class identification. Social mobility refers to both intergenerational (father's to initial occupation) and intragenerational (initial to current occupation) mobility. Socio-economic status and social mobility will be related to the proportion residentially stable, average number of moves per mover, and the proportion of movers who migrate.

STRATIFICATION AND RESIDENTIAL CHANGE

The first relationship to be examined is between education and resi-dential stability. These data are presented controlling for life cycle interval (constructed retrospectively) and whether a life cycle event occurred in that interval (Table 10-1). In general, these data show that higher education is associated with greater residential mobility for most life cycle comparisons, within all ethnic groups. For the 18-24 and 25-34 intervals, education is not related to geographic mobility for those without some life cycle event. However, for those marrying and/or having children in this interval, the most educated are the least residentially stable. For example, only 4 percent of the Catholics who had some college education did not change their residence at least once during the 25-34 interval compared to 19 percent of those who did not complete high school. The occurrence of a life cycle event does not affect the pattern for the 35-44 inter-val. For those with some and with no life cycle events in that inter-val, the more educated are most mobile. Less than 30 percent of the more educated Protestants with some life cycle event in the interval 35-44 did not change their residence compared to over 40 percent of the less educated Protestants. The respective proportions for Protestants with no life cycle events are 43 percent (more educated) and 57 percent (less educated). Catholics show the same pattern only for those with some life cycle event in the interval. A similar relationship may be observed for Catholic ethnics in this interval, without exception. For example, 10 percent of the college educated

Table 10-1. Percentage Stable, by Ethnicity, Life Cycle, and Education*

Life Cycle Interval** and Education	Protestants		Catholics		French Canadians	Irish	Italians	Portuguese
	Some	None	Some	None		Some Events		
18–24								
High	5	52	5	55	10	4	7	—
Medium	10	52	5	58	4	4	4	7
Low	6	52	10	56	6	18	12	8
25–34								
High	11	30	4	42	0	3	9	}18
Medium	15	8	13	53	11	6	14	
Low	16	36	19	38	18	18	17	29
35–44								
High	29	43	22	69	—	—	10	—
Medium	33	49	30	44	31	0	43	—
Low	41	57	41	53	50	25	50	20
45–64								
High or Medium		65	56		—	—	—	—
Low		51	45		41	—	58	—

*High = some college; medium = completed high school; low = did not complete high school.

**Life cycle interval combines age intervals with the occurrence of one or more family formation events (marriage and/or the birth of children) during the interval. The interval 45–64 includes both those who did and did not have a life cycle event in this life cycle interval.

Italians did not change their residence in the 35-44 interval compared to 50 percent stable for the least educated Italians.

Although the comparison is limited to Protestants and Catholics in the 45-64 interval (due to a small number of cases), the relationship between residential mobility and education shows a clear reversal from earlier intervals. For this oldest interval, the more educated Protestants and Catholics have higher levels of residential stability. This is, however, consistent with the literature noted earlier that the relationship between education and residential mobility changes direction over the life cycle.

In addition to confirming the relationship between education and residential change within ethnic groups, comparisons of the differential level of residential change by ethnicity may be made controlling for the effects of education. These comparisons show that the overall higher level of Catholic residential stability (see Chapter 9) is clearly limited to the least educated subgroup for the intervals 18-24 and 25-34 when a life cycle event occurs. Protestants are more likely to move than Catholics at all educational levels only among those without a life cycle event. The patterns for the later intervals are not clear. Similarly, many of the ethnic Catholic differences in residential mobility are eliminated when education and life cycle are controlled. The Irish have the lowest level of residential stability, Italians have the highest and French Canadians are intermediate only for those with some family formation event (mainly childbearing) in the 35-44 interval, when the effects of education are controlled. Thus, while some differences in residential stability remain within educational levels, a considerable reduction and blurring of ethnic differences in geographic mobility result when educational level and life cycle are controlled.

The same conclusions may be drawn when the average number of moves per mover is examined (Table 10-2). Generally, the more educated have higher levels of repeat mobility than the less educated. Data for the 25-34 interval illustrate these patterns. Protestants with some life cycle event in this interval who have more than a high school education move an average of 3.6 times compared to 2.6 moves for those with less than a high school education. Differences in average number of moves by education are even greater for those without some life cycle event in the interval—3.8 moves for Protestants with some college education compared to 2.2 moves for those with less than a completed high school education. There are some exceptions among Catholic ethnics within life cycle intervals, but the basic patterns may be observed.

In general, Protestants have higher rates of repeat mobility than

Table 10-2.   Number of Moves Per Mover, by Ethnicity, Life Cycle, and Education*

Life Cycle Interval** and Education	Protestants		Catholics		French Canadians	Irish	Italians	Portuguese
	Some	None	Some	None	Some Events			
18–24								
High	3.6	1.8	2.6	1.9	3.2	2.8	2.4	—
Medium	3.0	2.6	2.5	1.8	2.9	2.5	2.5	2.6
Low	3.0	1.7	2.3	1.8	2.5	2.3	2.0	2.4
25–34								
High	3.6	3.8	2.7	—	2.2	2.5	2.7	—
Medium	2.9	2.7	2.3	2.3	2.7	2.9	1.7	—
Low	2.6	2.2	2.3	2.0	2.3	2.6	2.2	2.8
35–44								
High	2.3	2.2	2.2	—	—	—	—	—
Medium	2.3	1.5	1.9	1.5	—	1.6	—	—
Low	1.7	2.1	1.8	1.4	1.9	1.9	1.6	—
45–64								
High	—			—	—	—	—	—
Medium	—			—	—	—	—	—
Low	1.8			1.8	1.8	—	—	—

*High = some college; medium = completed high school; low = did not complete high school.
**Life cycle interval combines age intervals with the occurrence of one or more family formation events (marriage and/or the birth of children) during the interval. The interval 45–64 includes both those who did and did not have a life cycle event in this life cycle interval.

Catholics for most levels of education, but some exceptions appear for the earliest life cycle interval when no life cycle event occurs. Italians tend to have lower rates of repeat mobility within educational levels, but differences are small with some inconsistencies when the effects of life cycle variables and education are controlled.

The relationship between education and migration is the clearest of the measures of geographic mobility examined (Table 10-3). For almost every comparison within ethnic subpopulations, the more educated are more likely to migrate than are those with less education. The range is impressive: 80 percent of Protestant movers in the 35-44 interval with some life cycle event crossed a county boundary, compared to 46 percent of those who did not complete high school; the respective proportions for Catholics (with no life cycle event) are 75 percent (high education) and 21 percent (low education). The same patterns characterize Catholic ethnics where comparisons are possible.

Almost without exception, Protestants migrate more than Catholics and Italians migrate the least within educational and life cycle categories. Differences between Protestants and Catholics are particularly accentuated when some life cycle events occur for the 18-24 and 35-44 intervals and when no life cycle event occurs in the 25-34 interval.

Unlike for education, the relationship between initial (and current) occupation and measures of geographic mobility is weak and less consistent. Protestants and Catholics entering the labor force at the highest occupational level are least residentially stable in the 25-34 interval when some life cycle events occur compared to those entering at lower occupational levels (Table 10-4). But these patterns do not characterize those with no events or the 18-24 or 35-44 intervals. The reversal of greater stability for the higher occupational ranks occurs in the latest life cycle interval, but only for Catholics. The number of cases is small for Catholic ethnics but the basic overall pattern may be observed, with some exceptions. As with education, the greater residential stability of Catholics than Protestants is reduced considerably within occupational levels and does not appear at all levels when life cycle effects are taken into account. Data on average number of moves by occupation (not presented) show differential patterns that are eliminated to a large extent when life cycle is controlled.

The proportion of all movers who migrate shows a more consistent relationship with occupation within life cycle stages (Table 10-5). A greater proportion of Protestants and Catholics in higher initial occupational ranks migrate than those in lower initial occupational

Table 10-3. Percentage Ever Migrate, by Ethnicity, Life Cycle, and Education*

Life Cycle Interval** and Education	Protestants		Catholics		French Canadians	Irish	Italians	Portuguese
	Some	None	Some	None	Some Events			
18–24								
High	75	57	46	51	67	48	39	—
Medium	56	53	26	40	33	16	16	39
Low	47	44	32	35	40	17	18	44
25–34								
High	77	—	52	57	50	52	50	—
Medium	54	67	32	27	39	41	14	—
Low	38	40	26	28	31	28	13	48
35–44								
High	80	75	28	75	—	—	44	—
Medium	50	26	27	25	—	21	13	—
Low	46	44	23	21	27	22	20	—
45–64								
High or Medium	—				—	—	—	—
Low	44			18	24	—	18	—

*High = some college; medium = completed high school; low = did not complete high school.

**Life cycle interval combines age intervals with the occurrence of one or more family formation events (marriage and/or the birth of children) during the interval. The interval 45–64 includes both those who did and did not have a life cycle event in this life cycle interval.

Table 10-4.   Percentage Stable, by Ethnicity, Life Cycle, and Occupational Rank* at Age 25

	Protestants		Catholics		French Canadians	Irish	Italians
Life Cycle Interval** and Occupational Rank	Some	None	Some	None	Some Events		
18–24							
I	9	51	8	65	0	8	7
II	15	58	10	56	5	10	20
III	3	54	8	54	5	—	10
IV	11	46	12	61	13	10	16
25–34							
I	5	38	5	—	—	0	7
II	17	36	14	67	7	12	12
III	15	38	18	45	18	17	19
IV	12	23	21	41	21	12	26
35–44							
I	20	45	33	44	—	—	—
II	35	39	32	42	70	12	18
III	58	59	37	49	47	—	46
IV	38	48	34	51	33	14	38
45–64							
I	—		—		—	—	—
II	57		64		—	—	—
III	40		53		—	—	—
IV	70		34		27	—	40

*I = Duncan scale values 59 to 97; II = 34 to 58; III = 18 to 33; IV = 1 to 17.
**Life cycle interval combines age intervals with the occurrence of one or more family formation events (marriage and/or the birth of children) during the interval. The interval 45–64 includes both those who did and did not have a life cycle event in this life cycle interval.

Table 10-5. Percentage Ever Migrate, by Ethnicity, Life Cycle, and Occupational Rank* at Age 25

Life Cycle Interval** and Occupational Rank	Protestants		Catholics		French Canadians	Irish	Italians
	Some	None	Some	None	Some Events		
18-24							
I	62	47	35	52	38	54	31
II	62	57	26	28	26	6	15
III	52	55	36	47	43	44	7
IV	54	60	29	31	44	—	27
25-34							
I	71	—	43	—	—	59	21
II	40	—	33	—	24	37	36
III	39	40	31	27	31	50	20
IV	51	20	29	25	47	27	6
35-44							
I	—	91	42	—	—	—	}36
II	71	38	27	44	—	29	
III	—	33	21	30	—	}15	}14
IV	39	36	30	20	43		

*I = Duncan scale values 59 to 97; II = 34 to 58; III = 18 to 33; IV = 1 to 17.

**Life cycle interval combines age intervals with the occurrence of one or more family formation events (marriage and/or the birth of children) during the interval.

ranks and this is particularly the case for the 25–34 and 35–44 intervals. For example, over 90 percent of Protestants in high occupational ranks who moved in the 35–44 interval crossed a county boundary compared to 36 percent of those in the lowest occupational rank (where no life cycle events occurred in the interval). The Catholic pattern in the 25–34 interval for those with some life cycle event is also illustrative of this pattern: 43 percent of those entering the labor force in the highest occupational rank migrated (of all those who moved) compared to less than 30 percent of those entering the labor force in the lowest occupational rank. Again, Catholic ethnic differences in migration are largely eliminated when life cycle and occupational rank are controlled.[a]

Differences in the residential mobility patterns for middle and working class ethnics are less consistent than either educational or occupational differentials. This may reflect the limitation of measures of current subjective social class when life cycle and migration patterns have been constructed retrospectively. However, for the strongest indicator of residential change, i.e., the proportion of movers who ever migrate, the patterns by religion are consistent (Table 10–6). The proportion migrant for middle class Protestants and Catholics is almost without exception higher than for the working classes within life cycle intervals. Moreover, Protestants are much more likely than Catholics to cross a county boundary when they move, controlling for social class and life cycle. Taken together, measures of socioeconomic status have a weak relationship to residential change when life cycle factors are controlled. Similarly, ethnic differences in residential change are blurred when the effects of socioeconomic status and life cycle are taken into consideration. The strongest relationships, and perhaps the most important theoretically for the study of ethnic continuity and community structure, emerge when education is used as a measure of socioeconomic status and for migration between country boundaries.

SOCIAL MOBILITY AND RESIDENTIAL CHANGE

The hypothesized positive relationship between social and geographic mobility is examined in Table 10–7. These data confirm the hypothesis in general but less clearly for intergenerational than for intragenerational social mobility and only for some life cycle

---

[a]Similar patterns emerge when current rather than initial occupational rank is examined and, hence, are not presented. Since current occupation needs to be controlled by cohort as well as life cycle, the number of cases becomes too small for detailed analysis.

intervals. For the early life cycle interval (18-24), ethnics who have higher occupational ranks than their fathers are the least stable residentially, except the Portuguese. The most residentially stable ethnics are those who have experienced downward occupational mobility (compared to their fathers). The Irish pattern is exceptional in this respect since it is the occupationally stable who are least residentially mobile: 51 percent of the Irish who have the same occupational rank as their fathers did not change residences in the 18-24 interval compared to 38 percent of those who were downwardly mobile and 28 percent who were upwardly mobile. The importance of these patterns for this life cycle interval should be emphasized. The measure of intergenerational mobility refers to the comparison of the occupational rank of fathers to the occupational rank of sons at age 25. Hence, residential changes in the 18-24 life cycle interval relate to geographic mobility *before* initial entry in the labor force. Thus, these data show the important role of residential changes in the process of occupational mobility between generations.

The relationship between intergenerational social mobility among ethnics and residential change is not clear for the 25-34 and 45-64 life cycle intervals and most of the differences are small. The pattern for the 35-44 interval, however, contrasts sharply with the 18-24 interval and is consistent with the changing relationship between social and geographic mobility over the life cycle. While differences

Table 10-6. Percentage of Movers Ever Migrate, by Religion, Life Cycle, and Subjective Social Class*

*Life Cycle Interval** and Subjective Social Class*	Protestants	Catholics	Protestants	Catholics
	Some Events		*No Events*	
18-24				
Middle	64	32	57	42
Working	49	32	48	39
25-34				
Middle	62	35	73	52
Working	43	28	38	18
35-44				
Middle	67	27	57	31
Working	30	25	30	16
45-64				
Middle	—	—	41	18
Working	—	—	38	19

*Middle = middle or upper class; working = working or lower class.
**Life cycle interval combines age intervals with the occurrence of one or more family formation events (marriage and/or the birth of children) during the interval.

Table 10-7.   Percentage Stable, by Ethnicity, Life Cycle, and Social Mobility

Life Cycle Interval and Social Mobility	Protestants	Catholics	French Canadians	Irish	Italians	Portuguese
Intergenerational Mobility						
18–24						
Upward	25	27	21	28	30	23
Downward	35	34	31	38	40	23
Nonmobile	31	32	26	51	34	16
25–34						
Upward	15	19	19	15	17	30
Downward	20	25	20	22	23	23
Nonmobile	11	22	20	12	23	29
35–44						
Upward	48	45	56	35	54	25
Downward	43	44	53	36	45	—
Nonmobile	43	43	40	17	59	17
45–64						
Upward	52	50	41	—	—	—
Downward	53	41	33	—	—	—
Nonmobile	62	50	50	—	—	—
Intragenerational Mobility						
18–24						
Upward	25	28	28	29	35	12
Downward	29	31	29	40	33	27
Nonmobile	36	37	28	41	43	7
25–34						
Upward	27	24	30	7	28	20
Downward	17	18	15	22	18	36
Nonmobile	9	21	18	6	28	20
35–44						
Upward	55	40	38	—	42	—
Downward	41	45	60	36	51	—
Nonmobile	38	35	39	6	55	—
45–64						
Upward	50	43	—	—	—	—
Downward	54	45	39	—	50	—
Nonmobile	70	52	56	—	56	—

are small, the pattern is that those who have higher occupational ranks than their fathers are more likely to be residentially stable in the 35-44 interval than those who have lower or similar occupational ranks relative to their fathers. The major exception is the Italians, where the most residentially stable are those who are downwardly mobile intergenerationally.

In sum, these data show a weak relationship between intergenerational social mobility and residential change that varies by life cycle stage. Of no less significance is the fact that geographic mobility differences between Protestants and Catholics and among Catholic ethnics are minimal or eliminated when the effects of intergenerational occupation change and life cycle are controlled. Indeed, Catholics are less residentially mobile than Protestants in the 25-34 life cycle interval but Protestants are more stable than Catholics in the 45-64 interval, when the effects of intergenerational mobility are controlled. There are no distinctive patterns of residential mobility among Catholic ethnics within social mobility and life cycle categories.

Turning to the relationship between career and geographic mobility, the patterns are somewhat more consistent (see lower panels of Table 10-7). Protestants and Catholics who are upwardly mobile intragenerationally are least stable residentially and those who are nonmobile in their occupational careers are most stable residentially, for the 18-24 life cycle interval. These differences are substantial: for example, only one-fourth of the Protestants who were upwardly mobile did not change their residence in this life cycle interval compared to over one-third of those whose occupational rank was the same initially and currently. This pattern characterizes only the Irish and Italian ethnics for this life cycle interval.

For the other life cycle intervals, the patterns are more complex. Indeed, upward career mobility tends to be associated with greater residential stability for 25-34 and 35-44 intervals. This relationship is clearer for Protestants and Catholics than among Catholic ethnic groups. The relationship between career mobility and residential stability in the later life cycle stage reverts to the pattern characterizing the earliest interval. For all ethnic subpopulations where data are available, career occupational stability is associated with residential stability in the 45-64 interval. These patterns suggest that residential mobility is associated with upward career mobility in the early and later life cycle stages, while residential stability characterizes the upwardly mobile in the family formation and family building intervals (25-44).

When the effects of career occupational change and life cycle stages are eliminated, Catholics tend to be more stable residentially than Protestants in the early life cycle stages while the reverse characterizes the later life cycle stages. Almost all the variation among Catholic ethnics is eliminated within life cycle and career mobility categories. Thus, the overall ethnic Catholic differences in rates of residential mobility—lower rates of Italian and higher rates of Irish residential mobility—reflect life cycle and social mobility effects rather than particular ethnic patterns. These results based on intragenerational social mobility are similar to those based on intergenerational mobility noted earlier.

Furthermore, data not shown indicate that when the effects of life cycle events within life cycle intervals are eliminated, no relationship appears between intergenerational or intragenerational social mobility and residential mobility for ethnic Catholics and the relationship is considerably weakened for Protestants and Catholics. The higher residential mobility of upwardly mobile (intergenerationally and intragenerationally) Protestants and Catholics in the early life cycle stage and their greater residential stability at later stages only characterizes those with no life cycle events.

There is also a weak relationship between repeat residential mobility and intergenerational social mobility among ethnic subpopulations when life cycle factors are controlled. Generally, ethnics in higher occupational ranks than their fathers are most likely, and those in the same occupational ranks are least likely, to be repeat movers. No patterns of repeat mobility and career social mobility emerge when life cycle factors are taken into consideration.

A more consistent pattern results when the rate of migration is related to social mobility. Upwardly mobile ethnics are most likely to cross a county boundary when they move and the occupationally stable are least likely to migrate within life cycle intervals. There are several exceptions to this pattern for both intergenerational and intragenerational social mobility when life cycle events are taken into consideration (Table 10-8).

Although the relationship between migration and social mobility reflects in large part life cycle factors, differences in the rate of migration between ethnic groups remain when these factors are controlled. For example, the rate of migration among Protestants is about twice as high as Catholics in the 35-44 interval within social mobility categories, when some life cycle events occur. This is true for both career and generational social mobility. Migration differences between Protestants and Catholics are smaller but in the same direction for those with no life cycle event in this interval.

imilarly, Italians tend to have lower rates of migration than the

Table 10-8. Percentage Ever Migrate, by Ethnicity, Life Cycle, and Social Mobility

Life Cycle Interval* and Social Mobility	Protestants		Catholics		French Canadians	Irish	Italians	Portuguese
	Some	None	Some	None		Some Events		
Intergenerational								
18–24								
Upward	60	47	32	44	40	24	24	46
Downward	54	59	32	37	39	27	22	42
Nonmobile	60	56	32	35	37	38	16	40
25–34								
Upward	61	74	34	46	31	39	22	44
Downward	40	36	31	23	42	39	16	—
Nonmobile	63	40	31	14	30	44	18	50
35–44								
Upward	54	46	27	24	20	33	25	—
Downward	68	44	29	28	45	23	19	—
Nonmobile	40	59	20	19	17	0	27	—
Intragenerational								
18–24								
Upward	63	62	23	34	15	40	29	—
Downward	59	47	34	40	46	32	15	31
Nonmobile	54	50	33	43	46	25	19	64
25–34								
Upward	50	—	32	46	36	46	23	20
Downward	49	40	33	22	43	40	19	38
Nonmobile	64	—	30	33	22	39	18	—
35–44								
Upward	40	44	33	26	—	—	—	—
Downward	57	45	23	19	31	21	20	—
Nonmobile	57	73	30	35	36	21	27	—

*Life cycle interval combines age intervals with the occurrence of one or more family formation events (marriage and/or the birth of children) during the interval.

Irish and differences are greatest for those who have the same occupational rank as fathers or the same initial and current occupational ranks.

CONCLUDING OBSERVATIONS

Three conclusions emerge from these data on the relationship between social mobility and residential change. First, most of the relationship between geographic mobility and repeat mobility, on the one hand, and intergenerational and career social mobility, on the other hand, reflects strong life cycle effects. Secondly, differences in the residential mobility of ethnic subpopulations are eliminated for the most part when social mobility and life cycle factors are controlled. Finally, migration differences are not solely the result of social mobility and life cycle variations among ethnic groups. This last finding is of particular importance since it highlights the fact that ethnic continuity and ethnic community structure continue to be differentially affected by social mobility patterns and distinctive ethnic factors. While movement within the community tends to be associated more with life cycle stages and events, residential movement that involves greater distances (as implied by crossing a county boundary) tends to be associated with the nature of the ethnic community, over and above life cycle effects.

It is clear, therefore, that the implications of residential change for ethnic continuity and community structure are complex and affected by family processes. Part of the difficulty in analyzing these implications rests with the use of cross-sectional data for investigating dynamic patterns as well as with the restrictions imposed by focusing on one geographic area. In an attempt to overcome some of these study design limitations, two additional pieces of information will be presented that are suggestive of the particular importance of migration for ethnic continuity and community structure. Data were obtained on the residential location of the children (of the older cohorts) who no longer resided with their parents. The proportion of children who left the area, when related to the socioeconomic status of parents, permits inferences to be drawn about the effects of selective outmigration on ethnic continuity. In addition, information on place of birth was obtained and may be subdivided into those born in and outside the study area. This, in turn, may be related to their socioeconomic characteristics in order to reveal the differential impact of inmigration on the socioeconomic structure of ethnic subcommunities.

The outmigration patterns of children show the strong effects of parental education on ethnic continuity. Overall, 40 percent of the children no longer at home have left the study area, but this varies significantly by their father's education. If their fathers had some college education, almost 60 percent had moved out of the study area compared to 35 percent of those whose fathers had not completed high school. Education, therefore, affects significantly intergenerational ethnic continuity through migration. This pattern, as shown in Table 10-9, characterizes the three religious subpopulations as well as Italian and Irish ethnics. The contrasts by education are impressive. Almost 90 percent of the children (of those not residing at home) of Jewish fathers with some college education have migrated out of the study area compared to 50 percent of those whose fathers did not complete high school. The respective proportions for Protestants are 72 percent (high education) and 40 percent (low education). Although the Catholic pattern is consistent, differences are smaller and reflect variation among Catholic ethnics. Italian and Irish patterns are consistent with the overall relationship—almost two-thirds of the nonresident children of Italian fathers with some college education left the study area compared to onefourth of those whose fathers did not complete high school. The French Canadian and Portuguese patterns are reversed—those whose fathers had lower education are more likely to be living outside the study area compared to those whose fathers had higher education. This may reflect the greater opportunities available in the study area for educated ethnic children among those subgroups characterized by generally lower socioeconomic status.

It is important to note that within each educational level, Protestant children are more likely than Catholic children to move out of the study area and Jewish children are the most likely to move out. Among Catholic ethnics, Irish children are generally more migratory out and Italian children most likely to remain in the study area. These intergenerational outmigration patterns reinforce the conclusion based on the analysis of migration among ethnic subpopulations.

The contribution of migration to ethnic community structure may be seen by examining average occupational scores (Duncan) of the lifetime inmigrants and those born in the area. The contrasts by cohort between Protestants and Catholics point to the fact that for the cohorts over age 35, Protestant inmigrants had higher occupational scores than Catholic inmigrants, while for the youngest cohort the pattern reverses (Table 10-9). Older Protestants who moved to the study area had an occupational score twice as high as older Catholic inmigrants, while younger Catholic inmigrants had an

Table 10-9. In and Outmigration, by Ethnicity and Socioeconomic Status

	Protestants	Jews	Catholics	French Canadians	Irish	Italians	Portuguese
Education of Fathers							
Percent of Children No Longer at Home Who Have Left the study Area (Father's Age 40 and Over)							
Total	47	72	36	33	41	30	38
Some College	72	87	57	36	67	64	—
High School	44	50	38	40	24	50	29
Less than High School	40	—	34	50	39	25	40
Mean Occupational Scores (Duncan) at Age 25							
Migrants (Born outside the Study Area)							
25–34	29	—	41	39	49	41	25
35–44	39	—	35	24	47	45	15
45–64	34	—	25	18	33	21	13
65+	36	—	17	20	25	14	11
Lifetime Residents							
25–34	37	—	41	36	40	47	34
35–44	39	—	31	25	44	31	12
45–64	32	—	27	24	36	22	18
65+	36	—	24	—	—	—	—

occupational score 30 percent higher than inmigrating Protestants of the youngest cohort. Such wide differences do not characterize those born in the study area. Moreover, comparing the occupational score of the inmigrants with those born in the study area shows that Catholic migrants and lifetime residents have the same occupational score, while Protestant inmigrants have significantly lower occupational scores compared to Protestants born in the area. These data reveal clearly the differential impact of migration selectivity on the occupational structure of ethnic communities.[b]

Most important in this context is the fact that the occupational status of young Catholics in the community is higher than for young Protestants (see Chapter 2). This reversal from the pattern characterizing the older cohorts has been affected by the selective inmigration of lower status Protestants and higher status Catholics relative to those born in the area. Furthermore, these findings are consistent with the patterns of outmigration of children and the changes noted earlier in conversion and social mobility for the younger cohorts. Taken together, these patterns suggest not only the deteriorating status position of Protestants in the area, but reveal clearly the effects of these changes on family and mobility processes. Conversely, the trend toward Catholic dominance, socially and occupationally, may clearly be inferred from data on structural changes in marriage, social mobility, and migration.

Irish inmigrants have the highest occupational scores of all Catholic ethnics for all cohorts and there is a clear increase in occupational level over time. However, inmigrants of recent cohorts of French Canadians and Irish have higher occupational scores than lifetime residents of the area, while the lifetime Italian and Portuguese residents have higher occupational scores than inmigrants of the youngest cohort. Thus, the contribution of Irish and French Canadian inmigrants raises the occupational level of their respective subcommunities, while inmigration reduces the occupational level of Italian and Portuguese subcommunities. Indeed, a comparison of average occupation scores of Irish and Italian lifetime residents points to higher occupational status among younger Italians than Irish. Since the reverse characterizes the relative occupational status of inmigrating younger Irish and Italians, the overall occupational distribution of those in the community (including both lifetime residents and inmigrants) is higher for Irish than Italians (see Chapter 2).

---

[b]There are limitations to this analysis since the data focus on lifetime migration and do not separate migrants who moved to the area as children and as adults.

Thus, these data on in- and outmigration complement the analysis of migration and social mobility. Taken together, the emerging pattern suggests that migration plays a significant role in the changing community structure of ethnic subpopulations and has important implications for differential ethnic continuity. Residential change for all ethnic groups is clearly affected by life cycle, stratification, and social mobility processes. Differential rates of geographic mobility within the community among ethnic groups are largely accounted for by these broader social processes. However, differential migration patterns seem to reflect specific ethnic factors that transcend life cycle and socioeconomic effects. Hence, there is an interdependence between ethnicity and migration: On the one hand, ethnic factors contribute to differential migration patterns and, on the other hand, variations in the level and type of migration have implications for ethnic community structure and continuity.

Chapter 11

The Ethnic Factor:
An Evaluation

Family and mobility processes are fundamental and pervasive features of human societies. Marriage patterns and mate selection, stratification and social mobility, residential concentration and geographic mobility are the foundations for understanding social life. Ethnic variations and changes in these processes provide the basis for analyzing ethnic continuity and the emerging structure of ethnic communities.

In the analysis of the ethnic factor in family and mobility processes, emphasis has been placed on ethnic variations, changes, and heterogeneity within ethnic groups. The isolation and identification of differences between ethnic groups, changes in ethnicity over time, and life cycle and social class variations within ethnic subpopulations allow for an examination of key analytic issues in the study of ethnicity. First, the most general question may be examined: Are there ethnic differences in family and mobility processes? Second, are there indications of convergences in these fundamental processes over time among ethnic groups? Third, which subgroups within ethnic populations are more receptive to family and mobility changes? Fourth, do ethnic differences reflect family life cycle and social class variations among ethnic groups? Fifth, what cultural and/ or structural features of ethnic subpopulations contribute to understanding the residual ethnic differences in family and mobility processes not accounted for by life cycle and social class factors? Finally, what are the implications of family and mobility patterns for ethnic continuity and the emerging new forms of ethnic community structure?

225

These analytic questions are elementary and have been discussed widely in the social science literature. However, surprisingly few systematic empirical investigations have focused in any detail on family and mobility processes among white religious and Catholic ethnic groups. The availability of an extensive body of survey data on white ethnics in Rhode Island, with details that allow for the retrospective reconstruction of marriage, family, social and geographic mobility patterns, and with correlative data on family life cycle and socioeconomic status, provided the unique opportunity for an analysis of the ethnic factor. While the patterns in Rhode Island have many parallels to other ethnic communities, every case study has unique features that make broad national generalizations problematic. Nevertheless, the richness of the survey material plus the assumption that it is more fruitful to identify the salience of ethnicity at the community (rather than at the national or individual) level, argued strongly for exploiting these survey data. Moreover, the fact that Catholics are numerically dominant in Rhode Island and that some ethnic groups located there had not been studied comparatively (particularly Portuguese and French Canadians) made the analytic potential of these data particularly valuable.

What are the major conclusions that emerge from the analysis of these data? First, and foremost, the evidence presented strongly supports the argument that ethnic pluralism is a continuing feature of community life in America. No analysis of family or mobility processes can be considered complete without attention to ethnic variations. To the extent that these fundamental social processes have implications for other social processes and for attitudes and values (that have not been considered in this study), the study of ethnic variation and change increases in importance.

The existence of ethnic variation in social processes does not however imply the absence of change. To the contrary. The cohort data showed clearly the multidimensionality of ethnic changes. Both the extent and pattern of ethnic change varies over time and differently among ethnic subpopulations and for the various processes analyzed. Hence, there are elements of continuity as well as change in ethnic variation that, over time, and in different social and economic contexts, result in changing forms of ethnic continuity and community structure. The changing nature of ethnicity cannot be viewed simply as an indication of the diminishing importance of the ethnic factor or of the "assimilation" of ethnic communities. Rather the manifestation of ethnicity changes as the broader society changes and new forms of ethnic identity and ethnic cohesiveness are emerging.

The evidence available also points unequivocably to variations within ethnic communities. Differences within the Catholic subpopulation are so wide that for almost all the social processes examined, Catholic ethnic variations are more substantial than Protestant-Catholic differences. Furthermore, social class and life cycle factors were found to be important differentiators within all ethnic groups. The variations within ethnic communities point to much greater complexities in analyzing the ethnic factor than previous research has implied. Nevertheless, it is clear that for many of the processes examined, social class and life cycle variations account in part for the patterns of ethnic differences. Although the data do not show that ethnicity is the most important or dominant differentiator of social processes, they indicate that ethnicity is one of several major sources of social differentiation. Indeed, the focus of this research has not been to identify the amount of statistical variance that ethnicity explains, relative to other variables. Rather, the objective has been to examine ethnic differentiation in the context of socioeconomic and life cycle changes so as to clarify the patterns of continuity and change characterizing ethnic communities.

Emerging from the analysis, therefore, is the importance of factors other than social class and life cycle in accounting for the continuing ethnic differences in family and mobility processes. These are factors that are more particularly associated with ethnicity per se. Part of these specific ethnic factors is cultural, but structural conditions play a significant role that has not been emphasized sufficiently in American ethnic studies.

These overall and abstract conclusions are only part of the generalizations that emerge from the analysis presented. The contribution of ethnicity to variation and change in family and mobility processes must be appreciated in the detailed and more specific relationships that have been uncovered. The highlights of these findings for family, social mobility, and residential change processes are presented below with special attention to the implications of the variations and changes in these processes for ethnic continuity and the changing structure of ethnic communities.

MARRIAGE PROCESSES

Ethnic groups share basic similarities in the extent, stability, and timing of marriage and in mate selection. Most ethnics marry, variation in marital stability is relatively small, age at marriage for men and women is concentrated within a narrow range, and there is a clear tendency toward increases in ethnic intermarriages and a decline in the salience of ethnic homogamy. On closer inspection, however, the detailed evidence shows that the processes that have led to these patterns vary substantially among ethnic subpopulations and the continuing ethnic variations in marriage patterns reflect important dimensions of structural pluralism. Indeed, the tensions between ethnic change and continuity are highlighted by the analysis of marriage processes.

In general, Protestants, Catholics, and Jews are characterized by almost universal marriage, but Catholics tend to have higher marital stability rates than Protestants, and Jews have higher levels of both marriage and stability when compared to non-Jews. Moreover, Jews marry at later ages and tend toward higher levels of homogamy compared to Protestants or Catholics. Delayed marriage among Jewish men and women is associated in large part with their higher levels of educational attainment; their lower rate of intermarriage, despite the relatively small pool of eligibles, reflect the cohesiveness of the Jewish community and the Jewish commitment to ethnic continuity. Unlike the national American picture, Catholics are more homogamously married in Rhode Island than are Protestants and the numerical Catholic majority in the state is clearly an important determinant.

Although there are patterns of convergence in these marriage processes among religious groups over time and within socioeconomic subgroupings, differences remain in the timing, extent, and stability of marriages and in the level of religious homogamy among the young, more educated, middle and upper classes. Differences among religious groups are further reflected in the differential exchanges between religious and educational homogamy. Jews and Protestants who marry out of their ethnic communities tend to exchange religious for educational homogamy. In contrast, Catholics who intermarry exchange relatively higher educational achievements for more prestigious (as indicated by higher aggregate socioeconomic status) ethnic status. Thus, an examination of the levels and convergences of intermarriage over time without attention to these selectivity and exchange patterns, particularly by education, misses one of the most significant differential features of intermarriages among religious groups. These exchanges imply different structural consequences for the composition and continuity of ethnic communities.

The overall comparisons between Protestant and Catholic marriage patterns obscure the major variations within the Catholic group. Indeed, Catholic ethnic variation in marriage processes is clearly greater than Protestant-Catholic differences. Differences among French Canadian, Irish, Italian, and Portuguese ethnics in marital separation, remarriage, celibacy, and age at marriage are large and there is little analytic justification in treating the Catholic subgroup as homogeneous in terms of these processes. For example, Italians, Portuguese, and French Canadians have high rates of marriage, but only Italians have low rates of separation. The Irish are similar to Italians in their low separation rates but have distinctive patterns of celibacy compared to all ethnic groups considered. The Irish not only have higher rates of nonmarriage but those who marry do so at significantly later ages than non-Irish Catholic ethnics. While there has been some convergence over time in these marriage processes, particularly among educated Catholic ethnics, differences are substantial when cohort and educational effects are controlled.

The continuing Irish patterns of celibacy and late marriage are significant indications of the persistence of ethnic characteristics. Removed by several generations and many decades from the conditions in Ireland that fostered these marriage patterns, and having experienced enormous social and cultural changes over the last century in America, these ethnic factors have continued to characterize the Irish. The consistency among late marriage, homogamy, and education for the Irish may have facilitated the retention of Irish ethnic identity without foregoing high status attainment and social mobility. The continuing emphasis on Italian family solidarity as reflected in marriage patterns (extent, stability, and timing of marriage, and in homogamy) is also remarkable evidence of ethnic continuity.

Ethnic differences in the extent, stability, and the timing of marriage are important in and of themselves as indicators of the changing pluralism of ethnic communities. Moreover, the direct effects on ethnic community structure and on the continuity of distinctive ethnic patterns may be seen in the relationship of these marriage patterns to indicators of community cohesiveness. For example, there is a clear fit between higher levels of education, late marriage, and ethnic continuity for the Irish. Marrying late is associated with ethnic residential concentration and implied community continuity for the Irish as well as Italians. Ethnic residential concentration among Portuguese and French Canadians, however, characterizes those who marry early. Hence, the relationship between education and delayed marriage among French Canadians and Portuguese implies diminished ethnic residential concentration; the same relationship between education and later marriage for Irish and Italians means continuing ethnic residential concentration.

Catholic ethnics have very similar patterns of religious intermarriage and the differences by religion in this case are more substantial than for Catholic ethnic groups. Nevertheless, Irish have significantly lower levels of religious homogamy than non-Irish Catholics. In general, as previous research has demonstrated, ethnic (as opposed to religious) homogamy is much less salient in America and ethnic homogamy has declined over time. Again, this is much less true for Italians than for the Irish. When educational levels are related to homogamy within ethnic groups, it becomes clear that the better educated Portuguese, Italian and French Canadians have lower levels of homogamy than the less educated. Higher education, however, does not lead to higher out-marriages for the Irish—as it does not necessarily result in later marriages.

Several points emerge clearly from these marriage patterns. Overall, ethnic homogamy has declined as the most important distinguishing feature of ethnic groups. Ethnicity in America is much less based on marriage within narrowly defined ethnic communities and the role of the intermarried is apparently being redefined in such a way as to allow for their ethnic community identification. Similarly, no strong or specific ethnic preference system in marriage choices seems to be emerging among Catholic ethnics and marriage selection is in large part tied in to educational-ethnic exchanges that are complex. These convergences and growing homogeneity among ethnic communities in marriage patterns do not necessarily imply similarities and uniformities. Substantial differences remain and continue to characterize ethnic communities. That these marriage differences reflect more than class and cohort variations among ethnic groups suggests that specific ethnic structural and cultural determinants are operating.

STRATIFICATION AND SOCIAL MOBILITY

Stratification and social mobility patterns are central features of ethnic community structure and have been considered to have the most important theoretical significance in the analysis of ethnic distinctiveness. The detailed analysis of ethnic variation and change in socioeconomic status has confirmed the centrality of education, occupation, and social class changes in the evolution of ethnic communities. In this context, two major generalizations emerge: First, ethnic groups are heterogeneous in terms of socioeconomic status and of mobility processes that have resulted in the contemporary social class configurations of ethnic communities. Second, social class factors are central for understanding ethnic diversity, accounting for a large part of the differences between ethnic groups. Nevertheless, ethnicity and social class cannot be viewed as synonymous or identical processes.

While selected socioeconomic subgroups within ethnic subpopulations have been more receptive to change processes and convergence between ethnic groups has occurred among the higher socioeconomic groups, differences between ethnic groups are not totally eliminated when the effects of social class are controlled.

There are many similarities in the general conclusions reached in our analysis of stratification and social mobility as with marriage processes. An overview of the stratification and social mobility patterns of ethnic groups places in context these similarities. The evidence clearly shows the higher socioeconomic status of Jews compared to non-Jews and Protestants compared to Catholics in terms of educational achievement, occupational level, and social class identification. The patterns of change over time in these characteristics have resulted in the growing socioeconomic similarity of the three religious subpopulations and the higher occupational achievements of young Catholics compared to Protestants. Among Catholic ethnics, the Irish are clearly higher for all the indicators of socioeconomic status, with the Italians at lower levels but closing the gap with the Irish. French Canadians and Portuguese have distinctly lower socioeconomic status. For the youngest cohort, French Canadians have higher occupational ranks and are more concentrated in higher social classes than the Portuguese, although they continue to have the lowest educational levels among Catholic ethnics. The socioeconomic gap among Catholic ethnics is greater than between Protestants and Catholics, despite general improvements over time among all ethnic groups. Moreover, the French Canadian–Portuguese contrasts in various socioeconomic measures, as the Protestant-Catholic differences in occupation and education, suggest strongly the different paths to occupational achievement among ethnics.

Despite convergences over time in socioeconomic status, there continues to be a wide diversity among all ethnic subpopulations— even for the youngest cohort. Furthermore, the differential processes and patterns of stratification and social mobility are more conspicuous than are the similarities. The fact that less educated Catholics end up in higher ranked occupations than similarly educated Protestants and that less educated French Canadians achieve higher occupation ranks than Portuguese points to the facilitating role ethnic communities play in the attainment of occupational position. Thus, the issue of a Catholic majority population is central not only in differential intermarriage levels but in stratification changes and the paths to Catholic occupational achievement.

Although in general Catholic ethnic variation in socioeconomic status is greater than differences between Protestants and Catholics (as was true for marriage processes as well), religion is a more important differentiator for one element of stratification—sex differences in educational attainment. Ethnic women are less educated than men but differences in the relative education of men and women are greater between religious groups than among Catholic ethnics. The particularly lower levels of education attained by Catholic women relative to Catholic men (and to non-Catholic women) and the fact that Catholic ethnics share this sex differentiation parallel the finding on the greater importance of religious in contrast to ethnic differences in intermarriage levels. Together, these patterns suggest that particular religious values associated with Catholicism may be important considerations in selected ethnic differences, particularly where religio-cultural traditions have been clear and central. Such a conclusion should not obscure the overriding fact that in most other areas of family and stratification processes, variations within the Catholic group are larger and cannot be explained by particularistic Catholic religious doctrines. Clearly, for Catholic ethnic variations—indeed for general Protestant-Catholic differences—the search for explanation must proceed to areas beyond specific cultural and religious values characterizing Catholic subpopulations.

To clarify these continuing stratification patterns differentiating ethnic subpopulations and to identify the processes that have resulted in the socioeconomic structure of ethnic communities, a detailed analysis of social mobility—intergenerational and intragenerational—was undertaken. The results of that analysis show that the processes of social mobility between and within generations are exceedingly complex, particularly when the variety of occupational and social class origins of ethnic groups are considered, when generational-age variations are taken into account, when the variations in ethnic experiences are substantial, and when major structural changes have characterized the occupational and social class distributions over the last half century.

While there are no simple ways to identify the social mobility processes characterizing ethnic groups, several important patterns emerged. When outflows from occupational origins are examined, Protestants seem to be more upwardly mobile than Catholics. However, this mainly reflects the higher socioeconomic origins and current status of Protestants. When the lower origins of Catholics are taken into consideration, it becomes clear that recruitment to occupational positions at levels comparable to those of Protestants involves greater upward mobility for Catholics, a pattern that is particularly conspicuous for recent cohorts.

Jewish patterns of social mobility differ significantly from those of Protestants and Catholics in the very large formation of new positions at the highest occupational ranks and the decline in lower occupational concentration. Jews tend to be located in the higher occupational levels in terms of origins, initial entry into the labor force, and current occupational status.

Identical patterns of religious differences in social mobility processes emerge when subjective social class origins and current identification were compared and reinforce the conclusions based on occupational changes between generations. While Catholics in higher occupational ranks tend to recruit from lower occupational and social class origins, Protestants tend to "inherit" higher occupational ranks and social class levels from their fathers more than Catholics. Both the occupational changes between generations and subjective social class data show the reversals of these patterns for the youngest cohort of Protestants and Catholics that clarifies the changing socioeconomic profile among the most recent generation of Protestants and Catholics.

Career and short-term social mobility differences also characterize Protestants and Catholics. Generally, career stability is much greater for Catholics than Protestants and upward career mobility characterizes Protestants of all cohorts more than Catholics. Short-term mobility differences between Protestants and Catholics vary, however, by cohort. Upward mobility over a five-year period is more characteristic of Catholics than Protestants of the youngest cohort, a pattern that is clearly a reversal of that found for the older cohort.

As with marriage processes and stratification, variations in occupational origins, intergenerational, career, and short-term mobility are substantially greater among the four Catholic ethnic groups than between Protestants and Catholics. Irish and Portuguese ethnics stand at polar ends of the occupational and social class origins continuum, with Italians and French Canadians in intermediate positions. Unlike the convergence between Protestant and Catholic origins, no consistent patterns of convergence have appeared among Catholic ethnics. To the extent that differential socioeconomic origins persist, and the current stratification of Catholic ethnics supports this assumption fully, ethnic differences in occupational and social class inheritance, recruitment, and social mobility will persist as well, at least for another generation.

Stratification and social mobility profiles of the four Catholic ethnic groups point to the greater Irish occupational inheritance at higher levels and their concentration at upper occupational ranks. The Irish have experienced the greatest upward mobility to the best jobs among Catholic ethnics but this rate of mobility has declined among recent cohorts, mainly because so few Irish have remained in the lowest occupational ranks. They have therefore experienced a transition over time from a pattern of greater occupational upward mobility to greater occupational inheritance. At the other end of the continuum are the Portuguese. This group has been least upwardly mobile and most likely to remain at the lowest occupational levels, despite the large pools of lower occupational origins to recruit into the higher ranks.

Differences between the social mobility of Italians and French Canadians are relatively small, but there has been a tendency for Italians to gain most in the lower white collar occupations (occupational rank II), while French Canadians have become more concentrated in the upper blue collar and lower white collar occupations.

These patterns of intergenerational occupational mobility are similar to perceived social class changes between generations. Both Portuguese and Irish have high rates of social class stability between generations, but for Portuguese stability is at lower class levels, while stability for Irish is at the middle and upper class levels. The process of social class changes for Italians and French Canadians varies by cohort: upward social class mobility is greater among Italians of the older cohorts, while upward mobility is greater among French Canadians of the younger cohorts.

There are also very large differences in the career and short-term mobility patterns of Catholic ethnics that again reinforce the need to examine heterogeneity within the Catholic subpopulation. Similar to intergenerational mobility, older Irish have experienced upward career mobility, while stability at high occupational levels characterizes more recent Irish cohorts. Patterns of career and short-term mobility among non-Irish Catholics are complex and are related to both initial occupational levels and cohort changes.

The statistical analysis of paths to occupational achievement summarizes some of these basic processes. Education, for example, contributes more to Catholic occupational achievement, while initial occupation and occupational origins are relatively more important for Protestants and Jews. Unlike other Catholics, occupational origins play a key role in the occupational achievements of Italians, again suggesting the importance of ethnic ties in the attainment of socioeconomic status. Most importantly, Catholic ethnic paths to occupational achievement are varied and complex and the relative influence of occupational and social class origins, education, and initial occupational level combine in a variety of ways to produce the differential occupational stratification of ethnic groups. Hence, the melting pot notion of occupational convergence is not only an inaccurate description of the changing stratification of ethnic groups but is inadequate as a basis for understanding the differential processes that have resulted in the socioeconomic mosaic characterizing contemporary ethnic communities. Ethnic pluralism in socioeconomic structure and process emerges clearly from our analysis.

Furthermore, there is no basis for assuming that these ethnic variations in stratification and social mobility will not persist in the future. Indeed, there is every basis for assuming the opposite: the differential structural processes associated with social class and occupational origins and the changing opportunity structures will continue to affect the social mobility and stratification characteristics of ethnic groups and these differential characteristics will remain a persistent feature of ethnic community structure. This emphasis on the structural determinants of ethnic stratification does not necessarily exclude the possible role of cultural values in sustaining ethnic socioeconomic variation. However, except for sex differences in education, there seems to be no basis for arguing that a "Protestant ethic," Jewish cultural traditions, or Catholic occupational values play a central role in explaining the changes in the socioeconomic structure of religious communities or accounting for the greater diversity in stratification and social mobility among Catholic ethnics.

RESIDENT CONCENTRATION AND GEOGRAPHIC MOBILITY

One of the structural features of ethnic community change and an indicator of ethnic continuity and cohesiveness is residential concentration. Changes in ethnic residential concentration and associated patterns of geographic mobility have been viewed as reflections of the diminishing role of ethnicity in American social life. However, an alternative view of these patterns suggests that residential concentration and changes may imply the emergence of new forms of ethnic identity and changing manifestations of ethnic commitments and cohesiveness. Although direct data to test the meaning of ethnic residential concentration and change are not available, detailed empirical analysis of ethnic variations in residential concentration and geographic mobility was presented that places in perspective the implications of these processes for ethnic continuity and community structure.

The highlights of the data on residential concentration of Catholic ethnic groups reveal that the Irish are least and Portuguese are most likely to reside in areas of high ethnic concentration. As with socio-economic stratification, the Italians and French Canadians are inter-mediate in their residential concentration. In addition to the doc-umentation of ethnic variation in residential concentration, several findings reveal the continuing but changing role of ethnic residential concentration. First, change in the residential concentration of ethnic subpopulations is not toward very low levels of concentration but to medium levels. Second, while the more educated and middle classes are less likely to reside in areas of high ethnic residential concentration, controls for education and social class do not elimin-ate the variation or extent of ethnic residential concentration. Hence, ethnic residential concentration is not a pattern solely of the older cohorts, the less educated and lower classes. Third, intermarried ethnics are more likely than nonintermarried ethnics to reside in areas of low ethnic concentration, but the intermarried of the most recent cohorts have tended to be more ethnically concentrated than the previous cohort. This change for the intermarried implies not only that intermarriage does not necessarily result in the total loss of ethnic identity but suggests that ethnic groups have changed in the extent of accepting intermarried ethnics as part of their communi-ties. Taken together, the analysis points to the persistence of ethnic residential concentration as an integral feature of ethnic community life that has changed over time but that has continued to be one of the major sources of ethnic continuity.

This conclusion regarding the change and continuity in ethnic residential patterns is clarified and reinforced by the detailed analysis of ethnic variation and change in residential mobility. Catholics are the least residentially mobile religious group and Jews are the most mobile within life cycle and cohort categories. In general, Catholics display much greater community attachments than non-Catholics, while Jewish community ties tend to be established later in the life cycle after a considerable amount of migration. As for other proc-esses that were examined, Catholic ethnic variation in residential change is greater than among religious groups. Italians have the highest rates of geographic stability and Irish are the most resi-dentially mobile—within and between counties—and have high rates of repeat mobility.

Although these patterns imply variations and changes in com-munity cohesiveness, particularly when cohort and life cycle effects are controlled, more direct relationships between residential change and ethnic continuity emerge from an analysis of geographic mo-bility among the intermarried and from an analysis of ethnic resi-dential concentration and change. With regard to intermarriage, the analysis points to the greater residential mobility of the intermarried than the homogamously married religious groups and greater residential change among intermarried Catholics than Protestants. The different residential mobility implications of intermarried Catholics and Protestants reflect the selectivity of Protestants and Catholics who intermarry, the greater cohesiveness of the Catholic community structure, and the fewer ethnic ties that intermarried Catholics are likely to have. Similarly, intermarriage does not have the same residential change implications for all Catholic ethnics. Intermarried Irish and Italian Catholics lose their distinctive ethnic residential mobility patterns. Indeed, it appears that when ethnic community boundaries are weak—as among the Irish—intermarriage has little effect on ethnic continuity. In contrast, where ethnic community boundaries are clearer and where communities are more cohesive (as among Italians), intermarriage loosens the constraints and residential mobility increases. The distinctive residential mobility among Catholic ethnics is weakened considerably for those who intermarry and greater homogeneity among intermarried Catholic ethnics emerges.

Furthermore, there is a clear relationship between residential mobility and ethnic residential concentration. While residential change may simply result in trading one community for another without affecting ethnic cohesiveness, the evidence suggests otherwise. The greater the residential change, the more likely ethnic solidarity and continuity will decline and ethnic residential concentration will diminish. Although life cycle and cohort effects appear to be relatively more important determinants of residential change, particularly mobility within communities, ethnic differences in residential mobility are substantial when these effects are eliminated and are related to the continuity of ethnic identity. The ethnic variation in residential change and the consequences of residential mobility for ethnic continuity are clearly associated with community stability between generations. There is a considerable ethnic variation in the extent of migration among the children of ethnics included in the study that has clear implications for the nature of ethnic solidarity in the coming generation.

The importance of socioeconomic status and life cycle are clearly evident in the analysis of ethnic variations in residential mobility. Generally, socioeconomic status shows a weak relationship to residential change when life cycle effects are controlled within ethnic subpopulations and ethnic differences are blurred within life cycle and socioeconomic categories. The clearest and most important relationship emerges when education and migration (between communities) are examined. Protestants migrate more than Catholics and among the Catholics, Italians migrate the least, controlling for education and life cycle; the more educated are more likely to migrate than the less educated within ethnic subpopulations and life cycle stages.

There is also a weak empirical relationship between intergenerational social mobility and residential change that varies by life cycle, and ethnic differences in residential mobility are small within social mobility and life cycle stages. But migration, unlike geographic movement within communities, shows significant ethnic variation— upwardly mobile ethnics are more likely to migrate and occupationally stable ethnics are least likely to migrate within life cycle stages.

Thus, the migration data indicate that ethnic continuity and the structure of ethnic communities continue to be differentially affected by social mobility patterns and distinctive ethnic factors. Movement between communities tends to be associated with the changing nature of ethnic cohesiveness.

These findings are consistent with the patterns of geographic movement between generations. Children of more educated parents are most likely to move out of the community, and intergenerational ethnic continuity is strongly affected by educational variations among ethnic communities. Catholics and Italian ethnics accentuate the tendency toward geographic stability between generations, even among the more educated. Jews, Protestants, and Irish show greater migration away from the community at higher levels of education. The structure of ethnic communities cannot but be affected by these patterns of selective outmigration. Ethnic communities are altered as well by the impact of inmigration selectivity on their occupational structure. In this way, ethnicity contributes to differential migration and differential migration contributes to variation in ethnic continuity and the structure of ethnic communities.

IMPLICATIONS

The analysis of ethnic variation and change in family and mobility processes is a necessary first step in understanding the dynamics of ethnic community change and in appreciating the multidimensionality of ethnic pluralism. The data analyzed have demonstrated the continuing but changing importance of the ethnic factor in a variety of elementary social processes. Moreover, there is a strong interdependence among family, stratification and residential mobility processes both in the patterns of ethnic differentiation and in the interactions of family variables (particularly life cycle and intermarriage), stratification and social mobility, and residential concentration and change (particularly migration).

These interdependent patterns of continuity and change in ethnic family and mobility processes have consequences for the study of the ethnic factor at many levels. Two questions are most appropriate at the community level: What are the implications of the various findings of continuity and change for these ethnic communities? How have these changes affected the larger community which forms the basis for the study? In addition, do these community patterns have implications for individuals—what choices and tradeoffs must occur as people try to make a life (and a living)? Finally, what has been learned about the ways in which ethnicity continues to remain salient, and how better might ethnicity be studied?

The most dramatic patterns of continuity and change emerged from the analysis of stratification and mobility for the three religious groups and four Catholic ethnic groups. Overall, continuity characterizes the Jews at a very high level of occupational prestige and class position. In contrast, the high relative standing of Protestants has been eroding for the younger cohorts while the upward mobility of young Catholics has been so vigorous that on some measures, young Catholics have higher standing than young Protestants (but not young Jews). This new success does not characterize all Catholic groups, however, since it is primarily the result of the recent achievements of a large number of younger Italians and to a lesser extent, the youngest French Canadians who have joined the Irish sons of an earlier generation of mobile Irish in high prestige occupations. The Portuguese, and many French Canadians, have, so far, been left behind in the lower ranks of occupational prestige and class position. As a result, sharp differences exist in class standing which continue to distinguish both religious and Catholic ethnic groups.

These class and social mobility patterns which have produced this hierarchy have affected the composition and continuity of the ethnic subpopulations in rather different ways. These differences are closely related to the different levels of education which characterize the ethnic groups. Education remains an important component of occupational success in any community. As such, it provides opportunity for those who remain, but since education is highly transferable, it allows many to take advantage of the opportunities which have emerged in other parts of the country. The Jews, Protestants, and Irish Catholics have achieved the highest levels of education. The high prestige levels achieved by many Italians and some French Canadians, on the other hand, are associated with substantially lower levels of education, suggesting that education, while useful, is not a necessary condition beyond a certain level, and that opportunities which may be connected with business and politics can provide avenues for many. These routes to occupational success, however, seem less transferable, and may reduce incentives to leave the community. The patterns of geographic mobility and the greater outmigration of the children of Jews, Protestants, and Irish seem to support this interpretation.

On balance, then, the migration and social mobility patterns of Italians are composed of elements which have had the greatest joint effect in promoting group position and continuity. The Protestant, Jewish, and Irish communities have experienced greater losses through outmigration as a result of emphasizing education as the means to occupational success. The combination of low education and low social mobility, together with the group disruptions associated with high rates of geographic mobility among French Canadians and Portuguese may have reinforced the low standing of these groups in the community.

The pattern by which ethnic family and marriage processes have influenced the ethnic subpopulations and the larger community provides a different dimension which both reinforces and clarifies to a certain extent the group positions which have resulted from social and geographic mobility. This is particularly clear for the patterns of intermarriage. To the extent that out-marriage can be interpreted as leaving the community for individuals and a lessening of group continuity, Italians again appear as the group with the strongest position and the Protestants the weakest. The other groups have intermediate intermarriage rates, although the Irish have been increasing group cohesiveness on this dimension, unlike other groups. In addition, it is the Italians who have the highest proportions married, indicating family, and probably group cohesiveness.

It is again education which operates to distinguish marriage patterns and group cohesiveness among ethnic populations. Higher levels of education are generally associated with intermarriage. Exceptions in this relationship are the Irish and the Jews, groups which are characterized by relatively late ages at marriage for both sexes. For these two groups, then, education has a contradictory effect on group cohesiveness, promoting continuity at the family level while disrupting community strength through its effects on migration. But for the other ethnic communities, education is doubly disruptive, since for Protestants and the other Catholic ethnic groups higher levels of education contribute both to intermarriage and geographic mobility. These relationships serve to underline the importance of the Italian route to social mobility which bypasses high levels of educational attainment. This pattern maintains greater cohesion at the family and community levels while allowing upward mobility.

Applying these relationships to individuals, it seems plausible to speculate that young Italians can find local economic opportunities, marry on schedule, and remain closely tied to their community, contributing to its strength and cohesiveness. College education entails the risk of out-marriage since many fewer Catholic women pursue college education, and Italian women marry relatively early. The need for college for advancement, however, seems less. But members of other groups probably face a less coherent set of choices. For Irish and Jewish men, occupational success without education is less common. Education does not mean out-marriage since Jewish men and Jewish women expect to marry after completing college, and many Irish women will be waiting until the men complete school. But education will also provide opportunities beyond the ethnic community, so that the community will suffer as individuals must choose between the success values of the larger society and the solidarity of remaining near relatives and friends. Individual and family values are coherent, but at some cost to community continuity. For French Canadian and Portuguese men, however, the choices seem most painful. To marry on schedule and remain within the community must greatly reduce opportunities for individual occupational success, since few avenues are open without education. Yet the pursuit of higher education risks an even more complete break with the community, since out-marriage rates are very high. So the communities must face the loss of their most successful members, many of whom (the intermarried), will have half their family ties in some other community.

The discussion of individual choices leaves unanswered many questions about the nature of the ethnic factor which need further research. The first is that we know very little about the choices which face ethnic women, or the effects of their choices on family and mobility processes and ethnic continuity. There are some indications in the patterns discussed above which suggest that this may be an important added dimension. Catholic wives of all ethnic groups have a much lower level of education than their husbands, and highly educated Catholic women are much less likely to marry than either other highly educated women or less educated Catholic women. And when such women marry, they are much less likely to marry Catholics. This suggests either that well educated Catholic women are less willing to marry at all, particularly with Catholic men, or are less attractive to Catholic men (or both). Does the structure of Catholic marriages differ in such a way as to deter women from higher education? How will Catholic marriages, and Catholics of both sexes, react to the increasing economic opportunities for well educated women? The economic contribution of women within marriage must also be considered. Some part of the assessment of subjective social class may have been based on a life style made possible by a wife's salary, and ethnic class differences may rest in part on differential labor force participation patterns of ethnic women. These are structural considerations which require further examination.

A second question for further investigation which this analysis has raised relates to paths to economic success that are not so clearly dependent on education. Such routes to occupational success are not very well understood. To the extent that they are based on local community ties to family and friends and the efficiencies of filling positions quickly with those who are near, such structures would seem to be unavailable to newcomers. Yet recently inmigrating Catholics and Catholic ethnics have experienced relatively high levels of occupational attainment, both in contrast to other cohorts of migrants in these groups and to recent Protestant inmigrants, a phenomenon which parallels the mobility patterns of Catholic ethnics in the area generally. This suggests that there may be a more specifically ethnic component to such opportunities which is transferable, perhaps through diffuse kin and friendship ties that extend quite widely. If so, such a process has served to reinforce the relative upward movement of the Catholic ethnic groups in the state. Research which can shed some light on this process might also reveal answers to a third area of concern: What is the meaning of ethnic identity for individuals? The answer to this question is frequently sought in adherence to ethnic cultural or national symbols and customs, in observances which could be tallied like the behaviors measured by such concepts as "religiosity." This is an approach which emphasizes abstract and individual considerations. But it may be that ethnic identity and affiliation have great structural value as well. When ethnic membership is described as providing a "sense of community" it may be that "community" means not only comradeship, but the greater ability to command resources—clients, jobs, promotions, nominations—a useful property which might very well explain the continued salience of ethnicity.

Future research must deal with these questions, whether the focus is on specific ethnic communities or on broader questions of social life. Research on other communities and on other ethnic subpopulations, as well as on the broader national American level, will place these findings in comparative perspective. Research that builds cumulatively on community variations and change and on more diverse areas of ethnic differentiation will refine, qualify, and generalize the changing role of the ethnic factor in American society.

Appendixes

※   *Appendix A*

Questions Used from the
Interview Schedules

Included in the survey questionnaire were a number of standard sociodemographic variables which have been used in this research. Age, marital status, place of birth, race, and educational data were collected using standard questions which need not be detailed here. However, the questions on ethnicity, on occupational and residential histories, and on subjective social class which form the basis of much of the analysis are complex. The key questions are the following:

Ethnicity
1. What is your religious preference?
2. As a child, were you brought up as a _____
_____ ?   (repeat denominational
preference)
3. Now, what is your $\begin{pmatrix}\text{wife's}\\\text{husband's}\end{pmatrix}$ religious preference?

4. As a child was $\begin{pmatrix}\text{she}\\\text{he}\end{pmatrix}$ brought up as a _____
_____ ?   (repeat denominational
preference)
For each of the respondent's: father, mother, father-in-law, mother-in-law:
5. What country did your _____ 's people come from originally? If 'America': Before that?
6. What was your (e.g. father) 's religious preference?

Male Occupational History and Origins
1. What is (your, your husband's) present job? I mean, what kind of work (do, does) (you, he) do?

247

(if not currently working):

2. What was (your, his) last job?

3. Five years ago (survey appropriate date), what kind of work (were you, was he) doing on that job?

4. At 25th birthday, what kind of work (were you, was he) doing on that job?

For each of the respondent's father, mother, father-in-law, and mother-in-law:

5. What was your _____ 's main job most of the time while you were growing up?

Subjective Social Class

1. There's quite a bit of talk these days about social class. If you were asked to use one of these four names for your social class, which would you say you belong in: middle class, lower class, working class, or upper class?

2. In what class would you say your family was when you were growing up?

Migration and Residential History

1. Will you tell me, in order, the states and/or countries you've lived in, starting with where you lived right after you were born?

2. Now, you told me you lived in _____ . Where did
                                    (state/country)
you live in _____ ? What cities or towns?
          (state/country)

(for each city and state, with due regard to 'first time', 'second time', etc.):

3. How many places did you live in _____ ?
                                (city, and state, if necessary)

4. What year did you move there, and when did you leave? We are especially interested in your moves within R.I.

5. What was the _____ city/town in which you lived
              (first, second, nth)
in R.I.?

6. In what year did you move there and when did you leave?

Number of Sample Cases

To simplify the tabular presentation accompanying the text and to avoid repetition, the number of cases on which the percentage distributions included in the text tables are based have not been presented in the tables themselves. Although somewhat different portions of the survey cases were used for some parts of the analysis, the population most commonly used was all white males aged 25 or older, who were in first marriages. (Whites made up 97 percent of the Rhode Island population in 1970.) The ethnic composition of this population by age appears in Table B-1. Some tables in the analysis appear for the wives of these males (e.g., education). The numbers differ very little by ethnicity from those presented for husbands, although the wives are, on average, somewhat younger.

These data form the basis of the analyses in Chapters 2, 4, 5, 7, and 8. Chapter 3, "The Marital Cycle," is based on the full white survey population over the age of 25, including the single, separated, divorced, remarried, and widowed, so the numbers are somewhat larger. In contrast, the analysis of residential changes in Chapters 9 and 10 is based on about five-sixths of the totals given in Table B-1, since information on migration histories was collected on only half of the cases for one of the three surveys (1969). Item nonresponse on specific questions also reduces somewhat the bases for particular calculations. Readers interested in the numbers on which specific statistics presented in the text tables are based and for which no exact number is presented in this table can obtain such information by writing to the authors.

Table B-1.   Ethnicity by Age

Age	Protestants	Jews	Catholics	French Canadians	Irish	Italians	Portuguese
Number							
Total	514	56	1,302	333	202	396	108
25–34	128	11	314	76	45	84	31
35–44	110	12	351	83	59	107	25
45–64	201	27	505	125	80	168	45
65+	75	6	132	49	18	37	7
Percent							
Total	100	100	100	100	100	100	100
25–34	25	20	24	23	22	21	29
35–44	21	21	27	25	29	27	23
45–64	39	48	39	37	40	42	42
65+	15	11	10	15	9	9	6

Bibliography

Abramson, Harold J. 1973. *Ethnic Diversity in Catholic America.* New York: Wiley.

Alba, Richard D. 1976. "Social Assimilation Among American Catholic National Origin Groups," *American Sociological Review* 41, 6:1030-1046.

Barth, Frederik (ed.). 1969. *Ethnic Groups and Boundaries: The Social Organization of Culture Differences.* Boston: Little, Brown & Co.

Bell, Daniel. 1975. "Ethnicity and Social Change," in N. Glazer and D. Moynihan (eds.), *Ethnicity: Theory and Experience.* Cambridge, Mass.: Harvard University Press.

Bernard, J. 1966. *Marriage and Family Among Negroes.* Englewood Cliffs, New Jersey: Prentice-Hall.

Billingsley, A. 1968. *Black Families in White America.* Englewood Cliffs, New Jersey: Prentice-Hall.

Blau, Peter M. and O.D. Duncan. 1967. *The American Occupational Structure.* New York: Wiley.

Bouvier, L.F. and I. Corless. 1968. *An Ethnic Profile of the State of Rhode Island.* Occasional Papers in Social Science No. 8. Kingston: University of Rhode Island.

Bouvier, L. and S. Rao. 1975. *Socioreligious Factors in Fertility Decline.* Cambridge, Mass.: Ballinger Publishing Company.

Carter, Hugh and P. Glick. 1976. *Marriage and Divorce: A Socioeconomic Study*, 2nd ed. Cambridge, Mass.: Harvard University Press.

Chamratrithirong, A. 1976. "Nuptiality and Migration in Thailand, 1970 Census: The Multiphasic Response Theory". Ph.D. dissertation, Brown University.

Davis, Kingsley, 1963. "The Theory of Change and Response in Modern Demographic History," *Population Index*, 29 (October).

Dixon, R. 1971. "Explaining Cross-Cultural Variables in Age at Marriage and Proportions Never Marrying," *Population Studies*, 25 (July).

Duncan, Beverly and O.D. Duncan. 1968. "Minorities and the Process of Stratification," *American Sociological Review*, 33 (June).

Glazer N. and P. Moynihan. 1970. *Beyond the Melting Pot*, 2nd ed. Cambridge, Mass.: The M.I.T. Press.

_____ (eds.). 1975. *Ethnicity: Theory and Experience*. Cambridge, Mass.: Harvard University Press.

Glick, Paul. 1957. *American Families*. New York: Wiley.

_____ . 1960. "Intermarriage and Fertility Patterns Among Persons in Major Religious Groups," *Eugenics Quarterly*, VII (March): 31–38.

_____ and A. Norton. 1973. "Perspectives on the Recent Upturn in Divorce and Remarriage," *Demography* 10, 3 (August): 301–314.

_____ and Robert Parke, Jr. 1965. "New Approaches in Studying the Life Cycle of the Family," *Demography*, II, pp. 187–202.

Goldscheider, Calvin. 1971. *Population, Modernization, and Social Structure*. Boston: Little, Brown and Company.

Goldstein, Sidney. 1969. "Socioeconomic Differentials Among Religious Groups in the United States," *American Journal of Sociology*, 74 (May): 612–631.

_____ and C. Goldscheider. 1968. *Jewish Americans: Three Generations in a Jewish Community*. Englewood Cliffs, N.J.: Prentice-Hall.

Gordon, Milton. 1964. *Assimilation in American Life*. New York: Oxford University Press.

Greeley, Andrew. 1974. *Ethnicity in the United States: A Preliminary Reconnaissance*. New York: Wiley.

_____ . 1976. *Ethnicity, Denomination and Inequality*. Beverly Hills: Sage Publications.

Hajnal, J. 1965. "European Marriage Patterns in Perspective," in D.V. Glass and D.E.C. Eversley (eds.), *Population in History*. Chicago, Illinois: Aldine Publishing Co., pp. 101–143.

Hodge, R.W. and D.Treiman, 1968. "Class Identification in the United States," *American Journal of Sociology*, 73:535–42.

Horowitz, D. 1975. "Ethnic Identity," in N. Glazer and D. Moynihan (eds.), *Ethnicity: Theory and Experience*. Cambridge, Mass.: Harvard University Press.

Kantrowitz, Nathan. 1973. *Ethnic and Racial Segregation in the New York Metropolis*. New York: Praeger Publishers.

Kennedy, Robert. 1973. *The Irish: Emigration, Marriage, and Fertility*. Berkeley, California: University of California Press.

Kobrin, F. and C. Goldscheider. 1977. "Ethnicity and Family Demography." Paper presented at the annual meetings of the Population Association of America, St. Louis, Missouri.

Lenski, Gerhard. 1963. *The Religious Factor*. Garden City, N.Y.: Doubleday and Company, Inc.

Lieberson, Stanley. 1963. *Ethnic Patterns in American Cities*. New York: Free Press.

Light, Ivan. 1972. *Ethnic Enterprise in America*. Berkeley, Calif.: University of California Press.

Mannheim, Karl. 1952. "The Problem of the Generations," in *Essays on the Sociology of Knowledge*. New York: Oxford University Press.

Matras, Judah. 1975. *Social Inequality, Stratification, and Mobility*. Englewood Cliffs, N.J.: Prentice-Hall, Inc.

Mayer, Kurt B. and S. Goldstein. 1958. *Migration and Economic Development in Rhode Island*. Providence, R.I.: Brown University Press.

Mindel, Charles H. and R.W. Habenstein (eds.). 1976. *Ethnic Families in America: Patterns and Variations*. New York: Elsevier Scientific Publishing Co.

Monteiro, L. 1976. *Monitoring Health Status and Medical Care*. Cambridge, Mass.: Ballinger Publishing Company.

Newman, William. 1973. *American Pluralism: A Study of Minority Groups and Social Theory*. New York: Harper & Row.

Oppenheimer, V. 1977. "Women's Economic Role in the Family," *American Sociological Review* 42, 3 (June): 387–405.

Organic, H. and S. Goldstein. 1970. "The Brown Population Laboratory: Its Purposes and Initial Process," in I. Kessler and M. Levin (eds.), *The Community as an Epidemiologic Laboratory: A Casebook of Community Studies*. Baltimore, Maryland: Johns Hopkins Press, pp. 212–232.

Parsons, T. 1975. "Some Theoretical Considerations on the Nature and Trends of Change in Ethnicity," in N. Glazer and D. Moynihan (eds.), *Ethnicity: Theory and Experience*. Cambridge, Mass.: Harvard University Press.

Prior, G.T. 1932. "The French-Canadians in New England." M.A. paper, Brown University.

Reiss, Ira. 1961. *Occupations and Social Status*. New York: Free Press of Glencoe.

Ross, Heather L. and I.V. Sawhill. 1975. *Time of Transition: The Growth of Families Headed by Women*. Washington, D.C.: The Urban Institute.

Runciman, W.G. 1966. *Relative Deprivation and Social Justice*. London: Routledge and Kegan Paul.

Schermerhorn, Richard A. 1969. *Comparative Ethnic Relations: A Framework for Theory and Research*. New York: Random House.

Smith, Judy. 1976. "City and Family: Italians and Jews in Industrial Rhode Island." Paper presented at the annual meeting of the American Historical Association, Washington, D.C.

Speare, Alden, Jr., S. Goldstein, and W. Frey. 1975. *Residential Mobility, Migration and Metropolitan Change*. Cambridge, Mass.: Ballinger Publishing Company.

Toney, M. 1971. "Catholic and Protestant Migration in Rhode Island." M.A. paper, Brown University.

van den Berghe, Pierre. 1971. "Ethnicity: The African Experience," *International Social Science Review*, 23, 4.

Yancey, W.L., et al. 1976. "Emergent Ethnicity: A Review and Reformulation," *American Sociological Review*, 41, 3 (June): 391–402.

Index

About the Authors

Calvin Goldscheider is Chairman of the Department of Demography in the Faculty of Social Science, The Hebrew University, Jerusalem, Israel and Adjunct Professor of Sociology at Brown University. He received his undergraduate degree at Yeshiva University in New York and his M.A. and Ph.D. at Brown University. He has also taught sociology and demography at the University of Southern California and at the University of California, Berkeley. His main interests have been in analyzing the junctures of social and demograpic processes, particularly the relationship between social change and population processes and the social demography of ethnic groups. He has published extensively in these areas and finds ethnic diversity and change a continuous challenge for sociological research in the pluralistic societies of Israel and America.

Frances E. Kobrin is Assistant Professor of Sociology and a member of the Population Studies and Training Center at Brown University. Her undergraduate work was done at Radcliffe College she holds a Ph.D. in ·demography from the University of Pennsylvania. Ms Korbin taught at Skidmore College before coming to Brown in 1974. Her fields of specialization and interest include development; the sociology of sex and age role changes; and the demography of household and family change. Work in this last area has included several publications and a conviction that ethnic groups provide an excellent opportunity to study comparative family demography.

A